TRANSPLANTED SHAMROCKS

RECOLLECTIONS OF CENTRAL OHIO'S IRISH AMERICANS

COLLECTED BY
JULIE O'KEEFE MCGHEE, J. MICHAEL FINN,
ANNE O'FARRELL DEVOE, KATHRYN HESS

outskirtspress
DENVER, COLORADO

CONTENTS

Ireland

Syracuse University Press, Syracuse, NY 2006

Collected stories compiled by

Julie O'Keefe McGhee, Chair
Anne O'Farrell DeVoe
J. Michael Finn
Kathryn McConnell Hess
William D. McGhee

Art Work Created By
Kathryn McConnell Hess

We would like to thank the following for their valued assistance in the formation of this book.
Karen M. Graham
Heather M. Mikolaj
Melanie D. Pratt
Donald M. Schlegel
Ancient Order of Hibernians Patrick Pearse Division 1
Catholic Record Society of the Diocese of Columbus
Greater Columbus Irish Cultural Foundation
The Daughters of Erin
The Ladies Ancient Order of Hibernians Countess de Markievicz Division 1
The Shamrock Club of Columbus
The Columbus Dispatch: McKinnon Article, Byrne Story, and Moran Story
Tim Puet, Catholic Times

Introduction

Information boards telling the stories of prominent Irish in Ohio's history were used in the establishment of the historic Irish marker, later installed on McPherson Commons in downtown Columbus.

As the boards were shown at public events, numerous people expressed interest in contributing their own stories to create a collection for publication. The Irish Family Story Project committee members agreed that the stories of our Irish-American families had not been told and deserved a wider audience. We realized that everyone has a story to tell. This committee hoped to compile enough stories for a book.

We requested anecdotes and memories from family histories that were thought provoking, colorful, humorous or sentimental. We suggested family gatherings and holidays as great sources for those stories about our Irish roots and immigration. After several years, we find ourselves with an excellent collection covering relations both current and past, some going back to their origins in Ireland. Also, many of the participants found this rewarding because it caused them to investigate their backgrounds in a way they never had before.

We hope that you find this publication as interesting and enthralling as we have in its completion.

Obverse Side

Reverse Side

Why we have collected these stories:
comments from the committee.

When I was a little girl I remember asking my grandma Bertha Voegelin O'Keefe if her mother-in-law, my great grandmother Mary R. O'Keefe had lived with her and my grandpa Jack O'Keefe. Grandma Bertha replied that yes, her mother-in-law Mary had lived with them.

As a child I loved stories, I still do, so I asked if great grandmother Mary had told any stories. Thinking about that fact I then remembered my Irish-Americans relatives who were always so garrulous and fun loving and I hoped that she would be a source of some good stories. My Grandma Bertha said that my great grandmother had told many good stories especially ones about the spirits and such that she, grandma Bertha, was afraid to go upstairs to bed at night. I was delighted with this bit of information. I then asked my grandma if she remembered any of those wonderful stories told by Mary R. O'Keefe. "No" was the only reply I got. I was so sad to think that all those wonderful stories were lost. My face must have shown my disappointment and my grandmother said she did remember one thing, that most of those forgotten stories contained a **MAGIC CIRCLE** and if you could get inside that circle you would be safe from harm. I mourned the loss of those stories but I remembered that Magic Circle. Now that I am grown I don't want to lose any more special stories and so I want the stories of the Irish-Americans of Central Ohio to be shared so that their stories with "Magic Circles" will not be lost.

In this book, Transplanted Shamrocks" we may have created our own **Magic Circle** of the love, laughter, sadness, strength and memories shared by the Irish-American friends and families of Central Ohio.

Perhaps we lost those stories because our great grandparents, grandparents and parents were not able to spend the effort and time telling and retelling their stories because they had another more fundamental job to do that consumed most of their energies; that job was survival and assimilation in a new country.

In this book we are doing what I wanted my grandmother to do; to share family stories. We are sharing the family stories because we can and we should. Our Irish ancestors made the journey here; built a new life and managed to preserve their heritage in a strange place. Now some of the Central Ohio Irish-Americans have taken this opportunity to share their stories. Perhaps this book is a way to thank our Irish ancestors for coming to America and providing their children and their children's children with a good life burnished with their Irish lineage.

Our book is an attempt to thank them for coming and doing their job.

Julie O'Keefe McGhee

Standing around at social events the Irish have a tendency to talk about their roots. With each conversation there is a story. Sometimes these stories are happy, sometimes they are sad and often they are amusing. All of the stories tell of the immigrant experience. All are important to the person to whom they belong. They are also important to all of us because collected together they make up the tapestry that is the Irish community in central Ohio.

There is a place on the Dingle Peninsula in County Kerry in the far west of Ireland. It's known to the natives of the area as An Clasach (the passage or channel). The location is not marked by any historical marker. It's just an ordinary place in the road at the top of a hill that anyone would easily drive by.

In the days when the Great Blasket Island was occupied, island people who were emigrating from Ireland would gather their family and take the rough boat ride from the island to Dunquin Harbor. From there the group would walk the road together to the top of the hill to the place called An Clasach. There they would say goodbye for the last time. The emigrant would walk down the far side of the hill to the town of Ventry where a train would take them to Cork and the boat to their new life in America. The relatives would remain at the top of the hill and watch as their brother, son or daughter passed out of sight before they returned to Dunquin Harbor and back to the island.

An Clasach was a place of parting. Knowing the significance of that spot you can almost feel the hundreds of stories that began from that point of the earth. Those who left would begin their stories; those who remained behind would remember the emigrant only from the point he or she passed out of sight.

What we have tried to do with this book is document the stories from this side of that long journey to America. We all stand on the shoulders of those who came before us. This collection of stories will be a benefit to those who come after us – those who will stand on our shoulders.

Hopefully, my involvement with this project has contributed a portion of preserving the memories and stories for the many families who shared their stories with us.

J. Michael Finn

All of us ask ourselves some time during our lives, "Why do I like this kind of music?" or "What did my ancestors do when they came here?"

Our decisions and desires, choices in a mate, how we raise our children and what career we pursue are all parts of our lives influenced by our families and what they have experienced. How we are raised and the values instilled in us create the way we respond to everyday life and its challenges and decisions.

Each generation affects the next, decade after decade, until it is your turn. Each generation is colored by what its growing children hear; the stories of our families' hardships, hopes, laughter and tears stick with us in our subconscious. Often, we dream during the night, seeing the familiar faces of our childhood in remembered poses. Sometimes our imagination, spurred by the brief references we heard but hardly noticed, completes the picture.

These stories and images, that we observe, read or are told, are the essence of our own history. They influence what we are and what we will become. We cannot ignore the lives that preceded us; and what shaped them.

This book was formed by our need to realize what has come before us. The valuable insights from this knowledge describe a people who fled their homeland by force or determination, desiring a better life for themselves and their descendents, claiming the very right to survive. How impoverished would our lives be without knowing what happened to them or how they continued in the face of adversity?

The research needed to create the Irish Historical marker, in celebration of Ohio's Bicentennial, opened many questions. Irish men and women who were prominent in the development of central Ohio founded institutions and accomplished achievements that are evident in today's cities and society. We drive by them, read about them, visit them and take them for granted. We cannot, however, take for granted the people who conceived them without losing a part of ourselves. Who, but us, can appreciate what they did, where they came from, what they survived and whom they loved and raised? We will not retain this knowledge, however, unless it is put on a page for the reading by the families who follow us and who will, in turn, wonder from what type of people they sprang.

We all need to know from where we have come in order to know where we are going.

Kathryn McConnell Hess

Growing up I had an Irish last name -O'Farrell- and red hair. My brothers are named Tim, Pat, and Mike. We learned my mother's maiden name was originally O'Toole and Mom might be as Irish as my Dad (but we had to whisper that at times). I knew all the Irish songs' "McNamara's Band" and "When Irish Eyes are Smiling".

But I learned what being Irish really meant when my daughter Katie became involved in Irish step dancing at the age of 8. I became involved in the Irish Organizations and there I learned the "real Irish music", the rich heritage of Irish dance and of our rich and ancient culture. I learned about Irish history and became, like my Dad, an Irish patriot!!! I felt a renewed sense of pride and love of my Irish heritage.

My involvement in this project grew from these experiences. Through this project I have learned much more about the courage and faith on my great great grandparents who came from Ireland. I learned how what we did and said in our family had its roots in Irish culture. (Aren't we the only ethnic group that believes our dead relatives hangout with us in Church, at celebrations, in the kitchen??)

This book is essentially the Irish immigrant story in the Midwest. These are OUR stories NOT stories written about us. It gives a personal/family look at the trials, tribulations and successes of the Irish in America. It provides a glimpse of the Irish involvement in the organized labor movement, local politics and religious practices. It was the Irish spirit that shaped these movements in Columbus and the Midwest. I am grateful to all who provided stories and to my son, Ben, who provided artwork for this project.

Anne O'Farrell-DeVoe

Life

And Its

Stories

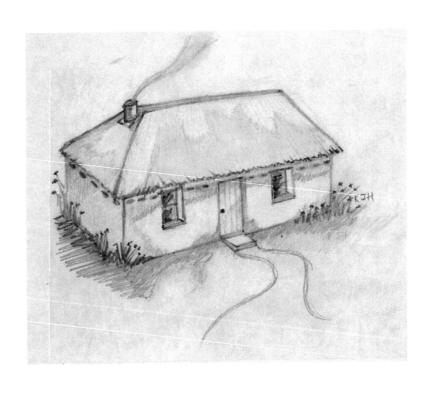

My Canty Family Story

Catherine Jane Adkins

My father John Canty was born in Kerry, Ireland on August 31, 1908. He came to America in the early 1920's. He stayed with his cousins, Nellie and Jack Barry who lived on First Ave. near to Sacred Heart Church. John got a job at Timken Roller Baring Company. He was there almost 50 years until he retired. My mother was Mary Ford. She was the youngest of 13 children, also born in Kerry, Ireland. She was five years old when she came with her parents to America. Later she went to Sacred Heart School and Business School just as I did.

My mother met my father through some of her older brothers who were not married at the time, and were still living in the area. I am the oldest of nine children most of them live in Florida now. But I have two brothers that live here in Ohio, John in Columbus and Tom in Powell. One sister, Margaret lives in a Senior Center in Mount Gilead, Ohio. She had three children, four grand children and one great grandchild. One of my nieces, Andra Williams Cotton, lives in Tennessee. She has eight children. She used to be an Irish Step dancer. All together now, I have nineteen great nieces and nephews and one great-grand niece. I have one son and no grand children.

My parents and all of my aunts and uncles and most of my cousins are now dead except for one older cousin in Illinois. But I think I might have some cousins in Ireland.

I am proud to remember that one of my first cousins was Father Larry O'Connor, a chaplain of the Shamrock Club and Fire and Police Department.

Hiram McDonald's Life and Hard Times

Dennis L. Anderson

Hiram McDonald came from a hardworking Irish family, and grew up in rural Pennsylvania, north of Pittsburgh. His father John, (born in Ireland, 1795) and older brothers dug iron ore for a living, to feed the furnaces of the day (before steel mills) in the area, and

Hiram continued to dig the ore after the family moved down the Ohio River, eventually settling down near Jackson, Ohio.

Hiram grew into manhood in Southeast Ohio in the 1850s, and eventually married Jane Rembey on July 4th, 1857, wed by Justice of the Peace for Vinton County, Joseph Kaler. T.M. Buskirk, Probate Court Judge, issued the marriage license in and for the County of Vinton, State of Ohio. This marriage is registered in Vol. 1, Page 120, of the Vinton County (Ohio) probate records. Their union produced three known children.

After the first two children were born, along came the Civil War. Hiram decided to serve the Union, along with so many others, and went to Camp Dennison, near Cincinnati. There, he enlisted in the 11th Ohio Light Artillery Regiment on Sept. 3rd, 1861. Just one year later, he was wounded at the Battle of Iuka, Mississippi, on Sept. 19, 1862.

Historical accounts say he was sent to an Army Hospital in St. Louis, Missouri, and from there to another Army Hospital in Columbus, Ohio, where he was discharged on June 29th, 1863. It was reported that he was shot in battle in the upper middle third of his right arm, causing damage to the brachial nerve, which caused partial paralysis to the muscles of the right hand.

The "wounded soldier" returned to his home and family in Southeast Ohio, where his third child was born 9 months later. He applied for his Pension, but re-enlisted before it was approved, stating that he had a wife and three children to care for, and couldn't work otherwise. During his second tour of duty, Hiram contracted Smallpox, and spent most of his time in the hospital or Prison Camp.

Hiram returned home again to care for his family as best he could. During the ensuing years, his wife Jane passed away, leaving him with the care and support of his three children. In an Affidavit sent to the Federal Pension Board by Mr. Nelson Richmond, he describes Hiram as a stout, able-bodied man that had worked for him digging iron ore before leaving for his service to the Union cause. Upon his return home, Hiram tried to return to work for him, but had been badly crippled, and his constitution was broken. Hiram was not capable of any type of manual labor.

Some time later, his small Veteran's Disability Pension approved, at the age of 47, Hiram re-married, on Jan. 25th, 1877, to Rachel Drake (age 19), daughter of David Drake and Nancy Ziegler, in Vinton County, Ohio, by Rev. John Gold. The same Judge that issued Hiram's first marriage license, Judge T.M. Buskirk, issued their marriage license Jan. 24th, 1877. This license issuance is recorded in Vinton County (Ohio) Probate Court records, Vol. 3, Page 334.

Over the next 2 1/2 years or so, Hiram and Rachel had two children, one of which was Alva Curtis McDonald, my great-grandfather. The 1880 Federal Census for Madison Township, Vinton County, Ohio, found on microfilm at the Ross County (Ohio) Genealogical Society on Nov. 20, 1993, shows that Hiram, age 48, was a laborer, wife Rachel, age 22, as "keeping house" and ill with the flu, Wesley, age 24, (step)son, laborer; Harvey, age 21, (step)son, laborer; Ella, age 17, (step)daughter, servant; Charles, age 3, son; Alva, age 1, son; All children unmarried.

Throughout the following years, Hiram tried to etch out a living at various menial jobs to support his growing family that would carry on his legacy and family name. He and Rachel had 11 more children, the last being born in 1902, when Hiram was 72 years of age, before he passed away the following year.

Rachel (Drake) McDonald lived on another 28 years, to finish raising her family in Vinton and Ross Counties of Ohio.

Many thanks to the Ross County Genealogical Society, Lilee (McDonald) Workman, and Janice (McDonald) Waits for their November, 1993, and May, 1991 input and assistance respectively, for details of this story.

Christopher Gets a Trophy?

Eileen Kelly Baesmann

I have always loved St. Patrick's Day mornings! My father (Sidney Kelly) would rouse the entire house by 6 am with his old

78 records of "Has Anyone Here Seen Kelly", "Harrigan", "When Irish Eyes Are Smiling" and "McNamara's Band". Although we knew we were special, because of our Irish Heritage, we never participated in any formal festivities of this day. Then the Daughters of Erin came along and changed all of that!

The Daughters of Erin was founded in the Fall of 1978 and while we did not join that first month with the founding members, my mother (Mary Louise Kelly), my sisters and I all joined within the first three months of its' existence. Mary Kelly Tisdale, Pat Thomas, Kathy Kelly and I were excited about the chance to join an organization with strong cultural and charitable roots.

The love of the Irish was instilled deep into the hearts of my four children and they looked forward to joining me every year as a member of the Daughters of Erin Clown Unit as we passed out candy on our parade walk down High Street to Broad Street or, so I thought!

My children and I were sitting at the dining room table one year shortly before St. Patrick's Day making our final plans for the big day. Christopher Michael burst into tears. At the age of seven, Christopher did not share my belief that no one should go to work or school on St. Patrick's Day. You see, my children were blessed with healthy Irish genes and never missed school because of illness. However, they had never received a "Perfect Attendance Award" from school. The only day they missed all year – yes, you guessed it – St. Patrick's Day!

Christopher had seen the trophies other students were provided with at the end of the year and wanted one too! My husband (Terry) and I had to do some creative scheduling that year in order to get a 1952 Fire Engine, three young clowns – Kelly, Joe and T.J. and ourselves to the procession on time while dropping Christopher off at school. Then we had to end our day at the Irish Family Reunion early so we could get Christopher home from school. I sure hoped that trophy was cast in solid gold!

Wouldn't you know, the end of the year came and there was no mention of a "Perfect Attendance" trophy. It seemed that due to budget cuts that year all Chris was to receive was a certificate in the mail over the summer! Suffice it to say; never again did any of us miss this celebration of our Irish heritage.

The Brady's (MacBrádaigh)

Morey J. Brady

The Brady family originated in County Cavan, Ireland; during the famine years my great-grandparents migrated to County Cork where the Brady family lived in Glengarrif. They migrated to the U.S. from Cork.

My grandfather, James Brady was born in 1870. He settled in DeSoto, Missouri; a railroad town of Irish emigrants. He was given a job as a fireman on the railroad because, a member of his family from County Cork, who was a railroader got him the job. He was a railroad engineer for the Missouri Pacific R. R. James Brady died in February 1897 when a locomotive boiler on his train exploded.

James Brady married my grandmother, Nell Howard; who was born in 1875 in Corofin, County Clare, Ireland. My grandmother, Nell Howard Brady's family was an old Anglo-Irish family. They married into families of O'Brien's and McCarthy's.

James Brady and Nell Howard Brady lived in DeSoto, Missouri. Two sons were born during this marriage. The first son was Edward, born in June of 1893; the second, my father, Morey Joseph Brady was born November 22, 1895. My father was only 13 months old when his father died in the train explosion; he never knew his father!

My grandmother's family owned a boarding house and her parents helped raise the boys after my grandfather's death.

My uncle, Edward Brady died of tuberculosis in 1916; he was only 23 years old. My father, Morey Joseph Brady, enlisted in the Army Corps of Engineers in 1917; he served in World War I in France. Upon his return he studied Civil Engineering and worked for the U. S. Corps of Engineers in St. Louis, Missouri. During World War II he was an officer in the U. S. Coast Guard and obtained the rank of Commander. He re-entered civilian life in

1946. He became Superintendent of River Navigation for the St. Louis District and was responsible for the river Channel and the locks on the Mississippi River from St. Louis to Memphis, Tennessee.

My mother was Lucia Ann Spring, born March 16, 1900. The Spring family were colonial people from Connecticut, Lucia Spring became a school teacher; teaching in southern Illinois. Her family was of English and Scottish background from Northumbria, Northumberland County, England and Glencoe, Scotland; they were Jacobites. My mother's family settled in Southern Illinois and they were farmers.

My father died in February, 1988; my mother died one week later. I am the only living child of this marriage. I was born December 17, 1936, in St. Louis. I had a sister who died as a small child.

I graduated from Christian Brothers College High School in 1955. I was educated at Quincy College, and Washington University in St. Louis, Missouri. I married Roberta K. Johnston on October 15, 1960; she was a registered nurse, with a Bachelor of Science in Nursing. She also graduated from Washington University. My wife died February 6, 2009.

My wife and I had three sons; Edward, Brian, and James. Edward and Jim are graduates of The Ohio State University. Ed is a project manager in the commercial heating and air conditioning industry. Jim is a social studies teacher at Westerville North High School. Brian is a graduate of Ohio University, Athens, Ohio. He is the General Manager of a logistic company, Building Systems Inc. in London, Ohio. We had four grandchildren; three grandsons and one granddaughter.

The Brady's have lived in Westerville, Ohio since January 1971. I entered the transportation industry trucking business in St. Louis. I became a Terminal Manager, a Sales Manager and a Vice President in the industry. Bobbi and I both retired in 1999. Bobbi was a school nurse at Westerville North High School for 14 years.

We enjoyed travel and Celtic History, having travelled to Ireland, Scotland, and England four times to renew our heritage.

Barretts of Glencastle, County Mayo, Ireland

Kathleen Robbins Brammer

My Great Grandparents were Patrick Barrett of Glencastle, County Mayo and Ellen Gaughan from Derrycorrib, County Mayo. Patrick married Ellen in Belmullet, County Mayo, Ireland on February 2, 1870. According to family stories, the famine in Ireland was only spoke of with bowed heads, and the soft words of "May God Rest Their Souls." Patrick Barrett's naturalization records from Marion County, Ohio, indicated the couple came to the United States shortly after their marriage in 1870. They lived for several years in the coal-mining region of Shenandoah, Schuylkill County, Pennsylvania until 1878. During the time that they lived in Pennsylvania there were uprisings and problems for the Irish Coal Miners, and it was during this time that the Mollie Maguires were organized. I have no information that Patrick Barrett was part of this group, but according to the records, there was a Patrick Barrett, which was a very common Irish name, that was a member. If there were hardships in Shenandoah, Pennsylvania for the Barretts, it wasn't spoken about. In 1878 the Barretts came to Marion, Ohio where there was work for Patrick as a laborer on the railroads. Census records after that showed him to be working in one of the many quarries that Marion, Ohio was known for. The two youngest Barrett children were born in Marion, Ohio; the youngest was my grandmother, Helen Cecilia Barrett Robbins.

I wanted to share a story about what happened to myself and my three sisters, Debbie, Maureen, and Judi, who visited Ireland in February 2004. It was a wonderful and eventful trip. We especially had planned to go to Belmullet where our Great Grandparents were married. Patrick Barrett was from Glencastle, and married Ellen Gaughan from Derrycorrib in 1870. That same year, they came to the U.S. to escape the famine that ravaged County Mayo.

Regarding our trip to Glencastle; we arrived in the early afternoon, midweek. We see there are a school there, a cemetery, some houses and a pub, not a lot more than that. We knew that pub would be the place to get information and talk with the town people, so we immediately stopped there. It is called The Full Shilling. We anxiously walk in; of course we were a little nervous, as the "all men" patrons gave us the once over. My sister Debbie blurted out: "Are there any Barretts in here" The bartender smiled, and waved his hand around the small bar. 4 out of 5 men at that pub were Barretts, and two of them were named Michael Barrett (our great-great Grandfather's name). We talked with all of the people there, they were so friendly, all of them. They did give us a piece of advice on the sly. When some from the Murphy family came into the pub, they advised us not to talk to them. They said, "The Barretts hate the Murphys, The Murphys are jealous because the Barretts are better looking." The Barretts offered to help us find a place to stay, they told us about others that would be good for family information, and one of them lead us on a wild goose chase up a mountain to see a Barrett man who, we found out later, had not come out of his house for 20 years. And there we were knocking on his door. (He didn't come out). The guys in the pub, I'm sure had a big laugh at our expense. We did go to a pub (McDonnell's) in Belmullet. I recommend this pub to all who go to Belmullet area. What a stroke of luck for us to go there. The bartender could not have been nicer. He bought us all a Guinness after finding out our family was from the area. We talked with him a while, told him about our ancestors and he said he knew of an older Barrett man who might know a bit of Barrett history. He offered to ring him up. He spoke with him a moment and handed us the phone. His name was Edward "Neddy" Barrett; he lived on Blacksod Bay in Derrycorrib. He was around 80 years old, and his wife was with him. I spoke also with their daughter who gave me directions to the house. We were invited to come by at 10am the next morning.

We found the directions to the Barrett home left much to be desired. There are no mailboxes with addresses as we are used to here in the U.S. The only directions were to "turn right at the yellow house, go three drives, and go up the hill towards the peat field, and turn left at the white home. In spite of the directions, we found it. We pulled in, and found the neat little home to be very charming on the outside, and we were nervous as to what might happen once the door is opened to us. The wife came to the door first, hugging and kissing each and every one of us as we entered their home. The old man then came in, he had a back problem which caused him to walk very bent over, and we were told that it was from working his whole life in the peat fields. (He reminded me of my Barrett grandmother right away). He also hugged us all. He kept saying over and over again that he couldn't believe that his Barrett family has come back to see him from America. They had a peat fire burning in their sitting room. They got out family photos for us all to see, and they got out the "good stuff' for us all to have a toast with a shot of Jamesons together. We had a two-hour visit with these nice people. They both hugged us and cried when we left them. What a wonderful experience. The Barrett family has lived near Glencastle, County Mayo for hundreds of years. I am sure that our Great Grandfather, Patrick Barrett was related to their family. I wish that everyone could experience that in Ireland. There is nothing like it. We certainly left Belmullet and Glencastle with warm feelings towards our Irish family that was still there. I heard last year that Edward "Neddy" Barrett passed away. He is, I'm sure, being welcomed by Patrick and Ellen Barrett with open arms and a shot of "the good stuff.'"

My Grandfather Frank McNulty

Jennifer McNulty Brockmeyer

I loved my grandfather, Frank McNulty. He was a marvelous, kind man. He did many things for the Columbus area people.

Grandpa was born in May 1895, his ancestors came from Ireland. His Irish father married a Shawnee woman from Urbana, Ohio. He never talked about it.

He had gardens, revealing knowledge from both of his parents. He always planted the three sisters as Indians do. He always fed native birds; my daughters still carry on this tradition. No one is complete without their ancestors' traditions.

He lived at 186 W Brighton Rd in Clintonville, Ohio with my grandmother Frances Casey. My brother Andrew lives there now.

Frank was the head of the Charity News for years; always at the corner of Gay and High Street, selling the Columbus Dispatch, which brought money to help the poor. He took me to their headquarters, as a small child to see what they purchased for the needy; coats, gloves, sweaters, hats, and lots of candy. What a worthwhile organization! I have a huge photo of my Grandpa pinning Charity News buttons on the famous radiomen "Amos and Andy".

I remember St. Joseph's Church and marching with my grandfather west on Broad St. and turning south on High St. to the Neil House hotel across from our State House Capital. My grandfather, Mike O'Keefe and Jerry O'Shaughnessy were at the lead of the parade with me at five years old. I was the first female to ever march in the St. Patrick's Day parade. What an honor!

He sold real estate, worked for Dan Royhan's Chevrolet and made whiskey in his bathtubs. When he passed away in May 1960 at age 65, John W. Galbreth, who owned the Pittsburg Pirates, then Steelers was one of the pallbearers. His good friend Jerry O'Shaughnessy buried him at St. Joseph's Cemetery.

Another good friend was Mike O'Keefe, who owned Forester's Restaurant, one block south of Lazarus, died the year before. Boy, did I love him too. I have such great memories of going to his restaurant with large black and white tiles on the floor. When you're little you remember stuff like this. Children love candy, he had absolutely the most beautiful display; children loved it, it was unbelievable. Mike had great soups and ham sandwiches. He was so nice, friendly to me, with his rosy cheeks and great smile. I miss him too.

My grandparents had four sons. Their eldest was Tommy, who won the Fulbright Scholarship. He sent me wooden shoes from Denmark, when I was 3. He was an architect, a teacher at Harvard, and MIT. He and his wife Mary Stevens created 'Living in Scripture' in a 1965 edition of "Life" magazine. They had 3 sons.

The second son was my father Frank, who graduated from Ohio State University in 1948. He was married to Beryl Preece from Wales; they met during WWII. They had four children. He was connected with Nationwide Insurance.

The third was John (Jack). I loved him and Tommy. The fourth was Charles who had three children. They are all gone now.

My parents had four children. I was the first, born March 10, 1947. I graduated from Bishop Watterson in 1965. Our 45th year is this year. I graduated from Ohio University sum cum laude in 1995 with a BSS in Native American Studies. My graduate work was in Cave Research. I've been a teacher, a speaker for Ohio History, and an artist. I live in the Hocking Hills.

The second daughter, Diane Kelch was three years younger. She was always late, marched in the parade.

Elysa Stuckey is the third, almost seven years younger; another marcher in the parade thanks to our Grandfather.

Andrew McNulty was born after our Grandfather died. He works for Nationwide; like our parents did. Our father never marched in the parade but Andrew does, along with some of the O'Shaughnessys.

I had four children. My three daughters Alyson, Elyse, and Sarah are the light of my life. They support me and always are in contact.

We're all grown up now. I'm getting old, two strokes will do that; but I always remember these memories from so long ago, and smile. That's what life is all about, isn't it!

Grandpa McGuire

Elaine Browning

My story, as of now, begins when my great-grandfather Henry Tish, a Mount Vernon teamster, married my great-grandmother Elizabeth (Jeffers) Tish from County Clare. They had two children: Bess and Paul. My grandmother, Bess, was born June 14, 1884. A few years earlier in County Cork, Ireland, my grandfather, Thomas, was born on August 23, 1878, to Timothy and Mary (Catrell) McGuire. I know he had at least one sibling, his sister Caroline. It was with her that Thomas immigrated to the United States sometime between 1884 and 1913. I can estimate the date of their immigration because on January 18, 1913, Thomas married Bess in Mount Vernon, Ohio. This union was a third marriage for my grandmother, Bess (Tish) McGuire. From her previous marriages she had two other children, Bill and Rosemond.

The story goes that Grandpa McGuire was a retired trapeze artist. He worked as a laborer but was unable to support his family, so he planned to try returning to the circus. He needed a place to practice, so he set up his equipment in Great-Grandpa's barn in Mount Vernon. As Grandpa McGuire was practicing (possibly without a net), he fell and was killed. I have never been able to verify my dad's story of how his father died, and I have yet to locate a death certificate in Knox County.

Several months later, on October 25, 1913, my father, Raymond, was born. For the next five years Dad and his siblings continued to reside with his mother and grandparents in Mount Vernon, Ohio. In 1918, my grandmother, Bess, and her brother Paul contracted influenza and died within one day of each other. It must have been a hellish time for Great-Grandma and Great-Grandpa. They were left to care for three orphaned grandchildren—Uncle Bill, Aunt Rosemond, and Dad—along with Paul's wife and their numerous children.

Dad attended school in Mount Vernon at St. Vincent de Paul Catholic Church until the eighth grade, when he quit and began to work with his grandfather as a Teamster. Dad's grandparents died prior to his fifteenth birthday, and he was left on his own. He was taken in by the Turner family and stayed with them for a couple of years until he went to work as a hired hand for the Brown family. On an outing to a dance hall called East Miller's, which was located in Morrow County, my father met Eva Bemiller, who he married on February 14, 1941. My parents moved to Richland County where they worked as tenant farmers on the Graham farm near Lexington, Ohio. I am the oldest of five children.

My Irish Roots

Molly Byrne

Molly Byrne sat down and thought about and then talked about her Irish Roots. Her family likely came from southern Ireland close to the coast. Her mother told her about "Black Irish": French and Spanish connections stemming from invasions by continental Europeans.

Her ancestors entered the United States by way of a seaport along our Atlantic Coast and Canada. The family then came to Columbus where her grandfather was the stationmaster at Union Station. Her mother attended Holy Rosary School and her father attended Aquinas High School.

Molly has developed an interest in her Irish heritage and increased her knowledge by reading quite a lot about Ireland in both fiction and history. She is proud of the influence the Irish have made on the country they adopted, mentioning their activities during the Revolutionary War and the Irish Uprising of 1798. Molly noted that while the early Irish immigrants were poor, they settled in and branched out. They have greatly influenced segments of American culture such as: the southern style clog dancing, which is a form of Irish Step-dancing; and fiddle music and bluegrass that we enjoy today.

Today, she and her husband Pat have a combined family of six children and, in the example set by their parents, have made an effort throughout their lives to involve the whole family in Irish culture and values of community service, faith, storytelling, music, dance and fun! Today's Irish culture for Molly is a harmonious blend of these.

"Gent From the Old Sod Seeking Strapp Kin"

Bob and Marilyn (Strapp) Cain

The highlight of the Strapp reunion in the early seventies was the sharing of a newspaper article from the Urbana Ohio News. In the usual course of events, the seeking of Irish relatives is initiated by the American descendants, but this scenario sparked excitement because it was just the opposite. My father Frank Strapp cherished his heritage and encouraged the commemoration of St. Patrick and all things Irish 365 days a year. The collective group decided that we should make an effort to reply to the article and find out what we could of this gentleman from the old sod. Dad's cousin, Jim Strapp, was assigned the task to contact the writer, and report what transpired, back to the group at the next reunion.

The writer was an illustrious character unsurpassed in his knowledge and love of his family heritage. His name was Finbarr O'Brien from a very small town called Tower Blarney, County Cork, Ireland, only about a ten-minute drive from the Blarney Castle. Since O'Brien is such a common name in Ireland, Finbarr decided to research his fraternal grandmother's branch on the Strapp side of the family, which originates from the Tipperary area. The search was a fruitful one, in that our families became united, first by letter (SNAIL MAIL AT THE TIME) and eventually by visiting one another multiple times both here in America and in Tower Blarney. Each correspondence, "Epistle" as Finbarr called the letters, was eagerly welcomed, cherished and shared with the extended family on both sides of the pond. The new e-mail is quick and easily accessible, but being able to touch the same page that your loved one carefully inscribed and forwarded, is incomparable and intimate.

Finbarr was well read and a great correspondent, with many relatives and friends throughout the United States and far away places. All of his letters were single spaced and typed on his old

UNDERWOOD. Some of the keys were slightly tipped, as the soldered repairs were not exactly square. He was, as the Irish say, a "Grand Fellow". He was well traveled, via his letters, and admired by his neighbors who knew of his expertise with the pen, as evidenced by his mailing and receipt of letters from all over. Finbarr was stricken by polio during the 1990's epidemic and wore braces and an elevated shoe. He walked with two blackthorn walking sticks, requiring physical stamina and great effort. He was anxious not to inconvenience anyone in his presence by being a burden and would join in the activity, no matter how difficult it was for him.

My fondest memory of that trait was our trip to the Blarney Castle. If you go there, you'll discover the very difficult circular stone access stairway to the top of the castle where the Blarney Stone is located. He joined with the group and made it triumphantly to the top with the rest of us. His wife, May, told us later, that he had never made the climb before but wanted to make us all feel welcome and appreciated.

Cousin Finbarr was an accountant by trade and retired from a local construction company as their business manager. He raised five children; one lives in Australia, one in Boston and three in Tower Blarney. He passed at age 82 in 2007. He left us with a legacy to fulfill: of finding, encouraging, and cherishing one another.

Thank you for finding us cousin Finbarr and filling some of the blank pages from our family history.

Her Irish Family Story

Agnes Dorn Carpenter

Agnes Dorn Carpenter told this collection of family vignettes and recollections to Julie McGhee on September 14, 2008 at Trinity School in Columbus Ohio.

In 1859 Agnes Carpenter's grandmother, Mary Durkin Kenny was born in Ballymote, Ireland. We are not sure whether Ballymote is in County Sligo or Mayo. Shortly after arriving in

New York she met and married Michael Kenny. Michael Kenny was also an Irish immigrant, a recent arrival in America.

In those day honeymoons were not common among the working classes and so Michael went off to work the next day swinging his lunch pail. Agnes recalled that her grandmother told her daughter and later her granddaughter that as she watched her new husband going off the work that she thought to herself "there goes the man I dreamt of marrying."

Eventually five children were born to Michael and Mary: Ellen, Anne, Margaret (Agnes' mother), Michael and Agnes. Agnes' mother Margaret was born in 1890 and so when Margaret's father Michael Kenny died in 1895, that left Mary Durkin Kenny with 5 young children with the oldest being about 9 or 10 years old.

In Columbus, the older children attended 2nd Avenue School and went to St. Francis Church on Buttles Avenue. With the death of her husband it was now up to Mary Durkin Kenny alone to care for her children and so she began to take in laundry, becoming in fact a true "Irish Washerwoman." Her oldest daughter Ellen (Aunt Ellie) had to leave school because someone had to help Mary Kenny with the pickup and delivery of the laundry. Mary Kenny now washed, dried, and pressed clothes in order to provide for her growing children. Ellen used a small wagon to pick up and deliver the laundry.

When Margaret Kenny was about 12 years old her mother's sister, Aunt Kate, left her teaching position in Ireland to come to America to help her sister, Mary Durkin Kenny, with her family. Aunt Kate stayed in Columbus with the Kenny's for about two years. When she returned to her home in Ireland she brought her niece, Margaret (Agnes Dorn Carpenter's mother) to stay with her for two years.

During her two-year stay in Ireland, Margaret Kenny learned many Irish songs that she would often share and that entertained the family. She did not sing those songs outside of the family but used her singing talents in the Holy Name choir where she met her husband Burley Michael Eshelman.

Mary Durkin Kenny was a widow for many years; her husband Michael had died in 1895 and she lived on until 1947, dying on January 6, the feast of the Epiphany. In Mary's later years her daughter Anne was her principal caregiver. Anne, while having to leave school early, as did Ellen, was self-educated and she achieved a good position at the Huntington National Bank. Anne is remembered as a loving aunt to her many nieces and nephews.

Mary Durkin Kenny never forgot her Irish roots; Agnes remembers going to visit her grandmother and Mary would always greet her visitors by calling out "Céad míle fáilte," when they would come in the door. At the time Agnes didn't know what the phrase meant but she knows it now, "A hundred thousand welcomes."

John Jack O'Keeffe

Patricia D. O'Keeffe Ciotola

My grandfather, John Jack O'Keeffe was born December 28, 1869 in Carrick-on Suir, Tipperary, Ireland. He came to America via Baltimore, Maryland in 1898 and joined the Army at the outbreak of the Cuban War. He was one of four specially selected sergeant-majors of the regular army to act as First Lieutenant of the famous 69th Irish Regiment, New York, but fearing his acceptance would debar him from active service he refused and went to Cuba as Commissary Sergeant and subsequently to the Philippine Islands. For his work he received special praise from the Adjutant General of Commissary in Washington.

He met my grandmother, Mary Ann Donnelly at Fort McHenry and married her November 20, 1898. Together they had three children; my father was the only son. My fathers name was John Thomas born 1902. John Jack returned home to Ireland to visit an ill brother and he himself died there shortly after he arrived in 1909. John Jack O'Keeffe is buried at Kilsheelan, County Tipperary, Ireland. My cousin Jack Anderson visited Grandfather's grave and we have a picture of that graveside visit.

Clearly it was Clery to Clark

Margaret P. Clark

My grandfather, Patrick Clery, was born in County Mayo, Ireland on May 28, 1858. He came to America as a small boy with his parents, James and Margaret Clery and a brother, named Louis. They settled in North Vernon, Indiana.

In those days the Irish were looked upon as the lowest of the low. No one wanted to hire them and they were a downtrodden race. When he was old enough to seek employment he realized his nationality was a detriment, or at least it was viewed as such by anyone who was looking for someone to hire.

Consequently, he legally changed his name to Patrick Clark. He married my grandmother, Mary Cassin in 1895 and they had seven children. He spent his life working on the railroad.

Of interest – there has been a Margaret Clery/Clark on the face of this earth since 1833. When I die this will be the last Margaret Clark!!

A bit of "trivia": In the book/movie "The Thornbirds" the name of the main character was Maggie Clery. Just think, that could have been a book about me!!

Mother and Son Share the Cody Family Story

Bob Cody

John A. Gibson wrote about his mother and their family's story: "I win, you lose." Do you remember those words we used when we play our childhood games? Well, sometimes we all lose. Such was the case when our Mother, Avalyn Laird Gibson died in early June 2000. She was 95 years old and the best of record searches tells us that at the time of her death, she had the greatest longevity of any member of the Michael and Anastasia Powers Cody family. She had faced much adversity in life, but true to the Michael and Anastasia Cody tradition, she persevered through it all.

She also had a historical memory that dated back to her earliest recollections of the Cody family in the early 1900's. She took pride in remembering Michael and Anastasia, their children, grandchildren, siblings and their descendants, and even in-laws and some of their family backgrounds. Cody family history was one, as she said, "of which all their family members can be proud." She would share those moments with anyone who took the time to listen. Ask Bob Cody. When he was initially putting together family information from Florence Cody's records, he called long distance to Mother, who was living in New Mexico. Bob said, after three hours on the phone he knew more than he thought he could ever know, and maybe more than he wanted to know. She literally brought to life the earlier generations of the Cody family through the stories and anecdotes she could recount so vividly. Such was Mother.

Mother was born near Marysville and lived in the area much of her life. As the Cody Clan in and around Union County dwindled, as did attendance at the family reunions, she made certain that all of us children attended the family gatherings. With great detail she would explain family relationships and our connection with them. She emphasized the importance of "family" and tried to instill in each of us a sense of family history. We spent much time with her Aunts Catherine Macken and 'Stasia' Grigsby, Uncles Ed, Dick and Jim Cody and with their children and grandchildren, the latter who were in our generation of Cody's. At the time it seemed boring, but in my later life, and to many others, it was a foundation to know who comprised the Cody Clan. When I moved to Wichita, Kansas in 1974, one of the first things Mother told me was to get in touch with Ralph and Ione Cody who lived there. She made a trip to Wichita from her home in New Mexico to see us, but spent considerable time with Ralph and Ione rekindling her "family ties." She seemed to know the whereabouts of many family members who were only a name to the rest of us.

In her declining years, Mother recognized her memory was failing so she made oral tapes of the family history and her reminiscences of the family. At the time of her death, she had difficulty remembering what she had for dinner, but the mention of Michael Cody or other family members, and she lit up like a

Christmas candle. With a wink and a smile, she could detail people, places and events, both humorous and poignant. Whenever we talked, one of her first questions invariably was, "Well, what's new in Marysville, and what do you hear from the Cody's?"

With ever-growing confidence, I remain heartened to assure her, "Mother, things are fine in Marysville, and the Cody's are still a close knit group."

Earlier John's mother, Avalyn Laird Gibson wrote her family story: "My maternal grandfather, Michael Cody, was born in County Tipperary, Ireland in 1833. When he was eighteen he, his parents, John and Margaret Croak Cody, four brothers, Thomas, John Jr., Edward, William, and two sisters, Bridget/Clara and Anna, emigrated to America. As the oldest son, he learned to work. Farm labor was in demand then, so that was what he turned to. When he was twenty-six, he had saved enough to buy a small tract of land about thirty acres. On it was a log cabin. Then Michael acquired a wife, Anastasia Powers, the daughter of other Irish immigrants, Jon and Catherine "Kitty" Connor Powers. Together they worked the land, purchased livestock, expanded the operation until they owned more than two hundred acres of fertile and well cared for land, and as much livestock as it would support.

"The family too increased with the years. Eight sons, John, Edmond, Michael T. William R. James, Richard, Emmet, Bernard, and four daughters, Margaret, Mary Laird, Catharine Macken, and Anastasia Grigsby, all lived to maturity.

"Mike never regretted leaving Ireland, although as long as he lived he thought of Ireland with affection. He was fiercely proud of the country he had adopted. "In the United States,' he said often, 'A man can be a man.' Over the years he changed in many ways, but his brogue never left him. He said 'Leftenant' for Lieutenant, and he never harnessed or hitched up the horses. He 'geared them up.' He was a strong Roman Catholic, and he adhered to its principles as well as some of the customs practiced by the Irish. He never ate eggs on Good Friday, although it was a fast day and meat was forbidden. Grandma [Anastasia] managed vegetarian meals.

Neither would he wear a hat in a funeral procession or attending a burial in a cemetery. It was a touching indication or respect that eventually led to his undoing.

"In 1909, when the two youngest boys were leaving home, one to a farm Bernard and the other, Emmet to go into a hat shop business with a cousin, William F. Cody. Grandpa sold the farm and livestock. Then he bought a substantial brick home in Marysville, 709 East Fifth Street. It was on a wide tree-lined street. He didn't become inactive. Each morning he read a chapter in the bible and prayers for the dead. Then he went outdoors to pick up any stray twig or leaf that had fallen, or removed dust that had invaded the barn at the back of the lot. Then he spent an hour, at least, reading the morning newspaper, interrupting his reading, usually with comments on the villainy of the human race. After his noon meal which was dinner, he walked uptown, almost a mile. If the weather was fine, he and four of his cronies assembled on the benches on the Union County Courthouse lawn, where they discussed politics, economics, and crops, for they were all transplanted farmers. If the weather was cold or rainy, the group met at a little neighborhood grocery that averaged about a customer an hour. At four-thirty the group dissolved. Grandpa stopped at Johnny Asman's to bring home meat for supper. He could never get over the miracle of having fresh beef every day. Yes, the United States was a wonderful country.

For several years Grandpa's appearance and habits did not alter. His carriage was as erect as in his youth, his mind as active.

"Then, 1915 ushered in bad news. His second oldest living grandson, Leland Laird, was accidently killed. World War I was in progress and Grandpa supported the allies. He was a violent partisan. The group at the courthouse broke up. Two of its members were pro-German. I'm not sure if it was ridiculous or pathetic, but it came about when Grandpa shook his fist under Nick Kiel's nose and said: 'If Germany is such a great country you should take your big mouth and your fat purse back to it. Have you no gratitude for the land that gave you the right to an opinion and a good living?'

"Early the next year, the husband of one of his daughters, Frank Mackan, Catherine's husband died leaving three children, two them were under school age. Grandpa promptly paid off the mortgage on the house, saying that he had given each of his sons a start, but he hadn't done much for his daughters. Now Kate would have a roof over her head. Then Grandma fell ill. Margaret, his oldest daughter had never married. She had taught school and then worked in a department store. She took over the household chores, and the care of her mother. The illness was a long one. Grandpa rejoiced over the armistice that ended World War I but his wife of nearly sixty years was slipping. She died a few days before Christmas in 1918.

Grandpa still took his daily walks. The courthouse group met again. Now the talk was mostly political. All were active Democrats. Nevertheless the record of each political aspirant was reviewed. They took the responsibility of voting seriously.

"The husband of my youngest aunt, James M. Grigsby, died suddenly on Christmas Eve 1919. He and his wife had just finished decorating the tree for Glenn and Joseph, their two young sons. They lived in Columbus twenty miles distant. Again, Grandpa went into action. Their house was a rented one, and the young man had no insurance. Anastasia shouldn't live in a city surrounded by strangers. She should be home with her family – at least until the shock wore off and she knew what she could do with her life. As soon as her husband was buried in the family plot in St. John's, now known as Our Lady of Lourdes Cemetery in Marysville, she should come home to Marysville. Arrangements were made to close her house and store the furniture in Grandpa's barn until the following spring.

"It turned cold the day after Christmas: first a blizzard and then temperatures of 10-15 degrees below zero. Some roads were impassable, but the main road between Marysville and Columbus were open.

"The funeral was at Holy Family Church in west Columbus. Grandpa planned to go. The family used every possible persuasion, then arguments. He was adamant. When he would not change his mind, the children conspired to get him into the most comfortable car for the long ride. In 1919, the most luxurious cars were drafty and the heaters were unreliable. None of this dismayed Grandpa. The church was even colder than the car, and draftier, for it was an old one. Riding back to the cemetery in Marysville he refused to put on his hat. He had never worn a hat in a funeral procession, and he wasn't about to begin now at the funeral of his youngest daughter's husband. He stood bareheaded at the cemetery while the prayers for the dead were said. If the wind had not been howling so that it drowned out some of the words, the chattering of teeth might have, but he showed no sign that the elements disturbed him.

Of course, the family adjourned to the old brick house after the burial. The customary visiting took place. The callers and family members disappeared gradually. After a light supper, Stasia said goodnight and took her little boys, Glenn and Joe Grigsby upstairs. She would stay with them until morning, for should they wake they would be frightened by the strange house. Poor children! They had enough confusion already.

"Grandpa retired a little earlier than usual. One son, Emmet, was staying overnight for he could not get a train to his home in a neighboring state until the next day.

"In the morning, the weather moderated a trifle. Grandpa resumed the usual routine, but didn't attempt a walk uptown. The next day, he suffered a chill followed by a rising temperature. Over his protests, his daughter called a doctor who diagnosed the illness as pneumonia. The following morning, Grandpa asked for a priest and the last rites of the Roman Catholic Church. When the priest was gone, he managed a few last words. 'I made my will right by the girls when Kate Mackan was left alone. Now I can die in God's own time, "which he did five hours later.

"Again, the Cody Clan gathered. Grandpa lay in state in the parlor. Three candles for the Blessed Trinity burned by at his head.

There were no flowers, for the greenhouse in town was in shambles. It seems that because of the extreme cold, the owner had over-fired the boilers and they had burst. All that remained were frozen plants, burst pipes and icicles.

"In keeping with family tradition, the dead were kept three days and three nights. As was customary at the time, someone sat with the dead. The family had discarded the Irish title of 'wake', which meant a deathwatch, but had been interrupted in some cases as a brawl. Each morning, a rosary was said by the family and callers.

"On the last night of the death watch, it was agreed that the sons and the two eldest grandsons should take part. By that time, the first shock and grief had passed. The gathering had taken on the character of a family reunion. Seven of the eight sons were still living, but John, who had died in his early thirties. They entered into the anecdotes and reminiscences about Grandpa until it seemed as if he might materialize at any time. Kind neighbors had provided enough food for a hundred. Ed, the oldest living Cody son, was delegated to keep the fire in the kitchen stove so that coffee was always readily available. Dick and Bernard had each brought a quart of their father's favorite whiskey. The evening that had begun in sorrow, mellowed. All had returned to the days of their youth when Dad was the law, the protector, and the counselor. With Dick's rendition of how Biddy Mackan insisted that he had put a spell on her cow: and she had called down disaster on him every time he passed her door. It was young Mike who urged quiet. He was in politics and didn't want the neighbors talking. Besides they were his neighbors, for he lived the third house over.

"As the crowd settled down, Will said, 'He was a good man. He lived by what he believed.' Then Ed spoke, 'It's too bad he couldn't be here. He would have enjoyed this.' The funeral mass was said the next day. The little church was filled; chairs were placed in the aisles; many crowded into the vestibule or stood on the steps outside.

"The sermon was based on Paul's First Letter to Timothy, Chapter 4, Verse 7; 'I have fought the good fight. I have finished the course. I have kept the faith.'

"Somehow, I feel that Chapter 5, Verse 8 would have made an interesting commentary: "But if anyone does not take care of his own, and especially of his household, he has denied the faith, and is worse than an unbeliever."

"Mike was a family man."

COINCIDENCE?

Ann Gentilini Cooper

Not being one who believes in coincidence, I believe the people we know or are aware of, the significant and even some of the insignificant, share our paths for a reason. Each weaves one or more threads in the tapestries that we name our lives. Threads light and dark, joyous and sorrowful intertwine as warp and woof overlap, twisting and turning in ways unexpected, in ways that take the design full circle. And so it has been with Bill and May; though I didn't know it until about 1990. Let's begin.

A funny thing happened one night in the late 60's, long after St. Mary of the Springs Academy had closed and shortly after the College of St. Mary of the Springs had become coeducational. One of the sisters made a frantic call to Bill, one of the maintenance men. "Come right now, Bill", she cried, "someone has stolen the Baby Jesus." Bill came and indeed, the Baby Jesus, part of a Christmas display was gone. Gone, too was the stone marker at the Sunbury Road entrance that read "School for Girls." Bill was asked to track down these items, but not to confront anyone, if he discovered them.

Discover them he did, in one of the dorm rooms. Waiting until the room became empty, he entered using his master key and removed the stolen goods. The sisters decided not to mention anything to the culprit. The Baby Jesus was put away; and Bill was told to take the stone and "break it to bits and use it in his garden." Yet one more time had Bill come to the aid of his employers.

25

Bill's employ had begun nearly 40 years before in 1929, at age seventeen. Borrowing his Uncle Robert's car, he drove from his home and began to mow the grass on St. Mary's campus in the summer months earning $15.00 per week. Bill never had another employer. He soon joined the permanent maintenance crew and continued to mow, fix, paint and take care of just about everything there was to mow, fix, paint and take care of at both the school and the Motherhouse. This care included the sisters.

In a time when the sisters were not permitted to drive, Bill became their chauffeur, driving them everywhere they needed to go -- to the doctor, to the dentist, and even to Somerset. His chauffeuring became so essential, that, when he received his draft notice for service in WWII, no one less than Reverend Mother, herself, personally petitioned the Draft Board for a deferment based on "necessity:" Apparently her arguments were persuasive. Bill never did get drafted.

He married and lived in a small house on St. Mary's campus. In time he started a family -- a son and a daughter. When his son developed a slight speech impediment, Sister Francis Xavier worked with him until he could speak well and rightly: His young daughter, Patricia Anne, made .her First Communion in the chapel. Afterward, surrounded by her family; she received many presents. One of her friends was a little Chinese girl, studying here and far, far from her own family in China. As Patricia Anne sat in front of all of her gifts, kind Bill noticed that the little Chinese girl had no presents at all. Without saying a word, Bill divided Patricia Anne's gifts in half and each girl had a very special day: Yes, Bill was extraordinary and his beloved sisters missed him greatly when he passed away in 1974.

When I think about my days at St. Mary's, I vaguely remember someone referring to a man named Bill. He blended in with other men doing chores around the Motherhouse and other buildings, mowing the grass, and taking care of the grounds. I remember catching sight of old nuns and young postulants and novices, wondering what their lives were like, as I daydreamed and stared out of classroom windows. I remember that everyone beyond that archway seemed to know each other well and. to be a sort of family; the maintenance men included. At the time, I didn't overly think about them. I was just aware of their presence.

I was much more aware of the woman named May. As a child, I remember hearing my mother speak about this best friend of hers. Just one year older than she, May arrived in mother's life when both were young women. Together they shared the joys of late girlhood, finding adventures in simple pleasures during the depression. They participated in many escapades -- once walking in the stylish shoes of the day from Peters Avenue, a street near Cleveland and 5th, to Mirror Lake on Ohio State's campus and back again. They soaked their much abused and sore feet in three separate dishpans of cool water upon returning to May's house. Inviting over their many friends, they rolled up the parlor rug and danced many a night away at each other's houses.

They saved their small wages, however, for their greatest pleasure of all -- the theater -- the Hartman Theater, to be precise, and many were the shows and stars they saw -- Paul Robeson, the famous Black baritone expatriate, who starred in Shakespeare's, Othello; Edith King, Victor Jorg, and Melvin Douglas, who were leads in the best stock companies of the day; and Maude Adams, who hailed all the way from the New York theater. Mother spoke so many times about May and the Hartman and the stars and the shows that brought so much joy to their youth.

May married Charles Weaver in 1933. She and he moved to Akron, where May got a fulltime job. Mom was working, too, and visits were few. Mom married in 1939 and soon was busy with a growing family: May; on the other hand, remained childless. When she was widowed early; she decided to stay in Akron, secure in her job and in her life there. May and Mom remained close, however, despite the distance. Whenever May visited her parents, she made an effort to contact Mom. Birthdays were always big days and not one would have been complete without a card and/or a call from the other. It was always a good day when Mom heard from May:

Mother's friendship with May Foley Weaver remained part of the backdrop of my childhood. Her presence was there, but I never gave it much thought. I graduated from St. Mary's, went to Europe, graduated from Ohio State, married, lived in several different states, had two daughters, got divorced, moved back to Columbus, and started working here. Throughout all of this time, Mom and Dad had remained in Columbus, and occasionally Mom still spoke to me of her dear friend, May.

In 1990 Mom was 79, able to get around, but clearly not doing so well physically. She moved slowly; but she still had a little of her sight. One day in spring, I mentioned to her that I would be presenting a workshop in Akron and I asked if she would like to come along. I told her that it would be an opportunity for her to see May again. We would stay overnight at a hotel in town; I would drop her off in the morning at May's house before my presentation, and pick her up at day's end for the return trip home. She was overjoyed and quickly called May to tell her about her upcoming visit.

With great anticipation each woman awaited "visit" day. It had been so many years since they had had a face-to-face visit and both were eager to see one another again. Things went just as we had planned. I dropped Mom off in the morning and when I returned later on I found two beautiful old ladies sitting in the soft late afternoon glow, each intently engaged in memories of long ago. When we finally left later that evening, they hugged each other tightly, each probably aware (and so it turned out) that this visit could be their last. May gave to Mom a Waterford crystal vase. Mom told me on the way home that she wanted me to have it, since she would never have gotten to see her friend so late in life had I not brought her there.

That day in Akron I learned that May; being Irish to her blood and bones, had a special interest in poetry: Indeed she followed Irish poets and writers avidly. After Mom died in 1993, I wrote and self-published a small book of poetry. On a whim, I decided to send May a copy: She was delighted and thus began .my own wonderful and very special relationship with Mom's dear friend, May.

May is now 91 years old. She has become my remarkably special and quite cherished friend. She calls and she writes, even though of late the writing has become more difficult for her. We check up on each other. We visit and when we do, we always have lunch at The Mustard Seed, a vegetarian restaurant in Montrose, not too far from her home. We talk about poetry and we share the stories of our lives. May reminisces about her girlhood with Mom and others whom I knew in childhood. We talk about places in Columbus, some of which are still here and some of which are gone. We talk of places we have been and things that we have seen. We talk of our families. I tell her of my children and grandchildren. I ask May to tell me again about hers coming to America from Ireland.

During one visit, she told me about her brother, Bill, mentioning that he had been one of the maintenance men at St. Mary's. She told me about all the mowing, the fixing, and the painting he had done for the school and for the Motherhouse. And all at once, I saw in my mind's eye that rear yard of St Mary's. Once again I saw myself back in that classroom staring out the window and hearing someone refer to a maintenance man called Bill. And all at once I knew. Bill Foley, May's brother, was Bill the maintenance man.

She told me about his children, of how Sister Francis Xavier had helped his son, and about Patricia Anne and the Chinese girl, and how Bill had helped each little girl have a special First Holy Communion day. She told me how Bill had become the "official" chauffeur for the sisters and how the Reverend Mother seemed to have played a role in persuading the Draft Board to grant him a deferment. She told me about the theft of the statue of the Baby Jesus and the removal of the "School for Girls" marker.

She told me that Bill had never broken up the stone marker to place on his garden, as the sister from long ago had suggested. Having obtained the written permission of the Mother General of the Dominican Sisters of St. Mary of the Springs, it will, instead, mark May's grave, when the time comes, acknowledging on the reverse side of the one reading, "School for Girls," her days among us. Fittingly the stone that marked the academy we knew and loved will rest quietly in disguised remembrance of that other time and place.

On one of my last visits, May gave me a lamp that Bill had made from the oak flooring of the Motherhouse. He and the other men had salvaged the wood from the old building just before it was torn down. That lamp lights my bedroom each night. It is the one I turn out before I sleep. It reminds me of May, of Mother, of St. Mary's, and it confirms my conviction that in all of life, there is no coincidence.

Patriarch Reveled in Customs of the Irish

Frank Copeland, Columbus Dispatch

As St. Patrick's Day step-dances its way into the limelight, I like to think of one-time Columbus leprechaun Murt Byrne.

In the early 1970s, when I met him, Murt stood out as an authority figure to be reckoned with.

Barrel-chested and imposing, he seemed to rule over a part of the South Side (where he lived) as well as a certain domain of county government (where he worked).

When an Irish minstrel once wrote, "He's got an arm like a leg and a punch that would sink a battleship," he might well have been referring to Murt.

A timid youth who was friends with his children, I simply sought the far edges of his peripheral vision.

In the late '70s, after the family moved from the South Side to the North, I didn't stay on the fringes of the Byrne household for long. Instead, I was swept in by his warm, gregarious nature.

And I quickly discovered that I had little to fear.

"The Old Man" would often hold court on the back porch of his home in the Clintonville neighborhood, with Irish music pulsing from a cassette player. Stories would be told and songs sung, with people wandering in and out.

The next thing I knew, I was throwing darts, buying Clancy Brothers albums and carrying a Shamrock Club membership card in my wallet.

Like many other Irish families, the Byrnes saw – and still see – St. Patrick's Day as the high-water mark of the year.

When March 17 rolled around, Murt would don a green corduroy costume and emerge as a jolly, twinkling-eyed elf.

He ingratiated himself to most everyone as the official Shamrock Club leprechaun, mugging for cameras and giving candy to youngsters until he ran out. A green spectacle of joy, he infected gatherings with the happiness he felt.

A devout Roman Catholic, he didn't miss Sunday Mass. A loyal son of Erin, he took several trips to Ireland and devoted himself to the Shamrock Club, serving as president and being honored by the club members as "Irishman of the year."

In the succeeding decades, the Byrne children and I grew up.

Then, one day, in the summer of 1983, Murt felt something in his mouth. The discovery marked the beginning of a years-long battle with cancer.

His first surgery hindered his ability to speak – especially hurtful to a man with a gift for blarney. Another operation left him without a portion of his jaw.

And he lost so much weight, he was hardly recognizable.

His true strength came to the fore during his illness: His family and extended family (the Shamrock club) rallied around him, and he found essential support in his faith.

Instead of letting the disease get him down, Murt seemed just to go on being Murt.

Though harder to understand, he always found a way to make himself understood. Though physically diminished, he never let his joyful Irish spirit be stifled.

In November 1995, a few days before Murt died, I saw him one last time.

He was at home in a hospital bed surrounded by his family, with Tommy Makem singing *Rambles of Spring* from a compact-disc player:

> *I've a fine felt hat*
> *And a strong pair of brogues*
> *I have rosin in my pocket for*
> *my bow*
> *And my fiddle strings are new*
> *And I've learned a tune or two*
> *So I'm well-prepared to rumble and must go.*

Looking up at me with those twinkling eyes, Murt pointed heavenward.

He had little doubt he was headed for a meeting with St. Patrick himself, and he was more than ready.

Brian Byrne, Murt's son shared a few more facts and reflections regarding his father and family history. His father's long 12 year bout with cancer did give Brian additional years and memories to share with his dad and now that he, Brian, is a father himself it put the family traditions of St. Patrick's Day and being Irish in proper order for him.

As to the family background Brian said that his grandfather Murdith "Pete" Byrne arrived at a Nova Scotia port from Ireland. Pete was a bricklayer/mason and found work in Chicago and eventually came to Columbus, Ohio. He helped construct the LeVeque Tower and Ohio Stadium. Pete decided to stay in Columbus, thankfully, because the boat going back to Ireland sank in route. Now you know more of the story.

A "Mixed Marriage" German and Irish

Annie Curran

My grandparents - George Pierce of the Railroad Pierces (but he was on a debit for Prudential Insurance!) was one of five Irish brothers - 1st generation. My Nana Tresa Sattler, was of German descent. They told stories of their school days when they walked to their own parish schools, which happened to be in the "others" neighborhoods. The German kids had to cross the Irish kids' neighborhoods to get to their school, and vice versa. Daily fisticuffs. They were each told to distrust each other.

When my grandparents married in 1907, it was considered a "mixed marriage" - German and Irish. Nobody thought they'd ever make it. They actually lasted 'til death did them part.

When I was a child in Lima, OH, I attended St. Gerard parish school, and the street names in my neighborhood were Murphy, Runyon, O'Connor, etc. Of course the kids' names were the same, or Sullivan, or Walsh, O'Brien .... adults hung out at Paddy Mac's ... At our house (and school) we sang all kinds of Irish songs, and at Christmas we sang Oh Tannumbaum .... these were the only "ethnic" activities my small family observed BECAUSE when my parents married, they decided that they would not just observe one of their cultures (both of them are half German/half Irish) BECAUSE of the prejudices they observed growing up in Toledo ... funny, huh?

My mom says that I am half and half, but Gerry, my husband, is a big whole .... !!

Papa always said:

1.   Never open a bottle unless you intend to finish it at that sitting.
2.   With some .people it is always an ass or an elbow (always something wrong about them...)

Poker Winner Gets the Funeral

Kathleen Hayes Davis

Around 1925 in Columbus Ohio, there was a group of first generation Irishmen who played poker together on a regular basis. Among these men was Thomas Miles McGurty, my maternal grandfather, who was a foreman for the Pennsylvania Railroad. Two of the other poker players were Mike Ryan of the Egan-Ryan Funeral Home and his friendly business rival Duke O'Shaughnessy of the O'Shaughnessy Funeral Home.

One evening Duke asked this question, "Tom, who is going to bury you? Will it be Mike or myself?" Tom thought a moment and then came up with this position, "Well, I've got an idea. Let's have you two play one hand of poker and see who wins the right to my burial." The game proceeded and Duke won hands down. In 1929 when Tom passed away, he was buried by the O'Shaughnessy Funeral Home. An Irishman is as good as his word.

The Columbus Blarney Stone

Mark Dempsey, Grandson of Edward "Red" Dempsey

In a quaint part of Columbus, known as German Village, lived a man named Jack Dempsey. Within his small backyard, family members and neighbor friends played baseball. These children would mark the bases except for home plate. There was a naturally protruding rock used as home plate.

Over the years, Mr. Dempsey grew tired of ruining his lawnmower blade on this protruding rock used as home plate. One afternoon, Mr. Dempsey began to dig the rock out of his yard in an effort to alleviate the stress caused while mowing the lawn. It didn't take long for Mr. Dempsey to realize the scope of the job was bigger than one man could handle.

Jack called his brother, Edward, known as "Red", to come over and assist him. As the two of them continued to dig, they had unearthed a four hundred pound behemoth. They celebrated their accomplishment by relaxing with a few drinks. At some point, they thought it would be a good idea to drag the stone around the corner to an establishment known as the Olde Mohawk Grill at Mohawk and Kossuth. So they loaded the dirty boulder onto a dolly and traveled the two blocks to celebrate their treasure.

Being that the owner was a Frenchman, Frank Brussard, the Dempsey brothers knew that their treasure may not be welcomed; so as they entered through the back door, hoisted the rock on the bar, at Jack's regular location, while no one was looking. Needless to say, the owner was a bit concerned having this very large and very dirty rock in his establishment and immediately told the Dempsey's to leave. They complied, leaving the rock behind.

The Dempsey brothers proceeded to the McSweeney household to tell Pat McSweeney what home plate had become and what they had left at the Olde Mohawk. Word spread quickly and the Olde Mohawk was the place to be to view "the miracle".

After several days of this large, dirty rock sitting on the bar, the owner had enough. He offered anyone in the bar free drinks for the night to anyone that could re-move the rock. At some point, an unidentified man of great physical stature, attempted to remove the rock from the bar.

He actually lifted this 400-pound rock off the bar. But his bravado was out-matched by the weight of the rock. He dropped the stone to the floor, which immediately gave way falling to basement below. This was a tragic situation. The Olde Mohawk was known for their turtle soup and, as legend has it, the turtles were from the Olde Mohawk basement. Rumor is that a turtle or two may have perished.

In the end, Frank Brussard convinced the four men to take their Irish treasure away from his establishment or face banishment from the Olde Mohawk. The Frenchman knew how to hit home and they removed the rock, painted it a disgusting green color and called it the Columbus Blarney Stone.

To date, the Blarney Stone has been an icon in the Shamrock Club of Columbus history. Regularly attending City Hall when the officers of the Club would meet with the Mayor of Columbus to have the Proclamation of St. Patrick's Day signed. In 1968, the Columbus Blarney stone was dedicated to the first Irishman of the Year and it has be-come the trophy for those who have received this coveted distinction from the Shamrock Club.

As these Irishman of the Year have been named, they have the opportunity to "maintain" the Blarney Stone for one year, usually placed at their office or favorite establishment. Throughout the years, it was a great honor of any establishment to have this local cultural icon as an attraction in their bar or restaurant.

Unfortunately, the security of the Columbus Blarney Stone was overlooked and on occasion, the 400-pound rock would come up "missing". It is believed to have come up "missing" for the first time in 1972, from the Clock Restaurant front window. (Known at the Elevator Bar today)

The endeavors of the Columbus Blarney Stone have a varied history and are the topic of many yarns spun over and over again. Some of the stories could be Chapter Two of this bedrock of a story in Columbus Irish history.

James Augustine Devine Sr.

James A. Devine Jr.

James Augustine Devine Sr. was born in Roxabell, Ohio on April 25, 1874. Roxabell is near the town of Frankfort about fifty miles southwest of Columbus. James' father, John Devine was the son of Richard Devine from County Derry Ireland and James' mother, Mary Goodwin came from County Longford, Ireland. John and Mary Devine had another son, named Michael. John Devine was a farmer who had "earned" the money to purchase his land by fighting as a substitute for another man in the Civil War.

Young James Devine will now be referred to as Jim, for that is how he preferred to be addressed, graduated from high school at the age of sixteen and worked on his father's farm for a few months and then became the deputy postmaster for three years. His next job was working for a Mr. Blue, who owned a mercantile and machinery business.

On October 30, 1895 Jim married Matilda Florence Coyner. Matilda preferred to be called Maude and will be referred to by that name. Maude and Jim had two sons; Richard and Thomas. In 1897 Jim was appointed deputy sheriff of Ross County and his family moved to Chillicothe. In 1900, he was elected sheriff – the only Democratic candidate elected in the county in what was a Republican landslide. Jim and Maude attended St. Mary's Church in Chillicothe where Jim's cousin, Reverend Alfred Dexter, was the pastor there.

While serving as sheriff Jim was responsible for the jail and the care of the prisoners, which included the preparation of their meals. One of Jim's favorite meals was potato soup that included turnips. His son, James Jr. attests to this food preference because he has written that as a child, when this soup was served, he had to sit at the table until he had finished his serving of soup, which he despised. Apparently there was one of the prisoners who also disliked potato/turnip soup and spilled his soup and turnips over the cell's floor along with some colorful language as to his opinion of Sheriff Devine's cooking skills. Now in the jails of those days there were no fire extinguishers on the walls instead they had long, big hoses on round cylinders with big nozzles. Sheriff Jim took the hose turned on the water and cleaned the cell floor; in the process he knocked the prisoner with the water's force from wall to wall. It was reported that no one ever criticized Sheriff Jim's potato/turnip soup again as long as Jim was sheriff.

In 1911, Jim was appointed by Governor Harmon to be examiner for the Ohio Building and Loan Association. After one year, he was appointed head of the department. Later he started working for the association in Columbus. The 1915 Columbus city directory listed him as an inspector for the Ohio State Department of the Building and Loan Association; at this time his residence was 1266 Bryden Road. Jim was a delegate to the 1920 Democratic National Convention in Chicago when the party elected Ohio governor, James Cox to run for president.

Governor Cox was trounced by his Republican opponent, Warren G. Harding who became president. After his defeat Governor Cox retired from politics. Then Jim became the executive secretary of the Ohio Building and Loan Association. Jim lobbied on the state and national levels for this state organization. He successfully lobbied against unfair taxation on dividends in Washington D.C. Details of her death is not known, but Maude died at the age of fifty on October 17, 1925 in Frankfort. She is buried at Green Lawn Cemetery in Frankfort.

Ann Florence Nerny was working in Columbus as the office manager for the Deshler-Wallick Hotel and at this time Jim booked a lot of convention and meetings there. The paths of Jim and Ann crossed and they started dating. In time they decided to marry and since Ann was close to a Reverend Charles Mulvey she wanted to be married at his new church in New York City. So on November 3, 1931 Jim and Ann were married in St. Vincent Ferrer Church in New York.

Ann and Jim moved to 2427 Brentwood Avenue in Bexley. They had two children; Mary Ann and James Jr. They attended Holy Rosary Church. Both Jim and Ann loved to laugh – Jim was a great storyteller. They were both staunch Democrats and F.D.R. supporters. They also shared a love of horse racing and gambling. They attended the biggest horse race of the century –The War Admiral/Seabiscuit race at Pimlico on November 1, 1938 betting on the winner, Seabiscuit.

Before the birth of their son, James Jr., Jim and Ann went on the trip to Ireland with their daughter, Mary Ann and a close family friend, Peter Dempsey. They had a wonderful time and traveled for three weeks. They visited family on the trip, but it is not remembered which branch. On this trip they hired a car and driver to take them through Ireland. They gradually made their way to the North of Ireland and about one mile from the Northern Ireland's border their driver pulled the car over to the area on the side of the road – got out – and started to walk away. Jim got out and accosted him and asked where he was going for they had not yet reached their destination near Belfast. The driver told Jim to drive himself and to pick him, the driver, up on the way back. When Jim asked the reason why the driver refused to take them to their destination the driver replied that he had a warrant for his arrest in Northern Ireland because he was an officer in the IRA. The driver said that he would see them in two or three days on Jim's way out at a certain pub in the town that they had just passed. Then the driver walked away.

The travelers continued on into Northern Ireland minus their driver. When they headed south again they returned to the village pub and their driver resumed his duties. The travelers returned home with an interesting anecdote to add to their memories.

In 1940 Jim had a stroke and was no longer able to work. He retired from the Building and Loan Association. Ann returned to work and they moved to Fairwood Avenue. In 1945 Jim suffered a massive stroke and was told that he would never walk again. But with a will to succeed he learned to walk again and he helped Ann support their children by taking a job as a night watchman for the Ohio Armory. He rode the trolley to work every night.

His daughter remembers a story from this time period. One summer in the middle of the night, Ann woke up her daughter. Jim had not come at his normal time and Ann was worried. Since it was summer, the windows were open. As they were getting dressed to go look for him, they heard his booming laugh. Jim had decided to stop off at a home about four doors down, where an Irish wake was being held for a neighbor. He had thought his wife would be asleep and he could just slip into bed a bit late. Anne was not pleased and Jim was in trouble.

Jim had a total of seven strokes- the last one was fatal and he entered a coma. He died at Columbus State Hospital on March 20, 1948.

James Devine led a full life from 1900 on he had been active in state political circles; he had been influential in the building and loan industry and had been a member of many social, fraternal and professional organizations. He is fondly remembered today as a charter member and the first president of The Shamrock Club of Columbus. In obituaries, two Columbus newspapers in giving a recitation of Jim's life facts also lauded his personal qualities and virtues giving good testimonials for a man who had led a rich and varied life. Jim and Ann had already decided that he would be buried next to his first wife, Maude. So he is buried in Frankfort's Greenlawn Cemetery.

The O'Farrell's – Famine Immigrants

Anne O'Farrell DeVoe

Only bits and pieces of stories are available from my father's side of the family. This may be typical of the Irish immigrants who left Ireland during the "Great Hunger", the 1845-1848 years of famine. During that time Ireland lost half of its population to death from starvation and illness and to emigration.

It took all their strength and courage to survive and come to America and make their way in a New World. There was little time to share memories or tell stories. And often the memories were so painful no one could talk about them. In America life was hard too so the Irish had to keep going just to survive.

My great great grandparents Bernard and Julia Conway O'Farrell were born in County Longford. They were married in Killashee Parish in 1839. They had four daughters from 1840-1845. They probably left Ireland in 1847, known as "Black 47", the worst of the famine years. They and their four daughters, aged two - seven, survived the crossing and settled briefly in Philadelphia. They soon made their way to Ohio settling in Chapel Hill in Perry County.

My great grandfather, James O'Farrell was baptized in the small Catholic Church in Chapel Hill in October of 1847. James was the first son, and Bernard and Julia went on to have four sons. Their births rounded out the family of four sons born in Ohio and four daughters born in Ireland.

My great grandfather, James married Bridget Haughran and settled in Corning, Ohio, a little town next to Chapel Hill. They had eight children, five daughters and three sons before Bridget died; sometime after 1885, when their youngest son, Bernard was born.

Charles James O'Farrell, my grandfather, was their oldest child. He was born in August of 1875. Little has been said about my grandfather's childhood. He did go to teacher's college in Indiana as a young adult and it was there that he met Jenny Mae Barnes. They both became teachers and eventually married settling in Corning, Ohio in the early 1900's. Charles and Jenny had two daughters, Genevieve and Josephine before they moved to Napoleonville, Louisiana where my father, Robert James was born in 1909.

In Napoleonville Grandfather O'Farrell was the lead schoolteacher but the family left Louisiana in 1913 after the death of their daughter, Genevieve from diphtheria. My father was four years old when they left and settled on a farm near Erie, Pennsylvania.

My grand father taught school in Erie and they farmed to make ends meet. Eventually in high school, my father was allowed to go to Erie Academy. He had attended the first eight years of school at his father's school and this new school was somewhat different.

After my Dad's youngest sister, Rosemary, graduated from High School in 1931 my grand parents returned to Corning. A monsignor from St. Mary's Parish in Lancaster, Ohio came to Corning that summer and recruited, my Grand father to teach math at St. Mary's High School in Lancaster.

Granddad O'Farrell was one of four men who started the Boy Scouts in Lancaster in 1931. He also taught my mothers siblings at St. Mary's. During a visit to see his parents in Lancaster, my dad saw my mother Helen Tooill playing tennis one morning before she went to work. The story goes that he was smitten and asked to be introduced! They married at the end of World War II at St. Mary's Church in Lancaster, Ohio!

My grandfather did not live to see any of his children marry; dying in August of 1940. His six grandsons and one granddaughter never met our grandfather "Professor O'Farrell". However we "inherited" his love and commitment to education. All of us were fortunate enough to attend college and many have obtained advanced degrees.

To avoid starvation and death, my great-great grandparents fled from Ireland. Their descendants have scattered across America but have prospered in this New Land.

I, Anne O'Farrell-DeVoe, great-great granddaughter of Bernard and Julia Conway O'Farrell of County Longford, am in awe of and thankful for their faith and courage to come to America to start a new life and for handing down to us our faith and our Irish heritage.

The O'Toole's Became the Tooill's

Anne O'Farrell DeVoe

My mother's maiden name was Tooill. The story we heard growing up was that Joseph O'Toole, my great grandfather changed his last name to fight in the Spanish American War. It seemed perfect to me because my father was an O'Farrell and with two "O" surnames I knew I was really Irish.

This story went unchallenged until the 1980's when a long lost cousin, George Snively, came to Central Ohio looking for a relative or two. His mother, Mary Tooill, of the Lancaster-Columbus area had relocated to the Southwestern United States before he was born.

George was surprised to find more than 200 Tooill relatives (and still counting). They are the descendants of Oliver and Clara Cooney Tooill. It seems that Mary Tooill Snively, George's mother was the daughter of George Tooill, my grandfather's older brother. Apparently George moved to Columbus where Mary was raised. George Snively and several of my Tooill cousins have filled in the real story of my great grandfather's name change.

My great great grandfather, Padric O'Toole was born in 1794 in Ireland; we are unsure of the county. Padric was forced into the British Army at the age of eighteen and forced to fight in the War of 1812 against the newly formed United States. He decided he did not want to fight against the Americans and left the British Army by hiding in a barn in upstate New York while the "Redcoat " British soldiers searched for him. He apparently was protected by the local Americans.

Padric remained in America and eventually found his way to Philadelphia. In Philadelphia he met Mary Anne Farry, Irish lass whose Irish county of origin we are not sure. Mary Anne and Padric married and moved westward.

They settled at Chapel Hill, Perry County in Ohio. Family history states that Padric was a craftsman making cabinets and other wooden furniture. Their son, Joseph O'Toole, my great grandfather was born in Chapel Hill. Joseph was a teenage when he went off to join the Union Forces to fight in the Civil War but his father, Padric, went after him. Joseph ran off again and again Padric went after him. The third time Joseph ran off, he changed his surname by dropping the "O" and changing Toole to Tooill. This time Padric did not find Joseph and he died before Joseph returned to Ohio.

Joseph met Rachel DuValle in Maryland and married her bringing his French-speaking bride back to Ohio. They settled in the Fairfield/Perry County area. They had eleven children but only even lived to adulthood. My grandfather Oliver Tooill was their youngest child. George Snively's grandfather was one of their oldest children.

Learning the "real story" of the Tooill name has had several consequences. Second and third cousins have been discovered in the Central Ohio area. My Tooill cousins in Lancaster were surprised to find that the O'Toole children they went to high school with are relatives. Our already large family had become much bigger.

A great, great granddaughter of Padric and Mary Anne O'Toole wrote this story.

The Canty Family

Eileen Canty Dine

Memories of our family and my childhood are some of my favorite. I grew up in a big Irish Catholic family of seven girls, two boys. I was the sixth of the nine: Catherine Jane, John Patrick, Margaret Mary, Mary Ellen, Patricia Ann, Eileen Frances, Rita Theresa, Michael Thomas, and Alice Marie.

Both parents were born in Ireland. Mom, Mary (Foran but changed to Ford) Canty, was born in Castleisland, County Kerry and Dad, John Canty, was born in Abbeydorney, County Kerry. Mom was 6 years old when she came to this country with her family. Dad was 22yrs old when he arrived, by himself, in this country. They both came by way of Ellis Island. My parents met at a party given in his honor to welcome him to America.

I remember a happy home, full of love, fun and Irish Music. Mom was always cooking, doing laundry and cleaning. She knew how to manage the family though. Dad worked two jobs so she was our "boss" and she knew how to assign responsibilities, so that no matter how young you were, you had a job to do. However, she also knew how to have a good time. She was very witty and full of blarney. She was like one of the kids and my dad used to say once in awhile that she was worse than the kids were.

Mom was a very funny lady. I guess you would have to have a good sense of humor to have nine kids. We had rules though, and we were pretty good kids...most of the time. We played many games outside with the neighbor kids and had to come in when the Angelus played at Sacred Heart Church.

After dinner, we all knelt down beside the couch or chairs in the living room, and prayed the Rosary. Prayer was number one in Mom's life and she did her best to make it number one in ours too. Often times, as a little girl, I would wake up early to go to the bathroom and I would see my mom kneeling beside her bed praying before everyone got up. That left a tremendous impression on me. She did that to her dying day. My aunt, who was a nun, used to say, "Your mother is a very Holy lady. She prays more than the nuns." It did seem that if mom prayed for something it always worked out for the best. We asked her to pray for us over the years, even as adults.

Dad was a hard worker and got very little sleep. You can imagine keeping nine kids quiet on Saturday morning so Dad could sleep in, but we managed. Dad played the accordion in his "spare time", with one of his Irish buddies who played the fiddle. We had many "sessions" in our basement with lots of music, singing, dancing and of course a few beers. My dad's buddy had been a dance master in Ireland and taught me my first steps. He would tell me in his thick, booming Irish brogue, "Your timing is perfect, I'd give ye' first every time!" That began my love of the dance.

It was not until I was 12 yrs. old though, that I actually became a part of a dance class, along with my sister, Rita Theresa. The Shamrock Club sponsored someone to teach us Irish dancing. My sister and I were picked among a group of 12 to dance at the Neil House at the Shamrock Club's St. Patrick's Day Breakfast. Unfortunately, that teacher did not last long and it was not until I was in my 20s that I found out about Ann Richens, from Dayton, Ohio. I contacted her and put her in touch with Joan Shanahan and Fran Murphy and they hired her to teach Irish dancing in Columbus. I enjoyed many years of dancing and wish I could still be involved with it, but age creeps up on you and other things become a priority. I am happy that Ann has made dancing so successful in Columbus and so happy that the Irish community is so strong. "Now," as Paul Harvey says, "you know the rest of the story."

I pray God's richest blessings on all who are so involved in the Irish community, keeping it strong and making your own memories. Do not ever forget to keep Our Lord number one in your life and He will make your life prosperous and then you will have good success.

Thanks for the opportunity to share a little about The Canty family

Julia L. Dorrian's Family Story

Julia L. Dorrian

The second to speak to the Catholic Record Society was Julia L. Dorrian. Julia is currently serving as a judge of a Franklin County Municipal Court. Julia acknowledged the presence of family members; father, Hugh Dorrian; mother, Janice Dorrian; Uncle John Dorrian; Aunt Nora Dorrian; and Aunt Mary (Dorrian)

Pulsinelli (married to Frank Pulsinelli). She noted that she is the daughter of Hugh James Dorrian and Janice Mary Flynn. Julia is married to David J. Robinson and together they have one son, Hugh Dorrian Robinson. Julia has three siblings: Margaret Macrina (Dorrian) Lombardo (married to Vaughn Lombardo); Mary Kathleen (Dorrian) Jeffrey (married to Dennis Jeffrey); and Hugh Joseph Dorrian (married to Poyee Poon). She has nine Dorrian nieces and nephews: Patrick, Grace, Bridget and Maggie Lombardo; Joe, Eileen and Thomas Jeffrey; and Catherine and Joseph Dorrian. Julia's other aunts and uncles were not able to attend: Julia (Dorrian) Hughes (now deceased); Sister Mary Macrina Dorrian, R.S.M.; Michael J. Dorrian (now deceased; married to Mary Martha Weber); Margory (Dorrian) Fadley (married to Richard Raymond Fadley, now deceased); Thomas Flynn (now deceased, married to Janet Harty, (deceased); Hubert "Bud" Flynn (now deceased, married to Arlene Skolinsky, deceased); John Patrick "Pat" Flynn (married to Audrey Wagner, deceased); and Richard Flynn (married to Mary Smith).

Relating to a question "How did your Irish Catholic family get into Politics?" posed by Pat Mooney, president of the Catholic Society, Julia said that she felt that one of the best things about running for public office is that as you are campaigning you are frequently meeting people who know other members of your big, Irish Catholic family. She says that she is always proud to be related to any of the Dorrian or Flynn family members.

In true Irish Catholic tradition she is named after her father's oldest sister, Julia, as well as her maternal grandmother, Lillian (Engel) Flynn. Lillian is Julia's middle name. Keeping up this tradition Julia named her 16-month-old son Hugh Dorrian Robinson. The afternoon of the Catholic Record Society Meeting Julia's husband David J. Robinson stayed home with young Hugh so Julia could come to the meeting.

Julia noted that many in Columbus know of and about the Dorrians so she started by sharing a bit about her mother's Irish

Flynn family roots. Julia's mother, Janice, came to Columbus from Yonkers, New York in 1964 when she married Julia's father, Hugh.

Janice Flynn Dorrian's family consisting of such wonderful Irish stock; Hogan's, Flynn's and McGuckins, all hail from the New Jersey and New York area. Janice's paternal grandparents, John Flynn and Bridget Hogan emigrated from Ireland around the 1860's. Janice's maternal great grandparents, Michael McGuckin and Susan McAvoy emigrated from Ireland around 1830. Various members of Mrs. Hugh Dorrian's family have a long history of public service. Julia's grandfather, Thomas Augustine Flynn, served in WWI and received a silver star for saving a comrade during military action in France. Julia had three uncles serving in the navy at the same time during WWII; their mother, Lillian, had a very anxious time with three sons serving at the same time. These same grandfather and uncles served as firefighters in Yonkers, New York and she has a cousin who is continuing the family tradition by currently serving as a Yonkers firefighter. Julia's brother carried on the family naval tradition by attending the Naval Academy. There are even a couple of the Flynn's in the funeral business in Yonkers. Uncle John Flynn founded the funeral home and his sons and grandsons now operate it. Certainly public service is strong" in both the Flynn and Dorrian families and that is part of whom she, Julia, is and that's why she wanted to share both sides of her family with the members of the society.

Coming back to the Dorrian clan Julia said that the Dorrians came to the United States in 1920. Julia's grandfather, Hugh Joseph Dorrian was born in Coatbridge, Scotland of Irish parents who had come to Scotland from County Donegal near Letterkenny Ireland. Hugh Dorrian first came to Halifax, Nova Scotia and then on to Pittsburgh by way of Niagara Falls. In Pittsburgh he met his wife Anne Agnes O'Flaherty who had come from Renvyle in County Galway. Anne came through Ellis Island to Pittsburgh because she had family member who had settled there earlier. Anne O'Flaherty worked for the Andrew Mellon family as a kitchen servant. Julia Dorrian's grandfather told her Father that if the Irish boys wanted to meet the Irish girls they would go to the servant quarters of the wealthy families.

At that time her grandfather Dorrian was working in a meatpacking factory in Pittsburgh. Her grandparents married and they moved to Wheeling W.Va. where seven of their eight children were born, including Julia's Father Hugh James Dorrian. They moved to Columbus in 1937 where their eighth child, her Uncle John was born. The Dorrians were raised at 740 Campbell Avenue in Franklinton, just west of the Scioto River Downtown, an area then referred to as "the Bottoms". Her grandfather worked at the David L. Davies meat packing plant located near what is now Dodge Park. Later Papa Dorrian owned his own grocery business, Dorrian's Market at St. Clair and Leonard Avenue on the near East Side of Columbus downtown. The Dorrian family attended Holy Family Church and the children attended Holy Family Grade School and Holy Family High School. Julia's Father Hugh and her Uncle John graduated from St. Charles High School.

Referring to her family's Catholic traditions Julia remembered that she was told by her father that his father used to tell him ..."Don't let anyone leave this door hungry." as beggars would keep coming by Dorrian's Market and her grandfather always gave them something to eat whether they could pay for it or not. Her Grandma Anne would say "Get your education, work hard and keep your faith in God." (A maxim later repeated by Julia's father, Hugh Dorrian, when he spoke to others in the group that afternoon.) Those philosophies or life lessons have remained with Julia.

Talking about the Dorrian family and politics Julia talked about her Uncle Mike Dorrian, a Franklin County Commissioner from 1969 through 1984. She recounted that in 1955 Mike and John Jones formed the Westside Democrats Club on the basement of a local establishment, Polly's Bar, on Sullivant Avenue. Julia's father, Hugh James Dorrian, joined the club and they were big supporters of Mayor Maynard E. Sensenbrenner. Mayor Sensenbrenner had an up and down career being elected first in

1950, losing a bid for re-election and then being elected again in the 1960's. In 1964 Mayor Sensenbrenner appointed Mike Dorrian as the assistant Safety Director for the City of Columbus serving with Fred Simon who was a long-time, good family friend. In 1968 Uncle Mike Dorrian ran for County Commissioner with Harold Cooper. They won that year which was a surprise because it was a Republican year.

Julia was born in 1965 and that was the year her father, Hugh Dorrian, first ran for office as City Auditor and that time he lost the election. The Dorrian family, are happy to say that he has won every election since that time. In 1966 he was appointed City Treasurer and he said he didn't want to take the position, But Mayor Sensenbrenner summoned him into his office and said to him," Dorrian, when you are called, you serve." Dad served. Julia went on to say that her father, Hugh Dorrian, feels that the two biggest influences leading him to follow a career in public office were his brother Mike and Mayor Sensenbrenner. After attending O.S.U. for two quarters, Hugh Dorrian went into the Army and when he came back he wanted to work for his brother, Mike Dorrian who had a bricklaying business at the time. His brother summoned him and told him that he, Hugh, was going back to college and he was going to get his degree. Dad did just that. In 1969 Dad ran and won the election for City Auditor and since that time he has served with five mayors and 44 Council Members including Jerry O'Shaughnessy and Maryellen O'Shaughnessy.

In true political tradition Julia remembers being born and bred in a political atmosphere. She remembered as a child being in the garage of her home where people were painting campaign signs. She felt it was like door-to-door Central working with the O'Shaughnessy's and the O'Grady's. As an adult she is still glad to be working with the O'Shaughnessy's and the O'Grady's and she is grateful for their support over the years. She first ran for an election in November 2003 and began her service as a Franklin County Municipal Court Judge January 7, 2004. Julia was recently re-elected in November 2009 to another six-year term.

HUGH JOSEPH and ANNA FLAHERTY DORRIAN FAMILY
JULIA DORRIAN HUGHES
MARGARET DORRIAN (SISTER MACRINA, RSM)
MARY DORRIAN PULSINELLI
MICHAEL J. DORRIAN – deceased
NORA DORRIAN
MARGORY DORRIAN FADLEY
HUGH JAMES DORRIAN
JOHN DORRIAN

Sister Mary Macrina (Margaret) Dorrian, RSM

We were born of Scotch-Irish parents who met in Pittsburgh, Pennsylvania, married, moved to Wheeling, WV, and thence to Columbus, Ohio. Dad left Coatbridge, Scotland at age 12 after the death of his father, to be raised by aunts in Donegal, Ireland. He came to America through Canada at age 20. Mom was born and raised in County Galway, Ireland and came the USA after the death of both parents. She came through Ellis Island, NY with her sister, Nora and brother, "Uncle Bobby", the youngest of 9 Flaherty children. They came in 1920, sponsored by another brother, Steve, who had preceded them to Pittsburgh.

In Pittsburgh, Mom resided with another sister, "Aunt Mary" and Jim Madigan on the third floor of their home at 84 Wyoming Street. When tears were dried, she took a position in the home of the prominent Mellon family in Pittsburgh as 'upstairs maid' and guardian of their children.

One story told of her meeting Dad when he came to the Mellon home with a Nursery to work in the garden. Thirst brought him to the kitchen door seeking a drink of water. He was instead welcomed into the kitchen for tea and a new friendship was born. Young immigrants from Ireland frequently met to dance and sing of their heritage on weekends and holidays.

Five years passed and their union was blessed in marriage at the Cathedral of St. Peter and Paul in Pittsburgh. The newlyweds found a home in Wheeling, WV where our great Uncle Ed's family had settled and "Aunt Nora" and "Uncle John" were welcomed. Dad started work at Schenk's meat packing plant where despite layoffs he stayed until it closed in 1936. During those years seven children were born in the Dorrian family. Wonderful neighbors, the Cannon's, helped Dr. Jones to deliver those born at home as midwife, then as barber, as grocer, as sponsors in baptisms, and as companions going to school (at St. Joseph's downtown), while Mom stayed at home with the youngest. These neighbors later drove us to our new home in Columbus where Dad had found work at the David Davies packing plant.

We lived next to Bellows Avenue School and had plenty of space to play ball or go to Sunshine Park for group exercises and games. We soon met neighbors of Irish, Italian and German backgrounds and again we were 'at home'.

Our youngest brother, John was born at Mt. Carmel Hospital, Columbus and what joy that brought to our home. Our Pittsburgh relatives continued to visit on special days, Halloween, Fourth of July, Thanksgiving, and even by surprise. There was always room for more in our home. It seemed there was always a pot of Irish stew, Irish soda bread and tea for the table. When our teenage friends came in the evening, we had tea and cinnamon toast and Mom would read the 'tea leaves' for entertainment. Dad loved 'good meat and mashed potatoes' for every evening meal as ten of us gathered round the table.

Holy Family Church and School were very much a part of our upbringing in Columbus. We grew in love of God nourished by our Irish parents and the Sisters of Mercy (founded in Dublin, Ireland), our teachers through grade and high school (for the girls) and St. Charles (for the boys). We are still an Irish family nourished by loved ones of Italian descent and the diversity of good neighbors and friends. May God bless us and remain with us forever!

My brothers and sisters can add to these stories and tell those of fondest remembrance as their families grew in Columbus, Ohio and Lakeland, Florida. My sixty-one years as a Sister of Mercy has increased my faith and love of family in our religious community and in my visits 'home again'.

A Dorrian Follow-up Story

Nora Dorrian

This follows up the Story of Sr. Mary Macrina Dorrian of her parents Anne Agnes O'Flaherty and Hugh J. Dorrian Sr. Mother Anne, when she came to Pittsburgh, PA., worked for the Mellon Bank family as a domestic maid as so many of her Irish friends had. Father Hugh held many jobs as most of the children were born during the Depression years with a High School education: a Butcher, a Grocer and in his final years a Realtor. They were disciplinarians.

Of the eight children born of this union, there were nurses, a teacher and coach, Realtor, a Franklin County Commissioner, City Auditor and a granddaughter who is a Judge in the Court system.

A Respected Man

Francis B. Doyle, Heather Doyle Fraser

He spent 44 years [from 1928 to 1972] inside the walls of the Ohio State Penitentiary and knew hardened criminals such as Thomas "Yonnie" Licavoli who was not only a gangster and a bootlegger, but also controlled criminal operations as the leader of the famed Purple Gang during the era of Prohibition in Detroit and Toledo. He also knew Dr. Sam Sheppard, an osteopathic physician and neurosurgeon, who was convicted of the infamous and controversial murder of his pregnant wife, Marilyn. There was even a television series and movie entitled "The Fugitive" that some folks believed was based on this unfortunate episode...but wait, before I go too far, let's start at the beginning!

His grandfather, Thomas, emigrated from County Longford, Ireland in 1850 and married Bridget Noonan in 1856 in Newark, Ohio. Bridget was born in Allen Creek, County Clare, Ireland in 1839. The boy's father, also named Thomas, was born in Newark,

Ohio in 1874 and married Mary Desport in Chicago Junction (nee: Willard), Ohio in 1897.

The boy -- we'll call him Francis -- was born in Deforest, Ohio in 1900; however, the family moved back to Willard when he was a young lad. He was the second oldest of eight boys. His boyhood was similar to many who lived in small towns at the turn of the century; playing baseball in the vacant lots, swimming at the "old swimming hole" next to the creek and working in the family garden. He also delivered the morning paper before school to the town folk to earn extra money for the family. He and his older brother Emmett made $35 a month delivering papers (6 paper routes). This was pretty amazing considering many men were working and supporting their families on $40 a month at that time.

The pastor of St. Francis Xavier Church in Willard was an Irishman, born in Ireland, by the name of Father Coan. He used to take walks every day and would pass by young Francis's house on the way out to the country. Father Coan was a big influence on young Francis and was very instrumental in his decision to move to Columbus in 1918 so he could attend The Ohio State University. Graduating in 1923, life moved on, as it always does, and our young Francis settled at the corner of Summit Street and Tompkins Avenue.

Fast-forward five years and life has changed a bit for Francis. Due to unforeseen circumstances, in 1928, he found himself within the walls of the Ohio State Penitentiary, but he was "released" shortly upon entering the prison. But Francis was getting a reputation around Columbus. People went to him for his "professional services" and they were never disappointed. If they had a problem, he would "take care of it." And so, Francis found himself in the prison again; this time for a longer stay. As I said, he spent 44 years inside the walls of the Ohio State Penitentiary.

Of course, now you may be asking, how could a young boy with such obvious advantages - a boy from a good family, a responsible boy who was heavily influenced by his parish priest, a boy who went to college in a time when most people didn't - how could this young man end up spending half of his life in prison?

Well our young Francis is none other than Dr. Francis J. Doyle. You will remember "Doc", as people affectionately called him, first visited the Ohio State Penitentiary in 1928. That had been to treat a prisoner who had an impacted wisdom tooth. The prison dentist recommended to Warden D. E. Thomas that Doc be brought in to do the surgery. By this time, after 5 years in his dental practice, Doc was getting a pretty good reputation in the Columbus area for working on impacted wisdom teeth. The warden acquiesced and contacted Doc. The surgery was performed and the prisoner recovered quickly. However, word spread within the prison population and before you knew it, many of the prisoners were requesting the professional dental services of Doc rather than seeing the state paid dentist. Warden Thomas allowed Doc to set up a private practice within the prison hospital. The prisoners could see the prison dentist for free or pay for Doc's services. And that is why Doc spent 44 years inside the walls of the Ohio State Penitentiary.

The story doesn't end there, though. He was the only dentist ever permitted to set up a private practice within the walls of the hospital of the old "Ohio Pen". During the 1952 prison riot, his office was the only one within the hospital which was not ransacked by the prisoners. Then in 1968, six prisoners entered the hospital at 10 o'clock in the morning and told Doc, "You need to get out of here because all hell's going to break loose." The six prisoners surrounded him and escorted him through the courtyard to safety. Within two hours another prison riot took place that required the services of the Ohio National Guard to regain control of the prison. This speaks of the respect and high regard the prisoners had for him.

Doc aka Dr. Francis J. Doyle, was past Grand Knight of Council 400 and Faithful Navigator of the 4th Degree, a member of The Shamrock Club of Columbus, and a Veteran of World War 1. He was the Honorary Grand Marshal (in memoriam) of the 2010

St. Patrick's Day Parade in Columbus and the father of The Shamrock Club Past President (2010) Francis B. Doyle...and now, as Paul Harvey would say, "You know the rest of the story!"

The Rambler from Clare

Mary Molloy Driscoll

Anne A. Gallagher was born in July 1903, Ennistymon, County Clare. Her birth date is in question because it was the same as her baptismal date. The parish priest explained that at that time people would take a baby from "the womb to the Church" to insure the infant's safe road to heaven.

At 13, Anne forged her father's signature to drop a class at school. That Sunday the Mother Superior and her teacher went to visit her father. Her career as a forger was over. Her choice was either: back to school and take the class, or go to work. So off she went to Lisdoonvarna and the Imperial Hotel.

For the next four years she worked at the Imperial, The Shelbourne in Dublin and then at Knappough in Clare. This was during the War of Independence. She became an adult watching the world explode around her. She told stories of seeing her friends terrorized and killed and of her mother having a bucket shot out of her hands by the Black and Tans.

Anne looked to America as a land of opportunity. December 1920 found her with enough money for the trip. Her father, the town tailor, sent a suit for her brother Patrick. Patrick was to meet her on the dock. She was told there was money sewn into the lining and to have a care. Waiting at the dock, a nun approached. Anne believed she was looking for donations and stopped her before she could talk, informing her she had "no change to spare". That nun was her brother Patrick, dressed this way on the run from the Black and Tans. So at 17 Anne left Queenstown (Cobh), on a ship to New York.

After arriving in Columbus, she stayed briefly with Tim and Anne Moore, also Clare people. She then met and married John Malloy, an immigrant from County Offaly. John was a railroad worker who also looked for a better life in America. John never visited Ireland again. "I didn't leave anything there," was his motto. Anne being the second of 18 children had numerous reasons to return and never let the chance pass her by. John referred to her as "the rambler from Clare".

Anne and John became the parents of three boys, Arthur, John Jr. and William aka Skin. They raised their boys during the depression era here, but found money to send home to help out. Anne and John both became citizens and reminded their family they were "Americans of Irish descent". They raised their sons with equal love for two lands.

On December 7, 1941, after hearing of the bombing of Pearl Harbor, John walked into the house and took all Anne's fine china out of the china cabinet. "John what do you think you're doing?" John's reply was, "I refuse to have anything in this house from Japan." Anne was 6-foot 1inch and well matched to any man. She retrieved her china and packed it away until her granddaughter married in 1975.

Skin served in the Korean conflict. He married Gail Devine in 1956. She was the daughter of Richard Devine and granddaughter of James Devine, first president of the Shamrock Club. Skin became part of the honor guard carrying the American flag. Skin and Gail raised 9 children with the same motto "Americans of Irish descent". They stressed the "American" as a privilege but also a duty and if you could serve this country, you did. Mike and A.J. were Marines. Pat and Bobby served in the Army as well as son-in- law Mike. Kevin Malloy (Mikes' son) was a Marine in Lima Co. in Iraq, and then Bobby had a year in Iraq too.

Anne and John found their opportunity in Columbus and put down deep roots.

My Fallon Family

Patricia A. Durbin

One of my earliest Fallon family memories is visiting Grandma's house at 475 South Ohio Avenue almost every Saturday morning when I was growing up. She was my Irish grandmother - Mary J. Bergin Fallon - or "Minnie" as practically everyone called her. My father, Joe, made the visit a weekly ritual for Mary Jo, and me while our mother did the marketing.

I loved to listen to the conversations whirling around me and to try to identify the changing faces of the uncles and aunts who were either living or visiting there. It was not until years later that I could figure out how they fit into the family. It was a certainty that my grandfather, Daniel J., had been dead for many years since my father was a boy of fourteen, on May 10, 1917 the date of his death. At that time, the boys of the family went to work; my dad did not finish high school as a result.

I never knew much more family history until finding some long-lost cousins at the March 17, 2008, Family Reunion at Vet's Memorial in Columbus. One of them, Dr. Tim Fallon, had discovered that his grandfather, Michael, and my grandfather, Daniel, had come to America from the district of Gort in County Galway.

Michael was older (b.1/21/1865) and Daniel the younger (b.12/7/1867). A record of naturalization for Michael was dated in November of 1890, which meant that the boys were only ages 15 and 13 when they came here.

What I know about Daniel's family is that there were eight living children at the time of his death in 1917. The cause of his death was "automobile accident" which is a curious fact in itself. Was traffic really that bad in 1917 or were autos just rather flimsy? Further research must be done. His profession was listed as Insurance Manager. The actual order of birth was listed in a family bible that became lost and I have not searched Columbus birth records to correct my memory. Sons Robert and Henry were either at the top or just under Marguerite or "Peg" as we called her. Then there was my father, Joseph, Mary, Daniel and John Francis or "Bud" Regina was the Baby Sister.

From the records of my newly found cousin, Dr. Tim, I learned that his grandfather, Michael J. Fallon married Rose Donohoe.

They had five children: Joseph M., Edward D., Mary B., Raymond P., and Charles B. It has always been a mystery to me why these cousins were not part of my father's extended Fallon family. The only explanation I consider probable is that after Daniel died, my grandmother and the older children were so overwhelmed at keeping the family together and fed and clothed, they did not maintain relationships with the "other" Fallons. My dad, Joe, always spoke of the "other" Joe Fallon as a distant cousin. Yet from the records I have, he was a "first" cousin, the son of Daddy's Uncle Michael. I wish I had paid better attention to family gossip sessions! Both Patrick and Jim, sons of Joseph M. attended Holy Rosary High School when I was there so I knew of a connection for many years.

Aunt Peg married "Mr." Brown; I never heard his first name mentioned. She always spoke of him as Mr. Brown. They had no children. I do not know what became of him. I only know that she became the head of the household at the time I was growing up because she worked for the State of Ohio and was the mainstay of family finance. She saw to it that Grandma was taken care of with the help of Aunt Genie. She enjoyed the spacious front bedroom in the house on Ohio Avenue and she let us peek into her cedar chest where all her cosmetics, jewelry and special treasures were stored. Regina slept in an alcove that adjoined Peg's room and was our special friend on adventures to the corner confectionery and even on shopping excursions "downtown." We WALKED all the way.

Uncle Rob married Helen McDonald and they were parents of three daughters: Helen, Jane and Mary Kay. When I was born in 1933, my mom and dad lived at 1787 Kent Street on the east side just down the street from Rob's family on the corner of Seymour & Kent. He was the first uncle I remembered because he often stopped at our house on his way to and from work always greeting me with "Hi, Baby!" For years I knew him only as Uncle Hi-Baby. He joined the Navy in World War II and it was then I learned his name was really Robert because we wrote letters to him when he served in Panama. He was discharged before the end of the war because he was over age. He came back to Columbus and worked in the Curtis-Wright plant for many years. His marriage did not survive the war separation and Rob later married Ethel. Our family kept in touch with his daughters. Helen married Dick Walters and helped me get a part-time job at the Columbus Dispatch where she worked. I spent many hours working with her during my four years at the College of St. Mary of the Springs. We stayed in touch until her death in 1989. Her sister, Jane, married Ed Hackett of Dayton; they were parents of six sons: Michael, Bruce, Terry, Kevin, Keith, and Dennis. Mary Kay died in 1976 survived by one daughter, Sherry. I was able to meet Sherry and four of Jane's sons when Jane died in March, 2008. These three cousins graduated from Holy Rosary High School, as did my sister, Mary Jo and I.

Uncle Henry Fallon lived at the Tuberculosis Sanitarium on Frebis Avenue at Alum Creek Drive where I first met him by waving from outside his window. Children were not allowed inside in those days. After World War II and the development of medicine to deal with this deadly disease, Henry came home to the South Ohio Avenue homestead to live. It was thought that he was no longer contagious. During those years he was at home, I delighted in listening to the lively discussions of politics, sports, and all the news of the day when we visited every Saturday. It was usually my dad, Joe, and Henry, but Rob joined in during several years when he also lived at home after his marriage broke up. To this day, I love to engage in such exchanges, as everyone who knows me at all would agree. The stricture to never discuss politics or religion certainly was not a rule of the Fallon family. They loved it!

Aunt Mary had already died when I was born. We knew her only as a beautiful dark-haired lady in a picture frame on Grandma's parlor table. I recall hearing that she had been married to James "Russ" Wiggins and she had died of meningitis in the early 20's. My long-procrastinated records-research would certainly enable me to find out dates of birth and death long lost in the family records.

Life And its Stories

My father, Joseph, went to work for the Walker T. Dickerson Shoe Company on Front Street as a very young man. He married Josephine Wittenmeier in June 1929, just before the fatal Wall Street crash. The fact that Dickerson's was a family-owned business enabled Daddy to keep his job; everybody worked without any bonuses or perks but with a salary at least. They survived the Depression by sharing meals with friends and vegetables from family gardens. Their first home was a small row house on 17th Street across from the original Josephinum Seminary. Their neighbors were devout Jewish immigrants from Germany and Russia. For many years our family visited them during our holiday seasons of Hanukkah and Christmas. Some of the recipes I still bake were those my mother learned from those good neighbors who shared with her when she was just a bride.

Uncle Dan Fallon did not live in Columbus during my young years. In fact, I really never heard of him until he returned during my grandmother's last illness in 1950. Uncle Bud, baptized John Francis, always lived at home. Bud also worked at Dickerson Shoes and went steady with a young woman, Loretta Glick, who lived next door on Ohio Avenue. Though I do not recall the exact date, at some point in the late 40's, Loretta, Bud and Regina contracted light cases of TB and Henry had to return to the sanitarium because he was once more contagious. By this time, I had a part time job at the local drug store on Saturday and my days of spending time at the yellow brick house on Ohio Avenue came to an end.

Uncle Henry's condition improved again and he was able to leave the sanitarium. He had fallen in love with Betty, one of his nurses, and when he was discharged, they married. Their one son, Patrick, has disappeared from our family knowledge. Uncle Dan also married Marianne and moved to Kansas City. When Grandma Fallon became ill in 1950, she came to stay with our family for several months until she died in June at the age of 92. Finally Bud married Loretta and we had several reunions with him and with

Rob and Ethel. After Aunt Peg's death in 1980, Regina moved to Kansas City with Uncle Dan.

Through the years, we shared stories of the Nerny's who lived across the street on Ohio Avenue and of the Feeney's who lived next door to the Fallon's. All of them attended St. John's Church and it was there that my mother and father met. There were always many stories about Father Burkhart. My grandmother's family, the Bergins, lived on 18th Street. We visited the Bergin's several times to meet many Bergin cousins, Bernie, Danny, and Margie. When I was just a tot, we often visited another Bergin cousin, Bill, and wife Lucille, who lived on the corner of Kent Street and Berkeley Road. He raised carrier pigeons in the loft of his garage. It is my hope that as these Irish family stories are shared some descendants will come together and fill in the many blanks in our histories. Denny Hackett, my Cousin Jane's son, shared a letter about Columbus dated 1876 by William McDonald, her maternal grandfather, to a friend back in Ireland. There is a wonderful description of Columbus that has special meaning as we celebrate the 200th anniversary of the city's founding in 2012.

"When I came here, the place I live in was 1/2 mile out in the woods. It is now about the center of the city. Columbus is the capitol of Ohio. The members of the Senate and House of Representatives meet here every winter and make laws for the state at large. The city boasts of all the finest buildings in the state. All of them are built in the last 8 or 10 years. Our new Lunatic Asylum is the largest in the states. It is 1 1/2 miles around it and four stories high. A new railroad depot was built last year about 650 ft. long. Stand at one end and you would not know any person at the other. Eight tracks run through it and all the offices and dining hall is under one roof. The roof is arched, made of iron and covered with tin. The city has a large foreign population. The Dutch is the majority and occupy the South end of town. The Irish is next and are to be found in the North and it is the most flourishing part of the city. Next summer we will build 4 miles of new street."

How fortunate we, the Irish of Columbus are, to have continued to prosper and help build this community in the spirit of our ancestors who risked much to come across the ocean.

An Irish Way Surprise

Mary Grace Edwards

I was 15 the summer I went to Ireland. I won a scholarship from the Shamrock Club of Columbus for the Irish Way Program. During my 5-week program, I lived with a family in County Mayo. They had a few cows but mostly made their living from equipment sales and an auto body shop. They were a normal Irish family with 4 boys and 1 girl. Also the Mother in law lived with them. I remember the guest room was not connected to the rest of the house, and was entered from the outside. Now is the heart of my story …

As you may know Ireland has a mild and damp climate. The summer I stayed with my host family was quite damp. One night the family decided to stay home after all the rounds of visiting and tea for the friends and family to meet the young American girl staying with them, namely me. On the television that night was a "B" movie, a horror movie called "Frogs". We all gathered around and watched. It was quite late when it ended. As the honored guest, I was to sleep in the guest room located outside the main house. There was no heat, but my "Mom" had a snuggly warm electric blanket on my bed for my comfort. Again, it was quite late and the movie was creepy and scary. It was about insects and reptiles growing in gigantic proportions; they were taking over the Island and killing everyone. When I pulled back my bed linen there was a **huge slug** laying in my bed. I, of course, screamed and everyone came running. It was too, too funny. I will never forget that summer in Ireland for the rest of my life.

A Questionable Vision of the Blessed Virgin

Steve Erwin

The essence of each story is genuine, as are the references to my family history. They're stories from my family, as passed down from generations ... but to work the Irish linkage in, I had to embellish a bit (but then what Irishman ever told a story without a little added blarney?).

No matter how long we Irish have been in America, we never seem to lose our native characteristics. My family immigrated around 1760. Our love for funny stories, music, jest, laughter and just plain old "blarney" are as intact as ever ... and they're just as wild and rampant as we find them in other Irish American families long separated from the Emerald Isle.

When I was very young, a story was told about a family friend, another immigrant Irishman, who sat in an old wooden chair outside St. Patrick's Church in Columbus on a warm sunny Sunday toward the end of World War II.

The Mass had ended and people were beginning to leave the Church in small family groups. Our friend was an amiable fellow, well known and liked by other parishioners, but he only occasionally attended Mass, to the scowling disapproval of his devout wife. He often simply accompanied relatives and friends; then he would wait outside for them if the weather was pleasant, while sometimes enjoying a beer or two.

On this bright sunny day, he'd enjoyed perhaps three or four beers. People leaving the Church became alarmed when they found him lying twisted on the ground. His chair was beside him, but crumpled and lying on its side. As the first few parishioners rushed up to see if he was hurt, he wobbled and rose awkwardly to his knees, all the while steadying himself on the broken chair.

His faltering words quickly spread through the gathering crowd that the Blessed Virgin had come down out of the sky and hit him in the face so hard she'd knocked his beer out of his hand, broke his glasses, shattered his chair and sent him sprawling to the ground. "Serves him right..." came an anonymous complaint from somewhere in the crowd, "... for missing Mass!"

He never changed his story, but the word from those who knew him was that, although no one had actually seen it happen, the "Vision" was more likely his wife, who'd waited for him in Church and then became aggravated at finding him outside after Mass. She'd meanwhile left the scene and walked home alone.

In this case, proof of a Vision of the Blessed Virgin is perhaps less important than its results.

Our friend became more faithful in Church attendance after this incident.

How the Skunk Boosted Church Stewardship
Steve Erwin

When the fish were biting, Great-Great-Grandpa would sometimes sit up fishing all night by the creek and bring his catch home for breakfast, just as his ancestors had done in Ireland.

Great-Great-Grandpa had a strange, old, magic walking stick. According to family legend, the walking stick, called a shillelagh in Ireland, had been passed down from his own Great-Great-Grandpa, who had immigrated to America from Ireland sometime before the American Revolution. One family legend even insisted that it had been made by the leprechauns. Whenever he went fishing, Great-Great-Grandpa would take his shillelagh along, and it would always guarantee a pleasant night and a big catch. On this particular occasion, Great-Great-Grandpa forgot his shillelagh.

It was a sultry summer night, and Great-Great-Grandpa fell asleep on the creek bank. He awoke suddenly to see a skunk, its characteristic white streak aglow in the lantern light, prowling around his tackle box. Not one to be crowded out of his favorite fishing spot by critters, Great-Great-Grandpa lunged at the skunk, determined to grab its fur and send it flying into the creek. He missed, and instead, flopped helplessly to the ground as he watched the skunk saunter off with a backward smirk and its tail high in the air. It wasn't but a few seconds before Great-Great-Grandpa realized the skunk had won this round.

Great-Great-Grandpa thought his luck had vanished because he'd forgotten to bring his shillelagh. It was very late, he hadn't caught a single fish, and now he smelled like a skunk. He returned home after midnight. His wife made him sleep outside by himself that night, and then only after bathing and burying his clothes in the yard by lantern light. He buried his wallet too, but not before removing a five-dollar bill from it. In those days, five dollars was a lot of money. As he handled the five-dollar bill, he thought no merchant would take it because it smelled like the skunk.

"Begorra! Will wonders never cease ?!?", exclaimed Father Murphy to himself at Sunday Mass. "Isn't that old Erwin sitting in a pew, and him wearing clean clothes ?!?" And to the good Priest's further astonishment, he could have sworn he saw Great-Great-Grandpa drop a five-dollar bill into the collection basket!

Now we'd always heard that skunks have no natural predators, except occasional careless dogs. Add to that one careless member of the Erwin Clan ... and maybe now it's clear why we rarely have any money.

Here's the historical info: My direct ancestor, Robert Erwin, arrived in Virginia around 1760 and stayed with other members of the family who had arrived as early as 1727. The family came from the northern counties of Cavan, Antrim, Down and Donegal, where, I understand, the British had confiscated some of their farmland. Erwins remain numerous in those counties today and are also related to the Irwin families in both Ireland and Scotland.

Ol' Uncle Liam Died at the Age of 98

Steve Erwin

Uncle Liam always insisted he'd live to be 100. He didn't quite make it, but he came real close. That's what's known as "Irish Time".

Ol' Liam used to say he'd go straight to Heaven when he died. No one believed that except him. If you listened to him for awhile, he'd explain. "Gettin' into Heaven is a lot like doin' things here on earth," he'd say. "You gotta be faster and smarter than everyone else, and you gotta' look for opportunities ... and then, when you see an opportunity, you 'pull a fast one'... and you get into Heaven." He said he'd just sorta' hang out around the Pearly Gates like he was prayin' the Rosary or playin' his tin whistle. Then when God and St. Peter weren't lookin', he'd make a mad dash and run through the Gate. No one would ever know.

Every morning, for as long as anyone could remember, Ol' Liam dumped a double shot of Irish whiskey in his coffee. He said that whiskey was what kept him alive and healthy. His wife said he didn't have that quite right. She said God wouldn't take him until he quit drinking that whiskey.

Well, one bright morning, just as sure as the birds were singin' in the trees, Ol' Liam poured his coffee and sat down at the table and drank it down. He forgot to put the whiskey in it. Well, God saw that as an opportunity! God "pulled a fast one" of His own and snatched Ol' Liam up before Liam could remember to go get his whiskey. God always outsmarts ALL of us in the end, even Uncle Liam.

Liam always said he had so many wives he couldn't remember them all. I think I remember about three of them or so, myself. He said he survived all his marriages because he didn't have them all at once.

We'll all remember Uncle Liam for a long, long time. He was always the first to admit that about half of his life was mostly blarney. Then another fourth of it was sorta' half true. The rest ... hell, he couldn't remember.

County Longford & Irish Magic

Jim Fath

Who ever goes to County Longford? It's not a hot spot of Ireland tourists' destinations. Well, we did and we had to play the part of "Dick Tracy" in the search for my Irish relatives.

Didn't know the true family name was "Hourican", changed to "Somers", by my grandmother when she arrived in America in 1892, or thereabouts. The name change was a common thing to do to separate yourself from other Irish immigrants of the same era.

Upon arriving in Longford town and being amazed by the wide streets, a walking funeral procession through the heart of the town at high noon, and more traffic seen in the few days traveling to Longford city, the journey had just begun. Longford is a larger than normal Irish town, not a village, not a crossroad, not a parish, but a thriving agricultural county capital with lots of activity and business and people.

The only clues Cathy and I had were unfamiliar names and unfamiliar phone numbers, but that is a golden start, better than most people have when tracking their ancestors in Ireland. Using a public corner phone in Ireland can be an experience, needing more patience than I can ever muster. Patience is something I have never had, that's why I am not a doctor. I don't have any "*patience*". I did have three names and phone numbers but I just couldn't connect with anyone.

My non-patient me said, "Let's go! These people don't exist or they don't want to be found. Who wants Yanks popping in on them unannounced?"

My Cathy started the "Magic of Longford". Resting my frustration with the phone disappointment, Cathy made the kindest suggestion a woman could make that any man could want to hear, "Let's go into this pub, have a pint, bowl of soup and bread, and try to figure this all out. After all, we have names and phone numbers; there might be something we just don't understand."

The "Market" pub/restaurant is a landmark in Longford, sitting on the corner of the public market square. First floor is the pub/restaurant; second floor the high-end, fashionable, fine dining restaurant. We were on the first floor and it was just perfect.

Upon ordering, the wait staff quickly learned that we were from the USA. They were quite accommodating, even though this was at the noon business hour. We weren't in a hurry, so we lingered through the lunch hour rush and, as the business slowed, the owner sat down next to us. His curiosity got to him. He wanted to know what brought a couple of Yanks to Longford?

Everything started to happen now. In the city of Longford, Hourican is a very good name, known for kindness, compassion and involvement in the community, especially in the harder times of days gone by.

Asking about the name of Patrick Hourican brought a surprise. The publican asked if he was the "painter". I didn't know if he was a painter at all .... house painter, car painter or what kind of painter. The publican said that he knows a Patrick Hourican, an artist, a painter of landscapes and portraits, and that his sister, Ann Brady, has a daughter that works for him in the evening, as a waitress at the upstairs restaurant. Magic!!!

Within one hour, the whole town knew that Pat Hourican had family from the USA looking for him. The phone call came into the pub from Pat and a time to meet was set.

We met Pat, his lovely wife Elizabeth, son John, and sister, Ann Brady. We had take-out Chinese dinner at their home. The Chinese was quite an extreme surprise. This day ended with new family and the promise that the next day would bring more magic.

Day two brought more surprises than ever, with a trip to the home ground. Augnacliffe is a small village in northern County Longford, with farmland and rolling hills full of streams. It's very interesting. It's all Hourican territory and really neat. Philip is a big name in the area. Everyone named "Hourican" has a name from the area where he lives: Philip of the "Pub", Philip of the "Valley", Philip of the "Hill".

One very kind and gentle, "Philip Hourican", owned the pub/grocery/carry out, one of two in this area, both at the same intersection. I don't know who owned the other pub, but the "Hourican Pub", and all the land behind it, was owned by Houricans for miles. And that is where the family homestead is located.

These Houricans are so very inviting and charming but aren't in on the family history. Tracking relatives and family isn't a big thing on their agenda. You have to dig information out of them.

We parked at the family church, St. Columbkille, which is surrounded by a cemetery. Most of the headstones were, of course, Hourican's. Pat introduced us to all of the deceased family with very interesting stories. He wanted us to walk through the fields to the old family homestead where the last two elderly aunts lived and died. You could look out across the fields and see the tiny little home.

At the end of the cemetery there was a ladder to climb down into the farm to begin the trek across several working farms. Pat had not taken this walk for some years and was not quite certain of the way. But, he did remember that there was a huge pile of rocks and a somewhat hidden small bridge to cross a stream that ran through the farm.

Well, the pile of rocks was a national treasure in Ireland.... a famous "Dolmen"...right there on the family property. I had never seen a dolmen, let alone ever thinking that I could stand right next to one. What a sight! But we still had to find the bridge, which we did, with a little brush and tree limb moving. There it was and ever more mysteriously hidden.

The house grew larger as we approached and the story about the two sisters unfolded, as we learned that they were spinster farmers raising chickens, cows for milking and a few small crops. All the business outside the farm was taken care of by the aunt Mary. Of the two, only Mary ever left that farm. In her whole life, the aunt Katie only got as far as the church. It is remembered by the locals that you would see her Wellys (rubber boots worn by most farmers) outside the church at daily mass.

The story goes: that Mary died from injuries in a rain and windstorm, when a gate was blown by the wind and killed her instantly. The surviving sister, Katie, died one year later by the very same circumstances with the same kind of storm. She was not killed instantly but lingered from her injuries. Pat remembered his father saying that she died from the broken heart because she missed her sister so very, very much.

This is the first of many trips to County Longford and to the countryside village of Augnacliffe. We have taken many, many, friends to this rural area of Ireland and all have become charmed and love the "magic" that begins in Phil Hourican's Pub.

Long Overdue Recognition

J. Michael Finn

The Ancient Order of Hibernians was the premier Irish organization in Columbus from the founding of the first division in Flytown in 1876 until its gradual demise in the mid-1930s. Many individuals contributed to the success of the Hibernians in Columbus. Many served as division, county, state and national officers or in the Hibernian Rifles (a military division of the Order). Information has recently been found concerning one of the unsung members of the early A.O.H. who worked to keep the Order alive in Columbus and to promote and document its history.

John Joseph Cook was born in County Louth, Ireland in 1851. He left the family farm in 1870 and with only a steerage ticket in his pocket, sailed for America, arriving in Boston. Cook said about his experience, "Twas a hard move for a gossoon only 18 to make, but in those days the oppression was so bitter! If you wore a green tie or whistled a patriotic air, into jail they'd clap you and you'd rot there."

Cook stayed in Boston for two years then moved to Columbus and started to practice his trade, that of a carpenter. He lived on Grove Street in the area known as "Irish Town." Soon he started building houses and in only seven years he had made enough money to return to his home in Ireland for a visit. "But back I came (to America) and that's the last I saw of my family – or old Ireland," said Cook.

In 1875 some Irishmen in the Flytown area of Columbus came together in Goodale Park and began discussing the formation of a division of the Ancient Order of Hibernians. Some of these men had come to Columbus from Sharon and Wheatland, Pennsylvania to work in the rolling mills that were located at the end of Goodale St. Their preliminary discussion led to action and in March 1876 the first division of the Ancient Order of Hibernians was formed in Columbus. It is unknown whether John Cook was a member of that organizing group, but we know that he joined the first division and was elected its first Vice-President.

Although the Hibernians first public appearance was in the July 4, 1876 parade that celebrated America's Centennial, the Hibernians were soon parading on St. Patrick's Day. In 1938 Cook said of those old days in Columbus, "In the 1870s there were 18,000 people living in this town, and they were all on the curb a-waitin' for the parade on St. Pat's Day. If you were Irish or had a dripit of Irish blood in your veins, you marched. If you didn't march, two broken legs was the only excuse that was taken. So you know that the parades were long. They all turned out – the Egans, the Ryans, the O'Shaughnessys, the Mulligans, the Joyces, the McCabes, the Crowleys, the Carrs, the O'Briens, the Murphys, the Caseys, the Sullivans and the Donovans. And what a brave sight they made on a fine day, led by a squad of cops with the map of Ireland written of their shiny faces, an' up front, the grand marshal astride a prancing white horse. The Hibernians were 700 strong then. Ah, for those days – but they're gone now... The younger folk, they don't join the Irish societies like they should. The parades are not what they used to be. But mind you this: The men you'll see in the Thursday parade are just as good Irishmen as the men of the old days."

Apparently, John Joseph Cook never needed an excuse for not marching on St. Patrick's Day. He marched in Columbus parades for 66 years. In 1939 at the age of 86 he was still marching. Cook was proud to report that he was the last surviving charter member of the Ancient Order of Hibernians, Division #1, founded in 1876. In his very long association with the Ancient Order of Hibernians he held many division, county and state offices. In 1938 he asked not to be re-elected as State Treasurer and County President. These posts he had held for 12 years. He always proudly wore his original A.O.H. ribbon to parades and funerals even while the AOH was in decline.

John Cook's major contribution to Columbus Hibernian history came in 1923 when he was asked to write the history of the Hibernians in Columbus for the State Convention Program. Columbus hosted the State Convention that year. He wrote about the first division and the first officers. He told about how the other divisions soon followed and the Order grew in members and strength. He also wrote about the founding of the Ladies Ancient Order of Hibernians in Columbus. Although it may not have seemed like an important assignment to Mr. Cook at the time, it was that convention program that surfaced from the corners of a musty attic in 1995. The program provided the present members of the AOH with John Cook's history of the Order's early years and provided the Order with information that had been lost for many years.

On St. Patrick's Day in 1938 the Columbus Dispatch did a feature article on John J. Cook. The reporter noted that it was often difficult to find Mr. Cook at home in the daytime. His wife, Marie Cook, would direct visitors to Grove Street or to St. Clair Avenue, where he would be working. At 85 he was still working every day, taking care of his numerous properties in that section of the city. The Dispatch reported, "He does odd jobs of plumbing, painting and otherwise keeps himself happy through labor." In 1938 he still drove his own car to and from work.

John Cook lived at 1038 Lockbourne Road in Columbus. He had four children, John Joseph Cook, Jr., Joseph P. Cook, Mary Louise Coffman and Ann Cook. In 1938 he had nine grandchildren. He was founder and first president of the Carpenters and Joiners Union, Local 200, which is still active today. He was a member of the Friendly Sons of St. Patrick, the Catholic Order of Foresters (50 years) and the Holy Name Society. He was also a charter member of the Shamrock Club. He was a member of Corpus Christi Parish.

According to the Columbus Dispatch he marched in the 1939 St. Patrick's Day parade. In 1940 the Dispatch reported that Mr. Cook was unable to march in that year's parade on the advice of his doctor. John Joseph Cook died on December 6, 1940 at the age of 89. "I am still, and always will be grateful to America," said Cook. The spirit of John Joseph Cook likely still walks in the parade to this day.

The Story of Dennis Shea

J. Michael Finn

Not all immigration stories have a happy ending. Some end in tragedy as this story of Dennis Shea indicates. The story was printed as follows in the (Columbus) Ohio State Journal, July 22, 1859:

In the year 1853, three brothers by the name of Shea (Patrick, John and Dennis) living in the county of Donegal, Ireland, having heard of a land of liberty where the down-trodden and oppressed of all nations are received and welcomed, tore themselves away from their aged parents, the scenes of their childhood, and the land of their birth, with the intention of making enough money to bring their loved parents to the country of their intended adoption. Two of them were men, but Dennis, the hope and pride of his aged parents, was but a boy of seventeen years, full of youthful ardor. After receiving the blessing of their parents, they crossed the ocean and landed in New York. They shortly started to find employment. The eldest stopped in New Jersey, the next found a place in Pennsylvania, and Dennis came to Ohio with an acquaintance, and found his way to one of our public works near Athens, where there were a number of his countrymen employed.

Not long after he arrived, on one of their holidays, two or three citizens were passing along the road, and found Dennis Shea with a dying man at a spring. Dennis carried him there, and was engaged in washing his face and cooling the temples of his dying countryman. Those who found him in this position charged him with murder, arrested him and conveyed him to Athens, and lodged him in jail. The man died without being able to communicate facts of the case, and the story of poor Dennis was not believed. He was tried at the March term of the Court in that county in 1854, found guilty of murder in the second degree, and sentenced to the Ohio Penitentiary for life. He arrived there on the 14th of April following; at that time but 18 years of age. Immediately after his confinement, he began to dwindle away, and he told the narrator of these facts that he could not survive a year, and wished his brothers to be kept ignorant of his misfortune and disgrace.

In the month of September following, he took to his bed, and sent a messenger to our informant. He wished for a priest and said he would not die without making his peace with God.

Father Meagher was sent for, and in the presence of the Warden, Mr. Wilson and our informant, he told his simple story. The dying boy was shrived (confessed) by the priest, said he would now die in peace, and in a few moments all was over.

He stated on his death bed (and it is substantiated by Lot L. Smith, Esq., a lawyer of Athens and formerly private secretary to Governor Medill), that there existed an old feud between what they call the Fardowns and the Corkonians – that a few of them had met near the spring on that day, in the temporary absence of Dennis, and had a fight when they left this man for dead and made good their escape.

Dennis came along a short time afterward, and found him, dragged him to the spring, and like the "Good Samaritan," was trying to restore consciousness to the dying man, when he was caught in the charitable act – his story discredited, hurried through the form of a trial – without money and without friends, and sentenced at the youthful age of 18, to drag out a miserable existence within the gloomy walls of the Ohio Penitentiary – and innocent too; who +wonders what he sickened – that he died?

The Tailor and the Detective

J. Michael Finn

Michael Burns, a native of Ireland, came to this country in 1853. He arrived in Baltimore, Maryland where he found work as a tailor, a trade he had learned in Ireland. He married Bridget Treahy in Baltimore and in 1861 they moved west to Zanesville, Ohio. He practiced his trade in Zanesville and eventually became a junior partner in the tailoring firm of Dennis & Burns. In 1873 Michael and his family moved to Columbus, Ohio, where he opened his own tailoring business at the corner of Gay and High Streets. His business grew and prospered.

Michael was a member of St. Patrick's Church and was active in several Catholic societies, including the Ancient Order of Hibernians and the St. Joseph's Mutual Benevolent Society. He was involved in local politics and served as Columbus Police Commissioner from 1878 until 1882. On February 18, 1880 he led the welcoming committee to Union Station when Irish politician Charles Stewart Parnell visited Columbus. Michael Burns died on February 9, 1892, survived by his wife and five children. At his death, the Columbus Dispatch described him as, "Staunch and loyal to his friends and devoted to his family and business." His funeral was held at St. Patrick's Church.

But, the Burns story doesn't end there. One of Michael Burns' two sons was William J. Burns. William was born in Baltimore in 1861. He came west with his father and attended public school in Columbus. He later attended business school and after graduation, joined his father's tailoring business, developing a good reputation as a tailor. His father's appointment as Police Commissioner in 1878 gave William contact with the Columbus Police Department. William's job was to cut and measure the uniforms for Columbus police officers. Through this contact, William developed an interest and skill in detective work.

Although never officially in the employ of the Columbus Police, William often proved himself useful as an amateur detective. The police, at that time, had no detectives and they often called upon William when they needed help to solve a mystery. William always maintained that, "There is no such thing as a mystery if you will only use a little common sense." Due to his success in solving local crimes, he was called upon by the Ohio Attorney General to investigate an Ohio election scandal. In the Ohio Tally Sheet Scandal he found that election fraud had taken place and he identified the men responsible.

As a result of his success in Ohio, in 1889 William Burns received a position in the United States Secret Service. He achieved great success, particularly in tracking down and prosecuting counterfeiters. In 1903 he resigned from the Secret Service and worked both inside and outside the government to solve several high profile national cases. As a result, he was hailed as, "The greatest detective, certainly the only detective of genius, who this country has produced." In 1906 Burns trapped and arrested the entire board of supervisors of San Francisco, in the act of committing bribery. In 1909 William and his son George E. Burns, formed the Burns National Detective Agency. In 1910 Burns solved the Los Angeles Times bombing case by arresting and bringing to trial the McNamara brothers, who were union officials (this case would mark Burns as an enemy of organized labor).

In 1914, in Georgia, Burns gathered evidence that cleared Leo Frank of the rape and murder of Mary Phagan in that famous case. Allegations were that Frank was prosecuted solely because he was Jewish. As a result of Burns' work on the case, he was almost killed by an angry mob in Marietta, Georgia. Leo Frank was taken from his prison cell by another angry mob and lynched.

In 1921 Burns was appointed by the U.S. Attorney, General Harry Daugherty, as Director of the Bureau of Investigation for the Justice Department. His most notable achievement during his term of service was the first successful prosecution of the Klu Klux Klan, an organization Burns came to hate as a result of their involvement in the Leo Frank case.

Unfortunately, Burns failed to detect the overt fraud and graft committed by the "Ohio Gang" in the Warren Harding administration and he left office in disgrace in 1925. In 1927 Burns received a sentence of 15 days in jail for contempt in the Albert Fall-Harry Sinclair criminal conspiracy trial. The Supreme Court overturned this conviction due to lack of evidence.

Burns was replaced as Director of the Bureau of Investigation by his assistant, J. Edgar Hoover, and the name of the department changed to the Federal Bureau of Investigation. Burns returned to his detective agency, where he continued to involve himself in famous criminal cases of the day. He often found himself afoul of the law through his zealous efforts to solve crimes.

William Burns died at his St. Armand's Key winter home in Florida on April 14, 1932 of a heart attack. He was survived by his wife Anna Marie (Ressler) Burns and six children. The detective business he founded is still in operation today. He was the author of "The Masked War" (1913) that concerned the Los Angeles Times bombing case and two works of fiction "The Argyle Case" (1913) and "The Crevice" (1915).

William J. Burns once said, "Every criminal leaves a track and if a detective fails to find that track he hasn't searched hard enough."

Would You Like to Go Have a Drink, James?
J. Michael Finn

My grandfather, James J. Finn, came to America from County Sligo in 1891. Landing in New York, he soon made his way to Cincinnati, Ohio, where his older brother Matthew was already living. Matthew had found good employment there working at the newly built Hotel Alms as a porter, and he promised to get similar employment for his brother.

James arrived in Cincinnati and took up residence in the same rooming house as his brother just north of downtown Cincinnati. When James arrived, his brother asked him, "Would you like to go have a drink?"

Now, you should know that Matthew was not a consumer of strong drink, having taken "the pledge" some years before. Knowing this fact, my grandfather was somewhat puzzled by his question, but he promptly replied, "I would."

The two set off for downtown Cincinnati. My grandfather was looking forward to sampling a few of the German beers for which Cincinnati was famous. After walking several blocks into the city, Matthew took him up to the Tyler Davidson Fountain, which at that time was a public drinking fountain.

"There you are," said Matthew. "You can drink as much as you like."

Matthew moved back to Ireland in 1895, but he would often tell this story to his family and neighbors in County Sligo. He would always laugh as he recalled the look of disappointment on my grandfather's face.

A Whale of a Story

Anne Flanagan

My grandmother was born Anna O'Toole in the rural Gaeltacht west of Clifden in an Irish-speaking family. She always referred to her childhood home as "cois na tra"—Irish for "near the beach." In fact, she said she could always see the water from their hillside home. Her mother's maiden name was King, and indeed when I travelled to Ireland some years ago, there were graveyards filled with O'Tooles and Kings all around that area (as Mike Finn may recall—he was with me and Pat on that trip).

Anna's father immigrated to Pittsburgh at some point to work in the mills, and a few years later when he had saved money for their passage, his wife and children also emigrated. In fact, the mother and children, including Anna, passed through Johnstown, PA, one day after the flood the famous Johnstown Flood (May 31, 1889). My grandmother was 10 years old at that time. That part of their journey the family knows to be true--imagine being in Johnstown one day after the flood!

But my grandmother was known as a "character" and great storyteller. Although she died shortly after I was born, perhaps her story of "Coming to America," as related to my older cousin when she was a little girl in the early 1940s, best displays this gift.

As they sailed across the Atlantic (so my grandmother claimed), their ship suddenly began to sink in mid-ocean. Frantic passengers started saying their Aves and preparing for the worst. But just as they were about to lose all hope, a whale swam by, and allowed the desperate travelers to get on his back. A few days later, after their remarkable ride, they saw the Statue of Liberty holding her torch aloft as their whale made its way into New York Harbor. (Oddly no newspaper reports recount the story!)

Of course my cousin believed our grandmother—for more than a few years! And perhaps that gift for telling a fine tale is in the genes! My Dad could certainly spin a yarn, as can my sister. And my Dad was able to remember and sing some of his mother's Irish songs, but sadly, he didn't really understand or speak the language. What a pity!

Bridget Doyle

Jim Flanagan

Bridget Doyle, my great grandmother, was born in Belfast, Ireland. After my great grandfather was set up in an electrical business and doing well, then Bridget joined him in McConnelsville, Ohio.

She was small, happy and possessed a strong wonderful voice. She sang hymns from memory at both Catholic and Protestant churches. It happened this way. She sang for the Sunday high mass. People attended to hear her belt out those hymns.

Word spread of her great talent. The Methodists asked her to sing at one of their gathering. That led to great grandmother singing at the early service for the Methodist church.

Not to be outdone, the Lutherans asked her to sing at their last Sunday service.

On every Sunday, Great grandmother Doyle, as long as she was able, sang at all three services. Needless to say, attendance was up at all the churches. Not a word was said against her. When she died all three pastors, Catholic, Methodist and Lutheran presided at the service.

The Night the Fireman Upset Grandmother Nell Flanagan

Jim Flanagan

My grandmother, Nell Flanagan, moved to McConnelsville, Ohio, after my grandfather died. She had an apartment on the town square.

She continued to work. After 20 some years as high school cafeteria supervisor, Nell took a job at the TB sanitarium outside of town.

She worked 4pm to 12am.

The volunteer firehouse was just next-door. She never minded the noise caused by the fire runs. However, she had requested they hold down the loud talking, yelling for the late runs.

This particular night, a call came in at 3am. The fire department boys made the usual amount of racket. Grandma got up and went over to the fire station to register a complaint. No one was there. That was not normal. They had left the doors wide open. Grandma felt they needed to be closed to safe guard the equipment.

She found a ladder and closed the doors. Not only had the firemen forgot to close the doors, they left the key in the main door.

Grandma Flanagan locked it and to teach those young men a lesson, she took the key with her.

The town was utterly amazed to find all the parking around the square taken up by fire equipment.

About 10 am, grandma appeared with the key. The embarrassed fire chief swore they would cut down the unnecessary noise on early morning fire runs.

You did not upset my grandma.

The First Columbus Feis

Linda Fox

Gary Fox's roll in getting the First Columbus Feis started was huge. And we all know the Columbus Feis for what it is today, and how the whole country wants to participate. They used his stages for many, many years because they were so perfect.

During the winter of 1981 Gary was asked to help with a project for the First Annual Columbus Feis at Saint Charles the following August. The dilemma was to build stages for the dancers (keep in mind Gary and Linda did not have any children having any interest in Irish Step Dancing). After a few weeks of conversation, discussing what had been accomplished in Dayton and about the concept they used, Gary came up with his design. As different committees embarked on promoting the First Columbus Feis it became apparent that eight stages needed to be built, which meant that eighty, or more, 4' X 8' sheets of plywood needed 2" X 4" bracing. While under construction, these were stored at Gary's warehouse and then transported to Saint Charles. Gary then was in charge to make certain the stages were level, safe, with no protrusions to trip a dancer and would not vibrate loose. The First Columbus Feis was a success which meant more stages were needed the following three years . . yes Gary was in charge of construction and installation . . . as a volunteer!

"Because We Are!"

Lynne Cahill Gatton

After much badgering by you, Julie, and my daughter, I have written something for the Irish book. If it isn't what you want, delete it, change it, or write a better one and pass it off as mine! For better or worse here it is:

We never talked about our Irishness when I was young; although my Dad's collection of Irish American records should have been a clue. Carmell Quinn's albums and Danny Boy by various artists were among them. At Corpus Christi School in

Columbus, Ohio, I was among mostly German students who happily took the accordion lessons that were offered there.

In the 60's, as a teenager, when the blond, tanned, California girl look was "in", I was a pale, black haired girl who definitely didn't fit the style. Sunbathe, as I would, it always resulted in burned skin and more freckles.

My father always assumed that we knew we were of Irish stock, apparently, since a couple of years before he passed away, I asked him directly, "How do you know we are Irish?" He replied in typical fashion, "Because we are!"

After my father passed away in 1977, I was determined to find out more about my Irish heritage. It was at this time, that I saw an ad in the Catholic Times for a newly formed group called The Daughters of Erin, for women of Irish descent and those who were interested in Ireland. My mother and sister joined too and, along with my two children, became very involved with the Irish culture. We are grateful to the many people who taught us about Ireland and it's people, and inspired us to learn more about the country's roots in language and the arts, as well as it's history.

Through talks and other communications with relatives, I now know that my great grandfather, Thomas Cahill, came to America from County Sligo in 1880, stopped in Boston for ten years and married Sarah McIntyre, who came from Prince Edward Island. They had one son in Boston, then came to Columbus where, apparently, an uncle was already living. Thomas' mother and younger siblings came to America and joined him in Columbus. Thomas and Sarah went on to have three other sons. The sons were Thomas, George, Martin and John, who was my grandfather.

John worked on the Hocking Valley Railroad, traveling through southern Ohio, where he met my grandmother, Brigid Barbara Gallagher whose family had come from County Donegal, who worked as a telephone operator in Nelsonville. She lived in Buchtel, Ohio and always called herself Margaret, which was her confirmation name. Perhaps she just liked the name, or perhaps the pressure to be seen as an American in the early part of the 20th century, was more important than taking pride in an immigrant heritage.

John and Brigid went on to have eight children: Thelma, Paul, Margaret, Richard (my father), Charles, John, William and Joan who was just a baby when John was killed in a railway accident at the age of 42.

My father, Richard, also worked on the railroad (now the C&O Railroad) for a time just before WWII and just after. He married my mother, Helen Marie Moore, before the war, where he served with the Army on the railroad in Burma.

I am one of three children. My older brother Richard Jr., now deceased, served in Vietnam with the Air Force and my younger sister Cynthia, lives in Pennsylvania with her husband and 5 children.

After belonging to the Daughters of Erin for many years, I joined the Ladies Ancient Order of Hibernians and am founder of the Irish Living History Society. I have also worked many years as a member of the Dublin Irish Festival Cultural Committee. My husband, Donald Gatton, has recently found that he too, has Irish ancestors. We suspect that my mother's father's family was also of Irish stock. But that will have to be another story; one that I look forward to learning and passing on to our children Mia Gilbert and Gabriel Gatton and our grandchildren, Kailee and Declan.

Eireann go bragh! (Ireland Forever!)

William McClelland

Karen M. Graham

William McClelland came from County Down, Ireland to Baltimore Maryland in about 1830 at age 16. His brother David and two sisters came a little later and found William in Baltimore. The two sisters later died in New York City during a cholera epidemic. David married Jane Hite or Haight in Baltimore and then moved to Guernsey County, Ohio. William followed. David and Jane had two daughters and then David died. Jane then married her brother-in-law William and had two more children (one dying in infancy). Jane then died and William married again. Then he died and the youngest, a daughter, lived with her step mother until her oldest sister got married and she moved in with them.

The oldest daughter Mary Jane married a Quaker and lived a modest life as wife, mother and grandmother. Mary Jane was my great great grandmother. Her sister Martha Anne (Mattie) married a minister, graduated from college, and traveled the world teaching temperance, in that order. Mattie at first used the name Mattie McClelland Brown. As she became more famous, her friends convinced her she should drop the "d" in McClelland to appear Scottish instead of Irish. So, Mattie McClellan Brown gave the suggestion for the WCTU and is credited with such even though Frances Willard and others became more well known.

CGrehan/Graham

W. Patrick & Karen M. Graham

I knew from my grandfather, James Graham, that he was born in Co. Kildare, Ireland. He was in his eighties and very hard of hearing when we began asking questions. He told us his brothers' and sisters' names, that his father was buried in Wellston, Ohio and his mother in Pine Grove. Grandpa was nearly 40 when my father was born, so he always was old to me. A few days shy of his 96th birthday, he died in a nursing home fire and to this day I regret not asking more questions.

Knowing grandpa was one of eight children, my wife and I set out to find relatives. Obviously grandpa hadn't kept in touch with any of them nor they with him. We obtained a birth certificate for grandpa from Ireland and found out he had been using his baptism date as his birth date and that our name was originally spelled Grehan. Also he had been born in Derrymullen near the Lowtown Lock in Co. Kildare. The area is still called "Grehan Gardens" because the family had a vegetable garden and shipped their wares on the canal boats. They were called by-traders.

After many years, we tracked down a cousin in Michigan who gave us a picture of grandpa and two of his brothers with a woman who owned a boarding house. She also had a newspaper article of her father and his 2 brothers (one being grandpa) who each thought the others were dead. One lived through the famous hurricane in Galveston.

Through an obituary in a Portsmouth, Ohio newspaper, another cousin was found. Someone in the Portsmouth Genealogy Society knew Madalyn Rase and gave her our letter of inquiry. We received a letter from her and she gave us her phone number. I called right away to make arrangements to visit her in Minford, Ohio. Later I learned that after inviting us, she panicked and told her grandson, Chris Konik: "I don't know if I did right or not, but I invited complete strangers to come visit." Needless to say, Chris was there when we arrived. We showed Madalyn old pictures, including the one from Michigan. She stated that the woman in the Michigan picture was her grandmother. Madalyn said she had another grandson, Dan and his family lived in Columbus and maybe we knew them. I think she was forgetting the size of Columbus. Lo and behold, we could see their home from ours and his wife is also related to my wife. She also gave us the name of another cousin, John Madden, who lived in California. Madalyn had a granddaughter who was leaving in a few weeks for Ireland to study and was going to try to find her Irish family. Right after we met Madalyn, she lost her husband Carl. I went to the funeral. She wanted me to be with her and to walk with her. Even though she had 7 children, she said I was her family. In her mid 80s she was able to travel to Ireland to meet second cousins and to see where her grandmother was born.

Unbeknownst to Madalyn, John Madden had actually been to Ireland to visit our relatives, but he was unaware of the extensive family in the USA. We shared info with Madden and he had an old picture of one brother and his family who stayed behind in Ireland. He had the phone numbers of some relatives in Ireland. That very day I called and talked to my Irish cousins. My wife and I had said if we ever found live relatives in Ireland we were going to visit them. Within 6 months we were there.

Life And its Stories

We took a genealogy book with us to Ireland to prove how we were related. We were all amazed at the family likeness in the pictures of our grandchildren and the young cousins in Ireland. We went to Church where my grandpa had been baptized. The Priest talked to us before Mass, and during Mass he introduced us and we had to stand up. After Mass, I asked him to bless my Irish Rosary. On future visits to Ireland, this same Father Fitzpatrick always remembered our names. One Irish cousin near my age, Fridolin, told me that when she was growing up several of her friends got gifts from their families in America. She always wished she had family in America. Another cousin had us over for dinner. Of course we had whiskey in our tea "to chase away the dew." Her brother called to say he and his wife were coming over to meet us. Immediately we were told to put the remaining food away and hide the whiskey.

We had trouble finding Pine Grove and my great grandmother's tombstone. Was Pine Grove a town? It wasn't on the map. Or was it a grove of pines? I decided to drive to southern Ohio (Ironton area) to see what I could find. Along the road there was a small sign saying Pine Grove. I turned that way, but couldn't find a town. I stopped at a general store (potbelly stove and all). I asked about Pine Grove. One old man in the back of the store said Pine Grove wasn't there anymore and directed me to a small church and cemetery. I walked through the whole cemetery looking for an old stone with my grandmother's name. Finally, I actually tripped over a newer stone and it was hers; Anna Grehan. I found out it was a newer stone because it was purchased when her 3 sons got together after all those years. The priest just happened to be there in the church that day and could read the German and Irish records. I also found out that Anna lost an infant child on the trip to America and died a year and a half after arriving. There were many strange coincidences doing this genealogy. We found exactly where our Irish family was a few weeks before Madalyn's granddaughter was going to study in Ireland. She was going to attend a college about 8 miles from her Irish cousins. Dan's wife Kim was distantly related to my wife and lived close to us. Thankfully the old man was in the general store and knew about Pine Grove. If I hadn't tripped over great grandma's tombstone I wouldn't have found her. And the priest in Pine Grove said he isn't at the church except for a few days a month and the other priest couldn't read the German and Irish records.

I was so excited driving home from Ironton after finding my great grandmother's tombstone. When passing St. Joseph's Cemetery in south Columbus where my grandfather is buried, I yelled out "Grandpa I found her." Just then the radio started playing Neil Diamond's Coming to America. I had goose-bumps and tears.

"That's My Son!"

Bishop James A Griffin

Michael Griffin, my great grandfather, came from Inver, County Donegal, to Baltimore in the early 1840s. His girl friend, Margaret Grogan followed a few years later, after he got settled, and they married. They moved to the western part of Virginia. In November 1855, Michael bought 300 acres in Fletcher's Run, near Orlando. This part of Virginia became part of West Virginia at the time of the Civil War.

Michael Griffin built a family Church, St. Michael Catholic Church on this farm. In 1916, my grandfather, James Griffin deeded this church, to the Diocese of Wheeling. In 1974, the state of West Virginia purchased the farm, to construct a recreation area, Burnsville Lake. The state moved the Church to a nearby Civil War battlefield park, Bulltown Historic Area.

While I was serving as Auxiliary Bishop of Cleveland, in the late 80's, we had a bad winter ice storm. Worried about my mother, who was almost 90 and lived alone in our family home, I got in my car and drove the treacherous twenty miles to her place.

She greeted me with a great hug and "Am I glad to see you!" Then, she explained. "That ice storm has frozen the roof drain on the unheated back porch. When the roof snow melts, it will come down on that porch and, with the drain plugged, the water will leak down on to the porch floor. I want you to go up there with a pry bar and unplug that drain."

I went to the garage, got the pry bar and a ladder, and climbed up on the roof and began to work on unplugging the drain.

My mother put on her coat and walked out into the back yard, so that she could see what I was doing, and, of course, give me directions.

During this process, our neighbor, a good Catholic lady, opened her back door to get her morning paper. She looked up, saw me, and exclaimed: "Is that the bishop up on the roof?" My mother turned to her and said: "That's my son!"

My brothers and sisters and myself still love to retell that story and my mother's quick reply.

John O'Neill

Patty and Maggie Grove

Our grandmother, Janet Scanlon, and her parents lived with her maternal grandparents, John and Mary Louise O'Neill. Grandma Scanlon was a great historian and kept newspaper articles and documents about her Grandfather O'Neill and growing up, we heard many stories and anecdotes about him. This is his story as passed down from Grandma Scanlon.

Grandfather O'Neill was born in Philadelphia and raised in Fredericktown, Maryland, but both his mother and father, who came to America in 1804, were from Derry, County Derry, Ireland. From an early age he was familiar with the institution of slavery and abhorred the practice. He studied law at St. John's College and was admitted to the bar at the early age of twenty. Soon after, he moved to Ohio where he met and married Mary Louise Searle of Newark. They settled in Zanesville where he practiced law with his father-in-law, Judge Corrington W. Searle and several other attorneys. In 1862, in the midst of the Civil War, Grandfather O'Neill, a Democrat, was elected the Congressional Representative for Knox, Licking, Coshocton, Guernsey and Muskingum counties.

During this time, he was also instrumental in raising a regiment of Muskingum County men to serve in the Civil War, but they never saw duty. After his term in Congress, he returned to Zanesville and resumed his law practice and also served for a period of time as the Muskingum County prosecutor. In 1883, Grandfather O'Neill was elected State Senator. During his terms as Senator, he was one of a committee of three that designed the circuit court districts of the state. He also introduced and pressed the passage of the bill that created the combined normal and industrial department at Wilberforce University. At the time, this bill was credited with saving the University. He later served many terms on the Board of Trustees for Wilberforce at the insistence of the faculty. One newspaper wrote "A devout Catholic and an ardent and life-long Democrat, there is no man in Ohio who has done more to promote the welfare of the colored people of the state or who has given more liberally of his personal means to assist the individual members of the race than Senator John O'Neill." This son of Irish immigrants had an immeasurable impact on the lives of many that may still be felt by their families today.

Grandfather and Grandmother O'Neill raised eight children, four sons and four daughters. One daughter married Dr. Jesse Magruder who was instrumental in the founding of St. Anthony's Hospital in Columbus.

Since Grandma Scanlon was raised in the O'Neill's home, most of their furniture was passed from them to Grandma's parents and eventually to Grandma. So, besides knowing many stories and the history of the Grandfather O'Neill, we grew up surrounded by his possession, which in a way was being surrounded by his presence. Today, almost everyone in our family has a piece of his history in their homes, whether it is a side tables, lamp or bedroom suite. Patty has his bed and dresser, Dorothy Gallen has Grandmother O'Neill's bed and dresser, Maggie has the dining room table and Jim Fichtelman uses the Mahogany game tables as nightstands. Several years ago our great nieces and nephews were sitting at Maggie's dining room table coloring. It struck us that this was the sixth generation to sit around the O'Neill's dining room table. And this generation will also learn the stories and be given copies of the articles and documents that Grandma Scanlon kept so that they too can be proud to be descendants of Irish immigrants.

Michael J. and Margaret Lynch Scanlon
Patty and Maggie Grove

In 1853, Michael Scanlon left his wife and new son in Ballylongford, County Kerry, and came to America to create a new life for his family. He found employment and settled in Somerset, Ohio. In 1854 he was able to send for his wife, Margaret, and son, Michael.

The ship Margaret came to America on, was to dock in New Orleans, but wrecked before reaching the harbor. Holding on to a piece of the wreckage, Margaret and her small son, Michael, were rescued. Another woman held onto the heel of Margaret's shoe, but slipped away when the heel broke loose. Several of Margaret's brothers came with her and together they made it up the Mississippi to Cincinnati and Margaret and Michael continued on to Somerset.

Michael and Margaret raised three daughters and four sons. When Margaret passed away, the article in the paper spoke Michael and Margaret as a happy loving couple. "In the early days love ruled the household of children, and not the rod. 'Honor thy father and thy mother' seemed an inborn principal in the children and they were deserving of honor." They passed not only their strong family love and loyalty to their children, but also their strong Catholic faith and Irish heritage. And each generation has continued to pass their teachings on to the next.

Their grandson, Anthony "Tony" Scanlon was one of the Charter Members of Shamrock Club. With Uncle Tony's full support, several of their great-great granddaughters were instrumental in the founding of the Daughters of Erin (DOE). Mary Margaret was a co-founder and Patty Grove and Dorothy Gallen were Charter Members. Great granddaughter, Mary Lou Scanlon

Fichtelman was instrumental in drafting the original Constitution and By-laws for the DOE. Today, Scanlon descendants remain active in the Irish community as members of the Shamrock Club, Ancient Order of Hibernians, Daughters of Erin and the Emerald Society.

Chasing Uncle Mike
A Writer's Search for His Desperado Namesake
By Mike Harden

Introduction

When Mike McGahan leaped out the back window of Lima, Ohio's Halloran Hotel, the first shot fired by waiting police officers shattered his wrist the instant his feet hit the porch roof below him. The impact of the slug drove a scalding tremor up his left arm, wrecking his balance long enough to send him tumbling over the eaves to the grass below. The cops might have finished him off as he scrambled to his feet, presenting his pursuers with a fish-in-a-barrel target as he fumbled for his dropped revolver, but the sight of yet another fugitive following Mike's plunge out the window distracted them. Raleigh Townsend, shooting wildly as he exited the Halloran, wasted no time catching up with his partner as the two dodged behind sheds and trees just long enough to squeeze off a few shots to delay their pursuers.

Ten minutes earlier, Mike and the four members of his gang had been savoring the good fortune of a surprising haul from their early morning heist of a tank-town bank across the state line in northern Indiana. Bursting in on a lone cashier and the bank's president, they forced the pair into the vault before relieving the Huntertown State Bank of more than $21,000 in cash and silver. Scooping up a pistol he kept secreted in the vault, the cashier fired two shots at the departing bandits, probably more to save face afterwards with account-holding townsfolk than to initiate a shootout. The four desperados, as newspaper accounts of the robbery would christen them, sped out of town, kicking up a wake of dust behind them. Once safely across the state line in Ohio, they rendezvoused with another gang member, ditching the Buick they used for the holdup and climbing into a Cadillac for the final leg of their escape to their temporary hideout at the Halloran Hotel.

At his headquarters in downtown Lima, Police Chief Jake Roush fielded a phone call from the sheriff of Allen County, Indiana. It came as no surprise to him that his law-enforcement counterpart thought the Huntertown job to be the work of the McGahan gang. Roush knew that Mike and his boys had been hitting banks in a four-state area for more than a year, and recently had been rumored to be hanging out across the rail yard at the Halloran and the Mihlbaugh rooming house next door. The chief assigned a pair of his officers to sneak a peek at the presumed hideout, but to do nothing that might flush the bandits out until he had returned from dinner. Patrolman Dick Watkins, a World War I cavalryman and expert marksman was joined by Charles Hamilton, another crack shot and one of the first African-Americans on the Lima force. The two found the Cadillac getaway car, coated with a patina of fresh road dust, two blocks from the hotel. Yet, even before Watkins and Hamilton identified the gang's car, neighbors along Vine Street had noted the arrival of five shifty-looking strangers who made their way to the hotel and the adjacent rooming house. Word swiftly leaked out from police headquarters, as well, and by the time Chief Rouse had polished off his dessert, a scattered band of concerned citizens and cop wannabes had begun forming a rag-tag posse on the south fringe of Lima. Armed with everything from deer rifles to pea-shooting, pawnshop .22s, they awaited orders from Roush.

When the chief arrived, bystanders reported that two gang members had entered the hotel, while the other three made themselves comfortable at the rooming house. Roush made his way into the boarding house surprising McGahan's lieutenant "Chicago Joe" Willis, who had been posted as a lookout.

"Throw up your hands or I'll kill you," the chief commanded.

Willis, his double-barrel shotgun parked against the wall several feet out of reach, obliged.

Hearing the commotion, gang members John Mason and George Donovan dashed up the rooming-house stairs to a second-floor window where they began trading fire with police outside.

McGahan and Townsend made their break, pausing only long enough to reload and to stash a bag of holdup money in a backyard cistern. With another ambush likely awaiting them at their Cadillac, the two began scouring garages for something to steal. Moving from Vine Street to Greenlawn Avenue, they came face to face with patrolmen Watkins and Hamilton. The latter leveled his .45 and fired a shot that shattered Townsend's shoulder before traveling through his lung and heart. McGahan, kneeling over his buddy long enough to realize the wound was mortal, grabbed his buddy's gun and rose, taking a slug from Watkins in his left side. He dragged himself behind a tree, trying to get is bearings as gunfire stripped the bark from his tenuous cover. By this time, the running gun battle had raged back and forth for almost 20 minutes. Chief Roush had been joined by the county sheriff, a deputy, the prosecuting attorney and a half-dozen railroad detectives. The next day's issue of the *Lima Republican Gazette* would declare—in what was likely something of an exaggeration—that "hundreds" of south side residents had thrown themselves into the manhunt. In any case, their number was sufficient that McGahan, fleeing in one direction while Donovan and Mason fled in another, had to contend with pot shots from behind every porch swing and pergola in the neighborhood.

When McGahan spied a car parked in a Greenlawn Avenue driveway, he made his move. Leaping into the vehicle, he was attempting to hot-start it when a bullet smashed through the windshield and lodged in the backseat upholstery. A second shot cracked the steering wheel as he clambered out and made for the street, taking yet another round in his left side. He spied a pickup truck whose 18-year-old driver had slowed to a crawl trying to make sense of the chaos unfolding before him. McGahan, leaping onto the running board, jabbed the nose of his revolver into the ribs of Lima resident Paul Phillips, commanding, "Drive like hell!"

Through smoke and spent cordite, his captive wheeled out of town, following a circuitous, back-road route through Delphos and Spencerville to Findlay.

Lima police surrounded Mason and Donovan, who threw down their guns and were hustled off to the city jail. They were not far behind their partner "Chicago Joe" nor much in advance of the body of Raleigh Townsend, which after examination at the jail by the coroner was trotted before the cell holding his three partners on its way to a nearby funeral home.

Between Delphos and Spencerville, McGahan, though unsure how much of a head start he had on trailing police, ordered Phillips to pull over at a spot where a small creek ran under the road. There, he bathed his wounds and tried to wash some of the blood from his clothing. He would make another stop at a brook to ease his wounds before he and Phillips reached the outskirts of Findlay. There, he stuffed a few bills from his pocket into his captive's hands, advising the young driver to tell police back in Lima that he had dropped him instead in the town of Ottawa.

Weak from blood loss, McGahan knew that not far from where Phillips had dropped him off, a criminal hangout known to the locals as "Dago Lil's" was probably the only place he might round up a physician who was not too discriminating about his clients as long as the money was right. Close to fainting from loss of blood, McGahan knew he had eight $100 bills in his trousers, money he had pocketed before stashing the bank's cash. He had always sworn that he would never be taken alive. Now, inspecting his wounds, he realized how close he had come to fulfilling that taunt.

Back in Lima, an enterprising undertaker had been blessed with an alluring attraction he was sure would draw curious locals to his establishment. Indeed, two thousand gawkers filed past the embalming table that held Raleigh Townsend's 25-year-old body even as a shady physician at Dago Lil's probed Mike McGahan's three bullet wounds.

Chapter One

I was nine years old the first time I took money to watch a man die. The pay wasn't much—a quarter, sometimes 35 cents—but the work was steady. For "Irish Bill" Murphy died with an arresting regularity during the childhood years I spent as his next door neighbor on the West Side of Columbus. Old Man Murphy lived with his sister Catherine in a pinched bungalow the hue of gray flannel, a place surrounded by an impeccably manicured privet. Neither Murphy had married, and each, clawing past the milestone of fourscore years, kept a white-knuckled grip on life purely for the sake of making the other miserable. Catherine was a dour stoic who shuffled over the linoleum from room to room leaving in her wake the mingled redolence of sauerkraut and sweat. The profile of her countenance bore a striking likeness to that of an aging Queen Victoria, had Britain's empress worn faded house dresses. Her brother Bill, a gangly, hawk-beaked fellow whose head was tufted with wisps of wood-smoke hair, was a drinker of good stout and player of ponies. He had burnished to a high sheen the exacting human drama of hypochondria. Though I was yet young, I had little trouble identifying the pair's indelible traits as I slogged for nickels and dimes filling their coal scuttle, hauling out ashes and running errands to the mom-and-pop grocery a few blocks away.

"That old woman's piss could etch glass," my father had once quipped of Bill's sister. She was not one to suffer fools gladly, particularly her brother. Thus, a yelped summons from Catherine through our open kitchen window sent me on the run to the Murphy's doorstep, where I was ushered in to take a seat on a straight-back chair a few feet from the bed where Bill, flailing at a tangle of sheets and pillows, had decided to die, though not without company. My vigil perch was much too close to a bedside stand upon which resided a tumbler half-filled with water and a China blue glass eye. Once Catherine had seen me to my deathbed station, she generally offered her benediction on the grimly comic tableau by sucking her teeth and turning her imploring eyes toward a framed print of Jesus, who--like a melancholy prom suitor proffering a boxed corsage--held out a heart licked with flames and capped with a rakishly-set crown of thorns. Her obligation to Christian compassion fulfilled for the day, Catherine retired to a back bedroom to whirl the dial of a radio the size of a confessional, filling the house with crackles and wolf whistles until the contraption fixed upon a distant signal and a tenor warbling something about a Paddy or a Sean climbing the gallows steps or falling off a barstool or putting a bullet in one of those goddamned English bastards who refused to give Ireland back to the Irish. While Bill's sister warbled accompanying too-rah-loo-rah-loo-rahs at the radio, I sat aside her brother's bed studying a lithograph depicting the sons of Erin battling their despotic neighbors in what was, so I later learned, a 17th century uprising that was ultimately crushed by Oliver Cromwell. I knew nothing of history then, though was hypnotized by the Irish lancers whose weapons, Old Man Murphy assured me, had been fitted with reversed barbs in order to make a one-two punch of skewering and disembowelment. Had the Irish lost the skirmish, the wall at the Murphy's would have been bare, but the rebels—strewing garlands of viscera--were whacking the Brits around like overstuffed pinadas. The lithograph possessed an oddly hypnotic effect on me, though like most of the trappings in the Murphy's home, I found it intimidating. It made me uneasy in the manner that the flaming heart of Jesus made me fearful, and the unseeing, blue orb in the water glass raised hair on the back of my neck.

At my elbow, Bill lay dying, his rosary entwining an arthritic paw as tightly as the rope of a punched tether ball. He had all the moves of a 19th century tubercular diva, tossing and moaning amid the covers strewn atop a berth too short for his rangy frame, the pale pecan halves of his hoary toenails peeking out beyond the wrought-iron scallops of the bed foot.

"I'm going," he episodically sighed, straining to prop himself up on his elbows before sinking in a feigned swoon back into the pillow folds.

"Jesus," he called.

Jesus, I thought. This had better be good for 35 cents.

When Bill had finished dying for the afternoon, he plucked a little spare change and pocket lint from his trousers and pressed it into my palm. Watching Bill die was nowhere as adventurous as serving as his guide dog. Too proud to accept the canine companion to which his diminished vision entitled him, he instead hired the eyes of neighborhood children to lead him four blocks to the bus stop and accompany him downtown on his weekly errands. He planted me on a seat beside him as the bus groaned away from the stop, and he waited for the driver to begin the obligatory, sing-song recitation of upcoming stops.

"Yale Avenue," the driver hailed, and though Bill could not see the storefronts and dowdy homes through his one, cataract-clouded eye, he would launch into a passionate recollection of the Great Flood of 1913, a deluge that had claimed dozens of lives in the low-lying "Bottoms" neighborhood of Columbus.

"Oh, Christ, it was terrible," Bill recounted. "Rain wouldn't stop that spring, and colder than a well-digger's ass, I tell you. The water came up, 10 feet, 15, 20 feet and still rising. People climbed to their attics and prayed through the night."

In the predawn of the flood's first day, a father of four fashioned a makeshift raft of bed slats and headboards, then floated his children away from the water creeping up the second-floor landing to the higher boughs of a nearby tree. There he lashed them to sturdy branches where, shivering in the March howl, they awaited rescue. The temperature plummeted. Help did not arrive until a half-day later when weeping firefighters in rowboats found the four small children, dead of exposure, bound to the tree. Only the father was revived. Downstream from the flooded bottomland of the Scioto River, four dozen bodies of the drowned came to rest amid the flotsam that settled among the headstones of the higher ground in Mt. Calvary Cemetery.

"Awful," Old Bill lamented, crossing himself as he did. "Just awful."

At Broad and High Streets, the main downtown crossroads of the city, I guided Bill off the bus and, clinging to a fistful of trouser leg, led him down past the State House to the office of his bookie. Before advancing age dimmed Bill's vision, he had been a railbird at Beulah Park, a thoroughbred track south of the city. Now, he was reduced to scribbling his picks on a scrap of paper around which he folded the bills of his wager, all of it tucked neatly in an envelope he slid under the teller-like grill fronting the work station of his bookie, a county employee whose legitimate job involved the selling of vendors' licenses. The man's face was half-shaded by a green visor, and dried crumbs of antacid dotted the creases of a perpetual frown. Although I accompanied Bill on dozens of occasions to place bets, I cannot recall my neighbor winning so much as a dollar on the ponies.

His wagers set, Bill would retire to one of his favorite watering holes, usually Ivan's, for a pint of stout. There, beneath the pressed tin ceiling, the carved walnut bar with its polished brass foot rail and scattered spittoons, he held court for whoever cared to listen on the scourge of Communism (which he found almost as loathsome as the British monarchy), the bungling of the Korean War or the state of the Cleveland Indians bullpen. In the golden arc of the waning day, he eventually nudged me toward the door, and together we would catch the west side bus home. Not once during our many forays did the old man breathe a word of his knowledge about my blood connection to the darker side of my mother's Irish kin. He knew the truth, most assuredly, for the Irish in Columbus were a clannish band of gossips and snipes, savoring the successes of local sons of Erin almost as much as they regaled in the misdeeds of its most fearsome ne'er-do-wells. In the half-lit taverns of the city's "Irish Broadway" neighborhood, the name that never crossed Bill Murphy's lips in my presence had become a household word.

Mike McGahan, my mother's most cherished uncle and my namesake, was either famous or infamous, depending upon one's view, but he was always respected. Newspaper headline writers labeled him a desperado. Crime reporters elevated his escapades to the level of high drama. Newspaper editors throughout the Midwest paired narratives of his latest adventures with a photograph of a menacing Uncle Mike whose countenance, even in repose, bore a defiant scowl that even Tinseltown outlaw Jimmy Cagney couldn't duplicate. The police feared Mike not because he was recklessly unpredictable, but rather because he was just the opposite. The cops knew that unless he was hopelessly outnumbered, he preferred to shoot it out with authorities even as his accomplices fled. Only now am I struck by the irony of the stunning differences that separated my mother's uncle from the boy she named in his honor.

Chapter Two

As a child, I ate fear for breakfast, lunch and dinner. It was my bedmate at night when the branches of winter-bare trees sharpened their claws against the windowpane. It dogged each trembling step I took accompanying my mother to the murky cellar to ignite anew the pilot light beneath an ancient lead-sheathed hot water heater. I was certain that behind that tank the dreaded hook-armed murderer lurked, salivating as he calculated the precise moment to leap from his hiding place and rip out our throats. Mortified by all things dark, it took all of my mettle to accompany my childhood playmates on their forays into the neighborhood's darkened garages, virtual troves of castoff junk—broken mantle clocks with enchantingly complex innards, weather-beaten baby buggies whose wheels and axles were prized for their utility when cobbling racing carts from junk lumber and orange crates. Those shadowy garages also served as the amateur theatres in which innocently awkward anatomical exhibits between pre-pubescent neighborhood kids assured that 4th graders got their first shadowy glimpses of one another's wedding tackle.

I had an inordinate, though hardly inexplicable, dread of sewers, having once been suspended by my ankles over the yawning mouth of one by my older cousin Jerry and a pair of his thug buddies. The mere thought of polio mortified me, for it was a cruel and capricious fact of life in my early 1950s childhood. The daily paper often featured photographs of small tortured faces peeking from what appeared to be monstrous barrels set upon their sides. I feared swimming pools, for adults seemed certain that, on the steamiest of summer days, they were a petri dish crawling with the bacteria of infantile paralysis.

At school, I cowered at the sight of a playground bully named Dickie. His black leather jacket, Marlon Brando motorcycle cap and duck-tailed coif could make any elementary school weakling quake. A toothpick sprouted from both downturned corners of a disapproving frown. The sort of apprentice hoodlum our parents warned us would come to no good, Dickie provided me an early lesson in the baseless nature of my childhood fears when I strolled out to recess one day to behold him sobbing inconsolably in the arms of a teacher. The sight measured 9.5 on the Richter Scale among those of us considered playground weaklings. A fissure of vulnerability had cleaved the pedestal upon which we had all been compelled to elevate a bully. I learned that a week before, Dickie's younger brother had perished beneath the wheels of a postal truck. The ponderous loss had unmasked a façade to reveal a child every bit as fragile and frightened as I was.

The thought of death mortified me. I feared hell. To me it was as tangible and real as my own neighborhood. Hell was a smoking, sprawling, sulfurous lake of fire in which the doomed of earth writhed in unrelenting pain, begging to be put out of their misery. Satan, seated atop a lifeguard's stand, waving his trident like symphony conductor's baton, laughed at the pleadings of the damned. I knew hell was real because my father had commanded his six offspring to attend the full-gospel fundamentalist church of his mother, a concession that served as a hedge against her badgering him to give his life to Christ. The congregation in which my grandmother was known as Sister Pearl converged several times each week in a former roller rink at which sinners had once done the devil's bidding in short pleated skirts. I feigned colds, flu, nausea and assorted irritable bowel calamities to escape Sunday morning services, though all to no avail. Sooner or later, a wheezing converted school bus driven by the bow-tied and buck-toothed Brother Burns, the pied piper of tongues-speaking, holy-rolling salvation, brought his rig to a halt in front of our picket fence to gather those Harden children who had sufficiently outgrown drooling and incontinence to know that they were damned if they didn't get right with God.

Sister Pearl, my grandmother was a short, stout woman with a parrot-like nose she couldn't resist dipping in other people's business. She wore sensible shoes, Woolworth dresses and kept her waist-length chestnut hair piled atop her head in an intricate braid that gave her the look of an aging *Star Wars* Princess Leah or an overworked loaf of challah. The church forbade women to cut their hair which, accordingly, required the application of such massive fogs of Aqua Net that—had helium been a chief ingredient of hairspray—would have lifted all of them to heaven before Sunday brunch.

The lone saving grace of those frightening Sundays was the bus ride to and from worship. In the long, looping arc that carried us to church, Brother Burns always stopped to pick up a honey-tressed, apple-cheeked Blanche Nair. Wherever she sat on the bus, I moved one seat behind. I loved the smell of her hair. White Rain? I can't recall, but I know that I was smitten the first time I saw her. Shy, saintly Blanche with her little white Bible embossed in gold with her name, became the unwitting author of yet another fearful specter in my life. Take an old school bus whose springs have witnessed 100,000 miles of bad road, drive it down brick-cobbled streets while a moonstruck lad on the cusp of puberty is inhaling the hair of the little girl in front of him, and a curious thing begins to happen. At first, I was not even aware that the tumescent yearnings straining at the wool pants of my hand-me-down suit had anything to do with my thoughts of saving Blanche from a burning tenement or pulling her out of the way of a runaway truck. Unfortunately, some dark hormonal lurking knew better. I arrived at the church one morning with a tent sprouted in the front of my trousers. Panicking, I was unable to return the pleasant smile Blanche flashed as she rose to exit the bus. Had she seen? Was that the reason for the smile? My God? I was sitting in front of the throne of God on a Sunday morning with a raging erection. Oh, yes, I would find out about hell soon enough. Satan had a particularly hot corner just waiting for me. I would stand there in my priapic shame naked for eternity. Removing my coat, I held it before me and tried to think about long division, the capital of Wyoming. Anything. As I descended the basement steps to my Sunday School class, the sight of Sister Whalen's pendulous goiter, a hideous thing over which we prayed every Sunday, did the trick. Swinging like an elephant's trunk, it saved me that Sunday. To me, though, it seemed that dawning puberty would be just another demonic presence for which I would eventually face exorcism.

My mother, all too conscious that she was rearing a son whose fearfulness had quickly earned him paternal chastening as a "pantywaist," tried to soothe my worries. Aware that I was having trouble falling asleep for fretting over polio, the rapture, the axe murderer under the bunk bed and my embarrassing new secret, my mother would smooth back my hair and comfort, "Mikey, try to think about bunnies." I would—rabid, 6-foot hares marching in lockstep toward my window as they fired up chainsaws.

My Uncle Mike would have been ashamed of his cowardly namesake. He was a street tough long before he reached his teenage years. The spawn of potato-famine immigrants growing up on the choked streets of downtown Columbus, he had managed to stir up enough trouble by 14 to be ordered by the courts to spend a year downstate at Ohio's Boys Industrial School. He was considered incorrigible, a hoodlum in the making, a smart-ass little Mick trying to make his bones on the mean streets of Columbus, Ohio.

Until the construction of Boys Industrial School in 1858, it was not uncommon that youthful offenders were simply dispatched to the Ohio Penitentiary, where they became easy prey for seasoned convicts. Only after a group of Ohio citizens concerned about delinquency and the social welfare of the immigrant poor traveled to France to tour its institutions did the state legislature move to establish a prison without walls or fences. The chief purpose of the new institution, unlike the finishing school for felons that the Ohio Pen had become, was to set young, malleable minds on a more socially productive course for life.

To my 14-year-old Uncle Mike, the pastoral setting of Boys Industrial School must have seemed like the other side of the moon after teeming, urban Columbus. Situated on the fringe of the Appalachian foothills, it resembled nothing so little as the reform school it was. A configuration of brick cottages held 40 boys each, along with a set of cottage parents, usually a husband and wife whose own children had been reared. In an era of stunningly primitive thinking about delinquency and rehabilitation, it was prescient of the institution's directors to assure that both a mature paternal and maternal figure would live in their company, mentor them and, perhaps most vitally, serve as surrogate parents. Mike needed that. His father James was beset with what the Irish euphemistically referred to as "the weakness." His drinking doubtless ate into the family's income, tainted his behavior toward his six offspring and left Mike with few models to emulate save the street-wise punks who had learned early on that, if you wanted to survive in the squalid slums of the city, you had to grab a root and growl.

Uncle Mike was logged into Boys Industrial School in 1903. The old registration book indicated that he was a mere 4-foot-10 and weighed 90 pounds. A thatch of ginger hair combed back in a pompadour rested above a pair of piercing blue eyes and the face of a pug. Even in repose, his mouth was set in a scowl. The admissions clerk duly noted that Mike used both profane language and tobacco, though he claimed to be temperate. The log reveals that his parents, James and Annie, had separated.

At Boys Industrial School, each newly arriving resident was informed that he brought with him a set of demerits. The number was based on the gravity of the sentencing offense. The catch-all charge of "incorrigibility" was sufficient to earn 50, perhaps 75 demerits. Incorrigibles, while hardly a menace to society, were a nuisance to the beat cops who knew they were up to no good. Uncle Mike's sin was burglary and petty theft. He could have stolen goods from a shop closed for the day or broken into a home and helped himself to lunch. The specifics of the crime have been lost with the records of the Columbus police court at which he was convicted. Suffice it to say, he likely carried at least100 demerits baggage when he arrived at Lancaster. A boy assigned to the industrial school was able to work off his demerits by adherence to the rules, diligent school attendance and satisfactory performance of daily chores. Much of the facility's 1500 acres not occupied by the bakery, kitchen, vocational workshops and administrative offices, was farmed by the boys, who also tended the livestock.

From the day the facility opened in 1858, military drill was a mandatory daily function for all young men. Indeed, when the Civil War broke out three years later, many of the youthful residents were released to join the assembling ranks of Union troops. Some of new recruits conveyed the bulk of their $300 enlistment bonuses to the industrial school, specifying that it be used to further the work of the institution should they not survive the war. Many did not.

In the 120-year history of the institution, more than 100,000 boys spent time there. Several years after Uncle Mike's 12-month stint, a Cleveland street tough named Lester Townes Hope was sent to the industrial school for truancy. Released after 8 months in 1918, he was returned the following year for the same offense, though he escaped during his second stint and was never returned. When, a few years later, he set his sights on a career in entertainment, it apparently occurred to him that Les Hope sounded more like a curse than a stage name. So Les, for his many decades in comedy, became better known to the world as Bob.

If Mike McGahan learned a trade at Boys Industrial School, it likely was not one he ever put to practice. Released after a one-year stint, he returned to Columbus and immediately fell in with his old friends along Irish Broadway or, as the police preferred to call it, the "Bad Lands." The 15-year-old Mike's father had completely vanished by this time, his mother and two sisters given over to seamstress work to keep food on the table. His younger brother, Ed, soon to be known to the cops as "Monk" McGahan, was apprenticing in Mike's footsteps. The McGahans were not lace-curtain, two-toilet Irish. The members of my clan were the "Shanty Irish," the famine immigrants driven from their home country less by politics than potatoes. A million and a half fled Ireland during the dark years, coming to America to help dig the canals which—because of the mortality rate in those festering holes—came to be known as the "Irishman's Grave." Many saw the United States as but a temporary state in their lives. They ached for their home country and longed for a time when they might return and wrest their Ireland from the British who had let them die like dogs during the famine. Instead, they poured the toil of their all-to-brief lives into the mines, mills and factories of the growing republic. They became fresh fodder for the Union cause in the Civil War, later becoming indispensable cogs in the machinery of the American Industrial Revolution. They saw themselves caricatured in the editorial cartoons of the era as tattered, drunken half-simians. The McGahans had arrived in the U.S. from Ireland's County Cavan a decade before the Civil War. At the time, Ohio was yet considered part of the western fringe of the young nation. Good farmland was available in abundance throughout the state and, though some among my far-flung ancestors embraced clearing the soil, breaking the furrows and celebrating the first gathering of crops, just as many headed for the big cities. The famine had schooled them in the cruel and capricious whims of nature.

The Columbus that was home to a young Mike McGahan was not one city, but two. To the patricians who drank and dined in the splendor of the rooftop garden of the Great Southern Hotel downtown, the Ohio capital was their oyster. They owned everything in the city from its numerous breweries to a score of buggy works that turned out 20,000 carriages a year. The produce of light manufacturing filled every consumer need from washboards to burial footwear. The barons who stood astride of it all collected politicians as some might rare stamps or coins. To them, leaders of city government and members of the state legislature served merely as chess pieces, pawns of their bidding when social reformers agitated too boisterously in the chambers of government for better working and living conditions for the have-nots. In Uncle Mike's youth, he had seen Columbus rocked by unrest and riots, bombings and beatings, during strikes against the city's streetcar companies as well as its many breweries. The improvements in labor conditions wrought by the strife were negligible when weighed against the toll they exacted in injuries and death, or the days of martial law when the sight of Ohio National Guardsmen prowling the streets in Stutz Bearcats affixed with hood-mounted machine guns became commonplace. In the waning years of the 19th century, although Columbus may have been the site of the nativity of both the American Federation of Labor and the United Mine Workers, the laborers whose toil lined the pockets of the city's burghers remained squarely under the thumb of management. Yet even the shapers of public opinion who sided with the capitalists were wise enough to see the eventual harvest to be gathered from the sowing of oppression. The sun had scarcely cleared the horizon of the new century when renowned social commentator and lecturer H.H. Barbour stood at the pulpit of the city's affluent First Baptist Church and implored the smug plutocracy seated in the amen pews to consider the young Mike McGahans being molded in the squalor of Columbus slums nicknamed Flytown, Milo, the Bad Lands and the Bottoms.

"What does it mean?" Barbour implored of the congregation. "It means that those who are to make up the Columbus of a generation hence, who are to be vastly in the majority here twenty-five years from now, are getting their education and forming their impressions of social conditions and having their characters molded amid influences of environment that make and can make only for evil. Trained in the nurseries of pauperism and crime, reared in rookeries where the sunlight is shut out, the foul air shut in, and modesty strangled, taught that there is no hope for them except in the overthrow of the existing order, what kind of citizens are they likely to make…?" If Barbour's listeners had wanted for a face to match with the grim prognostications of their guest speaker, they needed to look no further than the pinched and fight-scarred mug of Mike McGahan.

My Uncle Mike would spin a fuming pirouette in his grave were his namesake nephew to characterize him as a victim of life's circumstances, any more than were I to claim that he was simply born a bad seed. Plenty of his Irish contemporaries survived similar childhoods of want and privation; were reared in homes where family life was battered by the bottle, then turned out to make their way on streets where life was cheap and hope seemed a mirage. Unlike Mike, others swallowed the secular catechism of the American dream and lived out their lives as factory hands or mill workers so their children could become educators and clerics, maybe even social activists laboring under the conviction that a rising tide would lift all boats.

But Mike was not among them. He was away from Boys Industrial School just long enough to notch his 15th birthday when he held up a saloon-keeper and was dispatched by a judge to the Ohio Reformatory at Mansfield, a bleak, gothic structure of brick and stone which—decades after Mike had honed his criminal apprenticeship there—would become the motion-picture setting for the filming of *The Shawshank Redemption*. Fifteen years after actors Tim Robbins and Morgan Freeman put feet beneath Stephen King's fiction, I sat in one of the 8-foot-by-6 cells that was home to Uncle Mike for five years. A suspended steel grille held a wafer-thin mattress next to a rude toilet and a small wash basin mounted flush against a wall painted the dreary green of split-pea soup. A man confined to such a sunless warren might cling to the hope of pardon or waiting family in order to keep suicide at bay and sanity intact. Some found God inside the walls. I rather believe that my uncle survived by promising to plan his next heist meticulously enough to spare himself another ticket to the pen.

While Mike counted days at Mansfield, his younger brother Ed was providing authorities in Ohio and western Pennsylvania with yet another McGahan to trouble their days. Unlike his older sibling, who preferred to hit banks and saloons, Ed was partial to grocery stores and service stations. He reasoned, perhaps, that, while bank cashiers and bartenders had been robbed regularly enough to keep a revolver within easy reach, grocery cashiers and grease monkeys usually had no taste for gunplay.

As though two criminals at McGahan family reunions left such gatherings insufficiently armed, Mike and Ed's sister, Mary, accepted the marriage proposal of a rising young Columbus hoodlum named Pasquale Provenzano, alias Charles Provence, alias Charlie Dillon. Watching young Mary wed a desperado, Anna McGahan apparently decided to steer the fate of her two remaining daughters, Lizzie and Louise, toward more respectable suitors. To that end, she began scouring Columbus newspapers for their classified sections' precursors of what today are better known as "personals." A "lonely hearts" ad in the *Ohio State Journal* unearthed a 28-year-old farmer in upstate Medina seeking a steady, practical-minded woman to share his bed and bear his children. Lizzie, self-willed and wild, possessed none of the qualities Phillip Hand was seeking when he placed the advertisement. Moreover, she was 13 years younger than him. Undaunted, her mother coaxed her to a photo studio where she posed in a white, Gibson-girl dress. Anna penned a letter that knitted high praise and half-truths about her daughter and dashed it off to Medina, requesting in return a photograph along with firm assurances of the farmer's solvency. Not long afterward, the woman who would become my grandmother was married.

Comments regarding "Chasing Uncle Mike" by Julie O'Keefe McGhee

Mike Harden, a talented author from Columbus, Ohio, first became interested in our effort to collect and publish the family stories of the Central Ohio Irish in

2007. A columnist for the Columbus Dispatch Mike wrote two articles about our efforts and gradually he became interested in his own Irish background. This prompted Mike to give us the introduction and first two chapters of his book, Chasing Uncle Mike for inclusion in this book. Mike's book tells about his reconnecting with his own Irish heritage as well as the rough beginnings of many Irish-Americans in this country.

Thankfully Mike wrote his Irish family story before his untimely death on October 13th 2010.

Really Close Friends

Teresa Veeley Harris

In the late 1840s, two friends, Thomas Callahan and Patrick McCormick, left the land of their birth, Ireland, for America. Tired of the hunger caused by the Great Famine, they longed for the land of milk and honey that was America.

On the same ship were many people who had left Ireland on the same quest. Among them were two friends, Brigid Collins and Catherine McNerney. The four met and soon became close friends—so close, in fact, that once they arrived in America and settled in Kentucky, Tom and Brigid were married. Following suit, Patrick and Catherine were also married.

Tom and Brigid had three children. Their youngest, a son Michael, was born sometime in 1853. Patrick and Catherine had six children of their own. Their eldest, a daughter named after her mother, Catherine, was born sometime in 1854.

Michael, son of Tom and Brigid, married Catherine, daughter of Patrick and Catherine, sometime in 1873 or 1874. Michael and Catherine were blessed with six children. However, after the birth of their sixth child, a son James born on April 1, 1885, Catherine became ill. She died just nine days later on April 10, 1885.

Now Catherine had a half sister, Anne Laughlin, who was married to John Veeley with whom she had six children. Anne offered to take James who was only nine days old. Michael agreed, and Anne and John raised James as one of their own. James became so much a part of their family that he did not keep the Callahan name but took the Veeley name as his own. James was my grandfather.

The Visitor

Teresa Veeley Harris

The family of Catherine Thomas of New Lexington, Ohio ran a boarding house for workers in the area. During the winter and early spring of 1887 and 1888 a gentleman rented a room in the house. He was a tall redheaded Irishman, whose identity remains unknown to this day.

Catherine, who was 18 at the time, became smitten with this handsome stranger. When he left town, sometime in April of 1888, little did Catherine know at the time, that she was with child.

On December 15, 1888, Catherine gave birth to a beautiful redheaded daughter, whom she named Mary. Mary was my husband's Grandmother.

Luck of the Irish

Mary Ellen Sexton Hayman

My dad, Terence (Terry) Andrew Tackney Sexton, was born in Bailieborough, Ireland on March 14, 1874. Bailieborough is located in County Cavan, approximately 60 miles north of Dublin.

His parents, Andrew and Bridget had three children: Margaret (Maggie), Phillip and my Dad. Phillip was the oldest so he inherited the farm. His sister probably came over ten years earlier to America.

Dad told about traveling to this country below the water line (in steerage). He slept down there but spent all his time on deck because it smelled so bad below deck. My mother liked vegetable soup, but it was never served at our house. Dad said the smell of vegetable soup brought back memories of his trip over to this country. Ellis Island, to my Dad, was a very sad place because so many of the immigrants were sent back due to health reasons.

Before he was married, Dad wanted to go back to Ireland to see his family. Mother did not want to cross the ocean. He made the trip and had a wonderful time with his family. As he went to get to the boat to America, he missed the train and therefore, missed the boat, which was the TITANIC. He went back home and when he heard what happened to the Titanic he was afraid to come back to America. He stayed in Ireland a whole year. He spent his time going from castle to castle where they had beautiful gardens. He traveled by bike. The head gardeners showed Dad around and told him if you think the flowers are pretty here, I will give you a note to show at the next Castle.

A year later he returned to this country. He said when he left, saying goodbye was the hardest thing he ever did because he would never see any of his family again. He was fortunate because not many, who came to this country, got to return.

My father loved growing things and worked as a florist at various state institutions in Ohio. My mother and dad both worked at the State Hospital in Athens, Ohio. He was the head florist and she was a nurse when they met. He and my mother married in 1914. They came to Westerville, Ohio where my Dad had bought land. He wanted to start a greenhouse, but was unable to obtain water so he bought additional land and became a farmer. Mother had saved $1,200.00 and used it to build a new home. They lost two babies earlier and then I was born in 1922. They worked very hard, but were so happy to work for themselves after many years working for someone else.

In 1989, my husband and I, along with his nephew and wife, went to the British Isles. We had only one day to find my Dad's home. A Priest and another man who knew my uncle showed us the way. We found it! It had been abandoned. It had thick stone walls and a corrugated roof. We found the key to the front door and went inside. In the milk room there was a huge fireplace, a settle, table, chair and cupboard. I could not believe I was really there. We were very fortunate to find the house. My Uncle Phil and

Aunt Ellen had no children; so, to my knowledge, I have no relatives in Ireland.

While my dad never forgot Ireland, he loved America and was happy here. He continued growing plants and crops and stayed close to his Church here.

The O'Brien's, Campbell's and Mangan's

Joan Campbell Henderson

My grandmother Ellen O'Brien Campbell 1860 – 1943, came to the United States from County Mayo, Ireland with her parents James O'Brien 1839 – 1914 and Mary Mangan O'Brien 1835 – 1909.

Since I was not born until 1929 I did not know my great grandparents but do have fond memories of my grandmother since we lived next door to her until I was in the 4th grade and we moved into Springfield, Ohio. She baked her own bread and I sometimes helped her. She had a big coal fired stove with gas burners. She also taught me to sew. She had a black wool shawl she would put over her legs when we went out in the car during winter. In the back yard my father and aunts built a grotto for the blessed Mother and she would sit in front of it and pray with her grandchildren. She learned to read at St. Raphael's Catholic School in Clark County, Ohio. Her father was very proud that she could read to him as he could neither read nor write and signed his deeds with an "X".

When my grandfather died I remember the Mangan cousins came from Indiana and everyone stayed up all night listening to Pat Mangan playing the violin.

At Christmas Eve a lighted and blessed candle would be left burning all night to light the way for the Christ child.

My grandparents had one son and two daughters who never married and lived at home until they died. Uncle John had served in W.W.I. in France. He would entertain us with his step dancing. Aunts Margaret and Helen doted on their many nieces and nephews and told us stories of our great grandparents.

James O'Brien, at the age of 15 or 16 served in the Crimean War as a drummer- boy. The following is a verbal account of his experiences. "I joined the South Mayo Militia-Number 47 and was sworn in by Lord Sligo. The officers of this militia were: Adjutant Butcher, Colonel Palmer, Major Lynch and Doctor Burke. When in the Militia about two years was sent to Athlone and when the volunteer order was issued I volunteered for the Crimean War in 1855. From here I was sent to Bristol, England at the official barracks, under Colonel Ireland. Then I was sent to Crimea, as a member of the First division, at the camp of Fort Sevastopol on the vessel, Ironoka. Remained here about one year and then when Peace was proclaimed returned to England, received an honorable discharge in Bristol, was reviewed by Queen Victoria at Braurn's Down at Portsmouth, England and went back to Ireland in 1856."

James O'Brien was born in Ireland 1839, the son of Thomas O'Brien and Margaret Quinn O'Brien and married Mary Mangan in St. Mary's Church March 9, 1864 in Westport, County Mayo, Ireland. (Confirmed June 1993) Her parents were Patrick Mangan and her mother's maiden name was Basquill. At the age of 24 James and Mary now 29 and daughter Ellen age 5 immigrated to the United States. Before leaving, his wife Mary made a pilgrimage from their home in Westport, to Croagh Patrick. She climbed the holy mountain barefoot.

The O'Brien family sailed on the Steamship Erin from Liverpool, England arrived in New York on April 30, 1866. They first settled in Clark County, Ohio near George Rogers Clark Park, west of Springfield. In 1877 they moved to Sugar Grove Hill and built four houses on the West side of Omega Road. The two houses north of the first alley were in the family until 1987.

James O'Brien worked on building the railroad west of Springfield, and according to the 1880 census worked at the Malleable Iron shop. He had a pub in the front room of the family home on the SW corner of Omega Rd. and Columbia St. Later owned and operated a "Cigar store" at 504 Bechtle Ave. and a tavern at 500 W. Main St. now known as the 1200 W. Main. In later years it was known as Vollmers Cafe.

His family was members of St. Raphael Church and the other children were Margaret, Mary, Thomas, James and Michael.

Michael O'Brien was born around 1866 and died in 1930. He moved to Troy and married Tillie Goss. They had three daughters; Mary O'Brien Gibboney, Shirlee Ann O'Brien Fleming and Nancy O'Brien Baudrit.

Mary Gertrude O'Brien was born 1873 and died Sept.6, 1923 and was married to Francis Ed. Wm. Patton.

Thomas O'Brien was born around 1868 and married Ellen Smith. They had a daughter Margaret and lived on W. Main St. Margaret married a man named Heindel and lived on Moorefield Road. They had two daughters Margaret and Eileen.

James F. O'Brien was born April 1, 1870. He had a daughter Helen.

Margaret Josephine O'Brien was born Sept. 6, 1878 and married Davis Stewart. They had two sons, Charles and Eugene.

When James O'Brien bought the Sugar Grove property in the 1870's it was an abandoned brickyard. The deeds were given to the Clark County Historical Society. In 1998 Gene Stewart told my sister Marjorie that Billy Morgan's house was the first house built by James O'Brien, Sr. on Sugar Grave Hill. It was known as the "Blue" house built in 1877.

In 1993 I also climbed Croagh Patrick. I was much older than my great grandmother when she climbed Croagh Patrick. Since then my husband and I have gone back to Ireland four times.

Marjorie Kelly

Kathryn McConnell Hess

The Columbus Irish community all knew Marge Kelly as a lively, boisterous person. Upon her recent death in 2008, it came to light that many years ago, at the youthful age of 24 and while a nurse at Mt. Carmel Hospital, Marge took a two-week vacation to

Florida which included a three day trip to Cuba, with five other nurses.

The six girls took 22 hours to drive to Daytona Beach in two cars. Two days later they drove on to Miami Beach where they stayed with "Uncle John" Janakis, Agnes' uncle, who owned the Lighthouse Restaurant. Mr. Janakis provided all the meals for the girls while they were there and treated them to fun and sun.

After a few days they continued to Key West, where they caught a plane to Havana, staying for three days and two nights. For $56 each, they enjoyed their plane ride, hotel rooms, and three tours of Havana, which included two nightclubs (the Bamboo and the Tropicana), a cigar factory and a distillery for rum, the Cuban national drink.

They drank all the free rum drinks they wanted at the distillery as well as other sites along the way, sampling many varieties of the liquor at the curio shops. As was the custom, all the girls haggled to get the cheapest prices possible on their souvenirs, such as alligator belts and hand bags, hand-carved maracas and the five duty-free quarts of rum each was allowed to bring back into the States.

A wild time must have been had by all as the one thing they claimed to the Columbus Citizen reporter who did a photo-laden article on the trip was that, "the Latin men danced much better than Americans."

The entire trip cost each girl about $200. When they left Miami Beach for home, they had a total of $16 between them. The nurses were able to charge the gas for the two cars and by the time they reached home, they were prepared to plan another trip to Hawaii the following year.

We wonder if they ever made their second trip.

During her life, Marge's trademark was her many stylish hats, usually wearing one everywhere she went. In respect and memory of Marge, many women wore hats to her funeral service at St. Patrick's Church. We'd like to think that Marge would have been pleased and flattered and that we would have heard her loud laugh of enjoyment as well.

(The 6 nurses on the trip were Marjorie Kelly, 24, Agnes Janakis, 27, Margaret Ann Thurn, 23, Eileen Kress, 26, Naomi Evans, 23 and Rita Salvatore, 28.)

The Earrings

Kathryn McConnell Hess

The earrings led to the whole story. They rested in the same drawer, all my life, in the dull tin box with the finely perforated lid. A lock of hair, brown with just a hint of red, lay in the box with them, the pale blue ribbon tie barely fitting into the box.

The earrings resembled door knockers: a deep rich burnished gold color with ornate black enameled detail across them. They each hung from a heavy ear wire.

In the same drawer were the two portraits. Both daguerreotypes, their metal edges covered with curlicues, rest inside broken frames. The lids are gone; only the hooks from the original boxes remain. The man in his threadbare suit and collar, hair slicked down to his head, stares unsmilingly and directly into the camera. The woman, dressed far finer than him, glances slyly into the lens, the light glinting off the fancy jet beading of her satin dress with its high collar. Her hair is pulled up high on her head and falls in long finger curls, looking ready to bounce when she shakes her head. The same earrings, from the tin, dangle from her ears. This is Maria Gossit and Thomas Arthur Carnahan, descended from Irish immigrants.

When my mother died, it was crucial that I locate these earrings and photographs. Things had already been moved around by people preparing for the estate sale. I searched through drawers and boxes until I found them, with great relief, after several days.

What follows is as far back as my family has been traced to the original emigrants:

Maria Gossit and Thomas Arthur Carnahan married April 12, 1845 in Tuscarawas County, Ohio. They had children, one known by the name of Asbury (other children's names unknown.) One of these unknown siblings had Thomas Arthur Carnahan (who married Beulah Estelle Baird), Worthington Carnahan (who wed Mary M. Fisher in October of 1877) and other children (birth names unknown.) Thomas Arthur and Beulah Estelle had Neil, Esther Jeanne and yet another Thomas Arthur (known as Tommy) who died as an infant. Neil (married Lois Geitgey) had Mac, Rick, Alan and Greg Carnahan; Esther Jeanne (married Clyde Emerson McConnell) had Kathryn Jeanne McConnell.

Little more is known specifically about most members of this family. Esther Jeanne had an Uncle Toot (birth name unknown) who always carried wintergreen candy in his pocket for the kids. One of the siblings in the generation preceding Thomas Arthur and Worthington was a stable keeper who, it was said, trained his horses to return to his barn after they were sold, resulting in the rumor that he was a horse thief.

The house where my mother, Esther Jeanne, and her brother Neil were raised still stands in New Philadelphia, Ohio. It's at the top of a steep hill where my uncle Neil taught his little sister to ride a big old fashioned bicycle with no pedals, a huge front wheel and small rear wheel much taller than her. She launched herself down the road from the top of the hill even though her feet did not touch the ground. Apparently this created many near heart attacks for my grandmother Beulah as my mother shot across the well-traveled crossroad at the bottom.

A One-Way Ticket to Columbus, Ohio

Mary Higgins

One of my great uncles on the Nolan side (Thomas, Mark or William, depending on who tells the story) was the first of our Higgins family to come to the United States. After many generations had survived Cromwell, the Great Hunger and British occupation, the current generation saw little prospect of great success there. So, Mr. Nolan left Ireland for the United States.

He sailed across the Atlantic to New York City. The city was such a contrast to the green, rural west Ireland that he left. It must have been quite a change to see the many people, streets, and businesses there. This was not what Uncle Nolan was looking for and he decided to try another part of the country.

The family legend says that Uncle Nolan went to the train station in New York City and walked up to the ticket agent and said, "This is how much money I have. How far can I get?" The ticket agent sold him a one-way ticket to Columbus, Ohio.

Uncle Nolan must have found a job and a more comfortable way of life in Columbus. As he worked, he sent money back home for his other brothers and sisters to join him in America. His oldest sister, Sarah, married to Patrick Higgins, and their first born, Michael, came over thanks to Sarah's brother. Sarah and Patrick were my great grandparents, who made their life here, raising Michael and two other sons; Timothy and my grandfather, William.

Visiting "Ma-Mack" and "Pop-Mack"

Gene Hinterschied

Although my name is Gene Hinterschied, and I have a strong heritage on the German side of my family, I have an interesting heritage on my mother's side as well. Her name was Edith McQuaid, and she was born and raised in the town of Somerset, Ohio which is located in Perry County approximately 50 miles southeast of Columbus. She was reared in a stately home that was located a short distance from the town square. The home was beautiful inside, but revealed its age by a few remaining gas fixtures. It lacked plumbing, so it had an outhouse which accommodated six occupants at a time. This was necessary if you hoped to get the children to school on time. In each bedroom there was a fancy china container with a lid. This provided for a means for one to relieve himself or herself without making a trip to the outhouse. This was particularly important in the dead of winter.

In the center of the town square was an impressive statue of General Philip Sherman mounted on a stately horse. This statue was located in the center of a well kept grassy and floral area, the likes of which we would refer today as a "round-about". My mother's parents (my grandparents) were known to us kids as "Ma-Mack" and "Pop-Mack". My grandparents owned a farm on the outskirts of town and the only movie theater in town, which provided a comfortable living in their years of retirement. My family was there to help them celebrate their 50th wedding anniversary at the "Little Phil Inn", located a short distance from the famous statue of the General, for whom it was named. Pop-Mack owned a nice 1935 Chevrolet, which I was a passenger in a couple times. Mom-Mack was at the steering wheel and Pop-Mack was in the passenger seat with his spittoon between his feet. Clearly he had pretty good aim when he needed to expectorate. We dressed in our best attire on Sunday to go to Mass at the Catholic Church. Behind the church was a cemetery, where Mom-Mack and Pop-Mack lie in peace. I am very proud of my Irish heritage.

From These "Irish" Roots

Sister Margaret Hoffman, O. P.

James and Mary (Walsh) Handiboe who were my mother's mother's father's father and mother were born in Clara, Kings County, Ireland. They came to America by way of Canada and seem to have followed the canal system then being built. Apparently the men worked on the building of the canal and their families traveled with them.

James E Handiboe my mother's mother's father was born in Columbus, Ohio and was baptized at Holy Cross Church. He was a person who loved to sing. For a living he was a cornice worker. A cornice is a molding projecting along the top of a building or wall. James had five daughters and he gave them all nicknames by which he called them regularly. He called my mother's mother "Skip". He sang to his children and they sang to him. On the night that James died vey suddenly, his young daughter had been singing to him, "After the Ball," then a popular song.

Peter Gallagher my mother's mother's mother's father was born in County Tyrone, Ireland. He came to America with his wife and daughter and bought a farm in Logan, Ohio in 1844. The hills and trees of Green Township, Section 36, were beautiful, and there was a little church call St. John's very close to where they lived. Sometimes a traveling priest would come there to say mass and baptize the new babies born since his last visit. Eventually Peter had six children. When the Civil War came, he saw his son go off to fight. Thankfully, the war ended and he came home after only a few months. One day Peter had to chase a cow that had gotten out of the pasture. This running somehow contributed to his death.

Nancy (O'Brien) Gallagher my mother's mother's mother's mother was born in Ireland and came to America where she lived on the farm in Logan, Ohio. There she raised a family of six children and even buried one of them, a little girl, in a beautiful hillside cemetery. Nancy must have had a lot of trust of God to leave her home and come to a new one far away.

Katherine (Gallagher) Handiboe my mother's mother's mother was born on a farm near Logan, Ohio. She was baptized by a priest who took care of the people in a large area. He recorded her baptism in Lancaster, Ohio. She was the youngest of her six brothers and sisters. Their farm was in a beautiful hilly area even thought the land was mostly clay. The trees and wild flowers made the location peaceful. By the time Katherine was only sixteen, her parents had died. She lived for a while with her sister and her sister's husband. Later, she taught catechism to children in St. Patrick's Church in London, Ohio. Before long she met m mother's father, James. They were married in the St. Joseph's Cathedral, in Columbus, Ohio. Katherine was a very handy woman. She could sew and mend anything. Often she would take clothes that were too big and make them smaller for her children and grandchildren. She lived a long time without her husband since he died at a very early age. And she buried three of her five daughters very young. Katherine was a good woman. She treasured and helped the people she loved.

Susan Mary (Handiboe) Duffy my mother's mother was born in Columbus, Ohio. She went to Holy Cross School where everything was taught in the German Language. Even though she was Irish, she won all the prizes for spelling German. Susan loved to sing. She sang at home and she also sang in the choir at St. Dominic's Church. She helped in a millinery shop owned by her Aunt Molly Handiboe. The family lived in an apartment over that shop. For a few weeks in the summer, my mother's mother would go to Logan, Ohio by train some sixty miles away. There she would visit her many cousins in the small towns around Logan. On one such visit she met a young man whom she liked very much. He was from the small Ohio town of New Straitsville, where men mined coal. Some years later they married. One week before the wedding, my mother's father wrote a very loving letter to his bride. He said he felt that they were like "two souls with but a single thought." After they were married, the newlyweds traveled by train to Shawnee, Ohio and then by horse and buggy to the small mining town of New Straitsville. However Susan was happy when they could move back to her hometown of Columbic after several years. She missed the activity of the city. My mother's mother created a warm atmosphere in her home, and many of the neighboring wives would ask her opinion since she had the experience of raising her seven children. She later helped he grown children in their homes by willingly doing chores of peeling potatoes, rocking children, and folding laundry. My mother's mother loved to read and appreciated poetry. She was a person who took life as it came from God's hands and left the rest to Him.

John and Mary (McDonald) Duffy were my mother's father's father and mother and they came from Ireland. He was from County Monaghan and she was from County Louth. For awhile before coming to America they lived in England where he was a coal miner in a place called Newcastle, England, which is on the Tyne River. It was well known as a coal mining town. There is even a common expression used about this town. When a person has plenty of something already and does not need anyone sending him any more, a person says, "That is like sending coals to Newcastle." John brought his wife and children to America and settled in New Straitsville, Ohio in 1880. Here he worked as a coal miner. He bought a house for his family in that town. After Mary died, he gave the house to his newly married son, James, with whom he continued to live. He loved to take his grandson and namesake, John to the local gathering place and say "There are only two Jacks – 'ould Jack and young Jack." John died at home following an accident in the mine, in which he was hurt.

James Patrick Duffy my mother's father was born in Newcastle, England, but he was Irish. When he was told in America that he was English because of his birthplace he would cleverly reply, "If a cat has kittens in the oven, does it make 'em biscuits?" In America his family lived in New Straitsville, Ohio, a town where most of the men mined coal. It was hard, dirty work and many times the miners risked their lives by going into the deep mines. When he was a man, James met a young girl who as visiting her cousins in his valley. After several more visits James asked her to marry him. My mother's father was a very good man. He wanted to be a good husband and father. Sometimes he worried that he was not able to do enough for his family. After several years, my mother's father moved his young family to Columbus, Ohio. There he worked for the Ralston Steel Car Company, which made railroad cars. He put the parts together and later was the man in charge of keeping track of all the parts in the shop "store" and sending the parts to each part of the factory. He worked very hard and the men he worked with liked him very much. He bought a small house for his family in a neighborhood where all the people were from different backgrounds. Many were newcomers to America and all of them helped each other kindly. They had gardens, chickens, grape arbors, and they all shared information, advice and comfort. Whenever a visitor, whether family or friend would leave my mother's father's home, he would say, "Watch 'em shoes." This was his way of saying, "Take care," or "Watch your step." My mother's father loved to listen to the radio. He would often hear Father Coughlin speaking about social justice from Royal Oak, Michigan. He would often ask God to help the "Fighting Irish" to win.

Catherine Rose Duffy Hoffman, my mother, is a Columbus, Ohio woman who knows how to do many things. She can cook a meal for a large family within minutes. She has loved to read all her life. She enjoys reading mystery stories. She read to each of her nine children often and instilled in them a love of learning. As a student my mother was always at the top of her class at St. Mary of the Springs Academy. Though her family was poor during the Great Depression in America, she went to high school on a scholarship. My mother's brother knew my father in high school. Once at a high school dance which each attended with someone else, my mother and father danced together. That was the beginning of a three-year courtship. My mother worked for awhile, first as the priest's housekeeper at St. Thomas Church, then at the Felber Biscuit Company packaging cookies and finally at F.& R. Lazarus department store in the china and art gifts department as the cashier. Then when my mother and father were married she became a full time homemaker for her whole life. Kate is a very giving person. Many people ask her for help, advice and encouragement. My mother has many items in her home that other people consider old-fashioned. But whenever someone needs something unusual they come to her. People also give my mother many things they no longer want. They know that she will find a way to use them or pass them on. My mother always believes in making the world a better place. She reads about ideas to help the Earth and she does something about it. Kate is a warm vibrant, youthful-looking woman. She has a positive outlook and is quick to smile. Her children love to be near her even though they are grown. Her cheerful home is the setting for many large family gatherings. She loves life and she trusts God's providence to take care of everything. And he always does.

N. B. The stories in "From These Irish Roots" are from a family history book, "From These Roots" written by Sister Margaret Hoffman O.P. dedicated to her parents Catherine Rose Duffy Hoffman and John Valentine Hoffman, Jr. The stories we are sharing in this book are those of the Irish side of the family shared with us by Kathleen Hoffman Brewer.

How the "O" Got in the Ocean

Mary-Pat Brady Issenmann

Grandfather John Brady and his family came over from County Cavan, Ireland around 1882. One of the girls died and was buried at sea. They always said that was why when they got here they were just named Brady; they had left the "O" in the ocean (O'CEAN). That's how the "O" got in ocean.

My grandmother Brady believed in banshee's. When she said she heard a banshee, we knew we were about to hear of someone having died. Before she would throw out the dish water, Grandmother Brady would let out a yell to give "the little people" time to get out of the way.

When Lazarus department store was still downtown, they used to have a "Senior Tea" every year. Grandmother Brady would go every year and while there would help take care of the "old people" even when she was 92 years old. When asked why, she said she didn't want people to know how old she was and besides, "the old people needed help."

Another one: my mother told me that in her "reckless youth," she would take a trash can (a lot smaller and not as heavy as the ones these days) and climb a telephone pole and hang it at the top for a Halloween prank!

When my father was born, his family lived on Naghten Street, a couple blocks more or less west of St. Patrick's Church. While he was quite young, his family moved north to St. Peter's Parish in the Milo area. At Christmas time St. Patrick's put the Infant Jesus in a crib. My father didn't think the Infant should be down there all by Himself and alone, so he took his little wagon, went down to St. Patrick's, gathered up the Infant, put him in his wagon and took him to St. Peter's.

My mother had a theory that if you try to get to know people you won't hate them, even if they are English. My father worked for the Norfolk and Western Railroad. They put out a magazine every month with a "Pen Pals" section. My mother got me writing to a girl in England. My father didn't like it but accepted it. When I had packages to send to her, my father would mail them while I was at work. He would go to several post offices in other neighborhoods far from our house where no one would know him. He said he "couldn't be caught sending anything to England."

Patrick S. McAllister Carried a Cane

Martha E. Kelley

Patrick S. McAllister, my grandfather, was born in 1859 in County Antrim, Ireland. He worked in construction, learning a trade. He came by boat to the United States as a young man and continued to work and learn carpentry in New York.

He realized he was making very little money working for someone else, so he saved what he made and started out on his own as a contractor. He did very well. He moved to Columbus, Ohio. He built many Catholic Churches in Columbus; Sacred Heart, Holy Name, Our Lady of Victory, Immaculate Conception, and I don't know how many more. He also built his home, 1379 Wyandotte Rd., his son's home on Glenn Avenue and the home I grew up in, 1240 Wyandotte Rd., all in the Grandview area.

Several years he was in the United States, he met Catherine Scanlon, little Irish lass who had also made the trip by boat to the United States from County Sligo, Ireland. She was a cook for a wealthy family in Bexley. They courted and soon married. When the family she worked for went abroad for several months, they asked Catherine and Patrick to stay in their home while they were gone. So they had a beautiful little honeymoon while there!

125

They led a good life. They had seven children. A set of twins died when they were very young and one daughter died when she was eleven. The others lived long lives. Patrick lived to be 95 and Catherine died at the age of 90.

I remember in later years Patrick, on a Sunday afternoon, would go down to the YMCA on the street car and play cards with his "Irish Pals" and Catherine would go to visit her sister, Mary Ann (my mother) and then he'd come to the home and all the family would have dinner together.

Patrick always wore a black suit of clothes, and a tall black hat. He smoked a pipe and always carried a cane. He had one cane that had snakes carved up and down the sides and one had a section with little round balls that would roll up and down as he walked with it.

An Uphill Path

Father Raymond Lavelle

Fr. Raymond Lavelle grew up in Cleveland, Ohio the son of a police officer and Celia McNulty, an Irish immigrant from Achill, County Mayo, Ireland. His siblings consisted of three brothers and two sisters. A turning point in his youth occurred when he and some other boys were caught joy riding in a stolen car. They were fined, and placed on probation. He was keenly aware of the disgrace his actions brought not only upon him but upon his family. This episode has continued to remind him why parents challenge their children to find friends better than they are. This episode helped shape his future actions for he realized he couldn't expect others to care for him if he didn't care for himself.

Father Lavelle attended Cleveland Holy Name High School from 1944 to 1948 working at Stouffer's Restaurant as a bus boy. Thinking of possible careers in hotel management, sports broadcasting and sales as an aptitude test suggested but his career goals were switched by a teacher's suggestion in his senior year. Sister Owen Marie S.C. asked Father if he'd ever thought of being a priest and he weakly said "Yes" but he recalls that at first he rebelled at the idea. Sister Owen Marie persisted in her urgings and in time he came to accept the idea that his future was not to be what he wanted to do but what God wanted him to do.

Because of poor grades he was unable to study for a Cleveland diocesan priest so he went to St. Meinrad Seminary in Indiana. He paid his own way by working in the summers in a factory job, as a mailman, as a structural ironworker, and spending time on a tugboat in Lake Erie.

Still struggling with his studies in the seminary he resorted to praying to St. John Vianney, the Curé of Ars and St. Jude, the patron of impossible causes. Father did complete his priestly studies at St. Meinrad, St. Charles Seminary in Columbus, and St. Vincent Seminary in Latrobe, Pa. He was ordained on May 25, 1957 in Columbus St. Joseph Cathedral by Auxiliary Bishop Edward Hettinger.

Over the years Father Lavelle has ministered in the following parishes; St. Agnes, St. Dominic, St. Timothy, St. Phillip, St. Catherine, St. Matthias all in Columbus and St. Vincent De Paul in Mt. Vernon, St. Mary in Lancaster, St. Joan of Arc in Powell,.

Despite his acknowledged difficulties as a student Father Lavelle spent 10 years as an educator, teaching and counseling at Holy Family and Bishop Hartley High School in Columbus and Bishop Fenwick High School in Lancaster. He received a master's degree in counseling and guidance from The Ohio State University. Father commented that while working with students he both confronted and challenged them as priest and teacher and they both matured together.

Fellow priests whose remembered friendships that have helped enriched his priestly life are Msgr. Roland Winel, Father Robert Schmidt, and Father Tony Missimi. In fact it is Fr. Missimi who is said to have commented when Fr. Lavelle "officially" retired in 2000, "Lavelle, you didn't retire. You just relocated yourself."

Currently at St. Paul's in Westerville Father celebrates Mass where Father's career as a counselor and his Irish wit is often evident in his homilies and conversations for he brings home pithy and pungent ideas that leave his listeners with valuable thoughts to contemplate. (e.g." Another word for EGO is Edging God Out."). He helps with RCIA classes and prepares parochial school and PSR students for First Communion and Reconciliation. He also is chaplain at Mount Carmel St. Ann's Hospital in Westerville enjoying the fruitful and rewarding ministry as a chaplain while lamenting a decrease in bodily energy.

If he is remembered by others Father would like this phrase to spring to mind "He loved God and loved people" and that he tried to follow the words of St. John the Baptist who is recorded as saying "Christ must increase, I must decrease". (*This story is based upon Father Lavelle's notes and a story published in the Catholic Times by Tim Puet*)

Family History of Maureen Gillespie Lovell

Maureen Gillespie Lovell

My father James P. Gillespie, was born in McDonald, PA to Vincent A. Gillespie and Mary Mullen Gillespie. My mother, Ruth E. Duffy, was born in Steubenville, OH to Francis X. Duffy and Anna Margaret (Rodgers) Duffy. My paternal grandfather Gillespie worked for the Pennsylvania Railroad and eventually moved with his family to Steubenville where my mom and dad met in high school at Steubenville Catholic Central. My maternal grandfather Duffy worked mostly in retail, as his brother owned "Duffy's Motor Car." We were very close to my mother's parents, Mama and Dada, who were absolutely the best! Mama made the best meatloaf and Dada was always very proper, wearing a crisp, starched white shirt and gray felt hat every day... and when he drove, he wore driving gloves!

All of my grandparents were born in America but their parents all emigrated from the North of Ireland. The Duffy/Rodgers clan emigrated from Ballymageough, Kilkeel (near the Mourne Mountains), County Antrim and the Gillespie clan emigrated from County Armagh.

Transplanted Shamrocks

I was born in Steubenville and we moved to our home on LaBelle View in Steubenville when I was 3; that will always be my "home." I have wonderful memories of growing up. Our neighborhood was where everyone knew each other and summer was a time of sitting on the porch in the evenings and kids playing "re-le-vio". Christmas was always my father's favorite holiday and we would visit with family and friends each evening beginning several days prior to Christmas through New Year's. Christmas Eve always meant oyster stew for my father. Midnight Mass celebrated by the Pope on television was a must watch ... and my brother and I continue doing that to this day! And we always had a wonderful 2 week (or longer) summer vacation where we would travel and usually see historical sites which gave me my love of history. My father worked at Weirton Steel and my mother was a wonderful homemaker. She is a wonderful cook and baker (a trait I did not inherit).

I attended the only "real" Catholic Church in Steubenville, St. Peter's, where I received all of my sacraments, including the sacrament of marriage. St. Peter's grade school brings very special memories of the "Fighting Irish" and Mass every Friday.

In 1979, I moved to Los Angeles, met and married my husband and returned to Central Ohio in 1990. My brother and his 3 children also live in Central Ohio: Brendan James, Ryan Patrick and Claire Elizabeth.

A couple items of interest: One of my favorite stories is how my great-great-grandfather would stomp on the tiger lilies outside their cottage in Ballymageough, Kilkeel because they were orange! Also the maiden name of my maternal grandmother was originally McRory. However, the English made them change it to "Rodgers," so it wouldn't sound so Irish!

"On Again, Off Again, Gone Again Moran"

Barb Mangini

Our grandfather Pat Moran and his friend who came to Columbus, Ohio, Paddy Costello provided some great stories and here is one of them plus a bit more.

Grandpa Moran and his friends were born in Glasgow Scotland of Irish parents and they decided to come to this country after another friend, Mike Burke came back to Glasgow after a visit to America and told them about "what a great country it was....if the Blessed Mother was for hearing his prayers he'd be going back there one day soon". Mike went on to tell his friends that they had better come too for there is plenty of work in America. Mike told his friends, "You can come to Columbus, Ohio and ask for Mike Burke."

So Grandpa Moran came across the Atlantic to New York buying a train ticket to Columbus at Pennsylvania Station in New York. Grandpa Moran remembered it was a confusing place and that the conductors were "dirty heathens". The train stopped at Buffalo and Pat stepped off for just a few seconds to slake his thirst for the train ride had been so hot and dusty. The train pulled out and left him! Determined to reach Columbus he got back on any train that seemed to be going in the same direction – no ticket, of course! When the conductors would protest over his lack of a ticket Grandpa would protest that he had a ticket but he'd given it to the other conductor that had gone off and left him stranded. From then on his journey progressed in uneasy stages of off again, on again, off again. Five trains and four days later, he ended up in Marion, Ohio. His friend Mike Burke went to meet his train in Columbus. He waited and waited and finally gave his friend up for lost. After that there wasn't much that Paddy Moran did that surprised his friends and the name of "On again, off again, gone again Moran" remained.

A story was told of the time Grandpa Moran went into a barber shop and when the barber tilted him back in one of those new-fangled barber chairs he leaped up yelling and tearing the sheet from his neck. When he calmed down he explained that he thought the barber had seen his fat wallet and he thought the barber was going to slit his throat.

Grandpa Moran and Maggie, his wife were married over 50 years. Grandpa would tell the story of how Maggie, a new bride cooked a dish of sauerkraut for her new husband. The sauerkraut looked good on the dish but after his first taste Grandpa Moran grunted and complained that the cabbage was sour. Before Maggie could explain the nature of sauerkraut Grandpa had already dumped his plate into the garbage can.

In his sentimental Irish style Grandpa liked to tell how his friend Paddy Costello had hired a carriage pulled by two white horses for his and Maggie's wedding in Perth, Scotland. Grandpa Moran always joked that his Maggie wore the "britches" in the family but no doubt about it she was a good woman.

In true Irish style Grandpa had to celebrate St. Patrick's Day and they tell of the St. Patrick's Day dinner held at the Chittenden Hotel when the waitress place a cup of clear consommé before him and in a loud, clearly heard voice Grandpa announced that it was some tea and would someone please pass the sugar.

Grandpa Moran would take "the six Mentel brats" (his daughter, Mary Bernadette Moran married Ray Mentel), to the Neil House St. Patrick's Breakfast and one year, they split up the kids, so my brothers Mike and Pat were sitting at the next table, and one of the older ladies asked them their last name, and they didn't want to say Mentel on St. Pat's Day (Mentel being German, however, Grandma Mentel – was Maggie Ryan!).

Anyway, the boys said their last name was Moran, and it turned out, they had lied to my Dad's cousin! They really knew who the boys were!

Just like his long-lived marriage to Maggie; Grandpa Moran kept his good friends, Mike Burke, Paddy Costello, Ed Docherty, the friends he had known back in Glasgow and they had all come to America to work, raise their fine families and enjoy their friendship on this side of the pond. Grandpa Moran always said that his friend, Mike Burke, had been right all those years ago on the scaffold in Glasgow that America was a great country. Love the Irish!

Patrick's Shamrocks

Paddraigin Patricia Martin

By default, I inherited my great-grandfather Patrick's atlas of Ireland and his blackthorn stick. The story goes that he carried both with him when he left County Mayo to come to the United States. We don't know much about Patrick except that he survived the potato famine; he would have been four years old when it began. He had two sisters who remained in Ireland, three brothers who came here, and one who went to England. He was nineteen when he left home and never returned. Somewhere along the way he met and married Ellen Byrne from County Roscommon. They eventually lived in the Athens County area where Patrick was a coal miner. Ellen died shortly after the birth of their fifth child, Joseph. In my family there has always been one person most dedicated to their Irish heritage within each generation: my mother Kathleen, me, and now my son.

When I was going through Patrick's atlas, way in the back I found three pressed shamrocks, now brown with age but otherwise preserved. Somehow the thought of him picking them and pressing them into his book as he left his home and family for what he knew was the last time brought me to tears; in fact, it still does. How important that symbol must have been to that nineteen-year-old boy from County Mayo.

Searching for Patrick

Paddraigin Patricia Martin

On my first trip to Ireland, I was looking out the plane window and marveling at that spot of green floating in the Atlantic. More mysterious, even scary, to realist like me was the feeling that I was coming home. Yet, I wasn't really the one who was coming home. It was someone else, someone who had been gone for a long time.

Enough of that talk! After all, we realists, even the Irish ones, do have our reputation to uphold.

While we toured the country, I waited for that feeling to come back, but nothing more happened—no "aha!" moments, no sense of being there before. Even when we went to the town nearest to where my great-grandfather had been born there was no sense of returning. I told myself: "You see, it was just your overactive imagination and an all-night flight."

When we left two weeks later, I found myself again looking out the window and this time watching the green isle getting smaller and smaller as we climbed toward home. Unbeknown to me, tears were pouring down my cheeks. I felt such a loss: "I'm leaving, and I'll never be back again." Now where did those feelings come from?

That experience was the start of it. Patrick wants us to know him.

Who was this man who was my great-grandfather, Patrick Hoban? He came from County Mayo, near Kiltimagh. He was about four years old when the Great Hunger began. He had a brother who had immigrated to England, one to Seattle, and two to New York. His two sisters remained in Ireland. He was described as being short and witty. At age nineteen Patrick came to the United States, but I don't know where he entered the country. I suspect that he was a miner in Pennsylvania when he met his wife, Ellen Byrne, who came from County Roscommon. Ellen likely entered the United States through New Orleans, since my grandmother said she talked about the great Mississippi River.

After their marriage, my great-grandparents lived in southeastern Ohio where Patrick worked in the coal mines. My grandmother, Mary, was the oldest of their five children; they had three girls and two boys. Ellen died shortly after the birth of her youngest son, Joseph. Patrick never remarried. Ellen's family came from Pennsylvania and took Joseph to live with them near Pittsburgh.

Patrick tried to keep his remaining family together, but he was not able to do so. At the request of their pastor, the children were admitted to St. Vincent's Orphanage in Columbus, Ohio. My grandmother said that Patrick visited every weekend and brought them treats like oranges. She didn't have many positive stories to share about their treatment while living at St. Vincent's. As soon as she was old enough, she returned home; her brother and one sister joined her and Patrick in Glouster, Ohio. Her youngest sister, Catherine, joined the Benedictine order in Illinois.

Mary married my grandfather, and eventually Patrick moved with his son, young Patrick, and daughter, Nellie, to Illinois. We could never learn why they went to Illinois, but my brother may have discovered an answer after I had retrieved Patrick's death certificate and learned where he was buried. On a recent trip to New Orleans, my brother decided to take a detour through Springfield, Illinois, to see what additional information he could find. He found Patrick's grave and those of the two children who had moved with him. He also found young Patrick's obituary in which it mentioned that he had been a lifelong member of the United Mine Workers of America. There was a great deal of violence surrounding the unionization of mines, and my brother remembers my grandfather, who was a mine supervisor, carrying a gun into the mines. Young Patrick's active involvement in the union is probably the reason for the remaining family's move to Illinois.

I often comment that in our family there has always been one person who has been most interested in our Irish heritage. In my family it was my mother, then me, and now it is my son. I have a letter from my aunt Nellie in response to my request to know more about the family history. She said that she wished she had pressed her father for more information, but he did not talk about his time in Ireland. He gave her only limited information saying he knew when he left that he would never be able to go back.

So what do I have of Patrick, other than the feminine form of his name? I have the blackthorn stick that he carried with him to the United States. He also brought an atlas of Ireland, and inside it, pressed between the pages, were dried shamrocks. They never fail to bring me to tears when I look at them. He must have loved his country very much. I like to think that I also inherited his wit. When I stayed with my grandmother in the summers, I learned several Irish songs that she said she learned from her father. Only later did I discover that they were all songs of rebellion. Maybe that's why Patrick left Ireland.

I'm still searching for Patrick and only finding him in bits and pieces; but I know he misses his homeland.

John and Mary Find a Home
Julie O'Keefe McGhee

John Cronin was born in County Kerry, Ireland about 1828. In 1849, at the age of 21, he was one of the many Irish to leave Ireland from Cobh and come to the United States, escaping the hungry times in his homeland.

After coming to the United States, John likely worked at a variety of laboring jobs but there is no official record exactly how he earned his daily bread until, in 1861, he was working in Chillicothe, Ohio for the Marietta and Cincinnati Railroad (later became the Baltimore and Ohio Railroad).

In 1861, John Cronin, the railroad worker, was living in a Chillicothe boarding house along with other railroad workers. One evening John was lingering at the train depot and while he was there an incoming train deposited some passengers at the Chillicothe depot.

One of the passengers was Mary Bresnahan, from County Kerry, Ireland whose brothers had paid for her passage to come to the United States. As Mary stood on the station platform, she looked for her brothers to welcome her but she didn't see them. However, Mary noticed John on the platform and went over to ask him if he knew her bothers. John did! The Bresnahan brothers and John were in the group that lived at the same boarding house. John offered to take Mary to his boarding house and her brothers. Mary hesitated, for she really didn't know John. John left the station and Mary waited until he was about half a street block away and then she began to follow him. John did lead Mary to the boarding house and her brothers.

The family isn't exactly sure how long their courtship lasted but on June 10, 1861 John Cronin and Mary Bresnahan were married in Chillicothe, Ohio.

John and Mary raised a family of 6 children and, although some of their children traveled many places, they all loved Chillicothe as their home. However their parents, John and Mary Cronin, to my knowledge, never left Chillicothe again because they had found a new home in which they were content. Mary's brothers, though, later traveled on and settled in Kansas.

Mary died in 1895 and John died in 1907. Two people who came from the same Irish village met and married in Chillicothe, Ohio after finding a home in a place far away from their birthplace.

Some people will travel a long way to find a spouse.

The Irish Things I Kept

Julie O'Keefe McGhee

When I was a child, around about mid March every year, we always got out a box from a drawer in my home. The box contained the pins, ribbons, and other items we would always wear on St. Patrick's Day, the seventeenth of March, both to church and to the parade. Over the years the ribbons would get a bit faded and frazzled, the pins might be dented and scratched, but it didn't seem to matter; for out came the box each year for those pins and ribbons to be worn again. The ribbons and pins may have shown the passage of time but my memories of my Irish and Irish-American forbearers are the things that seem always green and they don't fade with time.

I remember my father singing," The Minstrel Boy" with gusto and a bit off-key, assuring me that it was the best Irish anthem ever, and my Aunt Mame would croon equally off-key, "I'll Take

You Home Again, Kathleen" and "Believe Me, If All Those Endearing Young Charms".

I remember visiting St. Margaret's Cemetery in Chillicothe and seeing the Cronin family plot with an extra stone to commemorate a visiting relative who shares a grave site with my grandmother, Alice. Keeping the family together was important.

I remember John and Mary Cronin's youngest child, Mary Elizabeth, known to the family as Aunt Mame, and to generations of children in Ross County as Miss Cronin. She taught for 52 years until, at age 70, had to leave the profession she loved. This first generation Irish-American made her mark on hundreds of children and their families. She influenced me in my love of learning and family pride.

I remember my father taking me to Mount Calvary Cemetery in Columbus to see the grave site of his grandparents, whose substantial stone stands alone in a seemingly empty plot. I found out later that area is filled but, evidently, the rest of the clan couldn't afford to have tombstones.

I remember my great uncle Declan, whose name was changed to David by a recruiting officer believing there was no such name as Declan. He stayed David for the duration of a military career but, upon retirement, David changed that name back to Declan, reverting to his original Irish name.

I remember Foersters, a local German-American establishment, sold green candy snakes in honor of St. Patrick's Day. This was because my Irish-American father, Michael O'Keefe, who managed and later owned Foersters, had those candy snakes made to celebrate the Irish holiday and a bit of his heritage.

I remember the story of a cousin who had a swastika tattooed on his back in a youthful impulsive moment; but his grandmother had that swastika changed to a shamrock prior to military service. He's kept that shamrock and it's still a bright green.

I remember reading, over and over again, the pale green book about Ireland that my father had bought for me shortly after my birth. I still have that book. He bought many other books which started me on my passion for books...many of them about Ireland.

I remember my father and his brother John's sibling rivalry over The Friendly Sons of St. Patrick vs. The Shamrock Club. Uncle John, a charter member of the Shamrock Club, won that contest, for the Shamrock Club is still going strong and the local unit of the Friendly Sons of St. Patrick is no more.

That memory box holds many green memories that I'm proud to keep.

McKearneys in Moy, Ireland

Colette M. McKearney

During the First World War, Tom Walsh, my father's first cousin, was stationed in Germany when he received a two-week furlough. He decided to go to Ireland to look up his family's ancestors. With the help of a Dublin hotel manager, he located the village of Moy, in County Tyrone, on a map. He recognized the village name from the letters he had addressed to be mailed to his grandmother as a child.

When he arrived in Moy he found eight families, five of whom were named McKearney, living in the village. At first, because of his uniform, they would have nothing to do with him. When eventually they realized that he was not British but American, they sent for the oldest woman and the oldest man in the county to determine where exactly Tom belonged. He was taken to a farm named Moy Grange about a mile outside the village. As he walked in the door he spotted a picture of his grandmother (my great-grandmother) on the wall. He had taken it himself in 1910. Also on the wall was a picture of his uncle (my grandfather). It was at that moment that he felt as if he were home. With his relationship to the family now clear, the man who had taken him to the farm told him the story of what happened to his great-grandfather.

The farm had belonged to his great-grandfather, Tom McKearney, who was nicknamed Broad Tom. He lived on the farm with his wife, Mary Lennon McKearney, and a member of her family, Mary Ann Lennon. In 1837, Broad Tom was working his farm when British soldiers came on horseback and started shooting at him as if he were game. Tom was killed. His wife continued to live on the farm for several years after his death. When the potato famine began, she left for the United States with her three children. She settled first in Rochester, New York, and then in Cleveland, Ohio. One of her children was my great-grandfather, James Quentin McKearney, born in 1832.

During the 1980s, as I was working on the family genealogy, I wrote to the Bishop of County Tyrone searching for the local church in Moy. About a week later, I received a friendly letter from Bishop Daley of Londonderry explaining that bishops were not assigned in every county and that Tyrone was part of his diocese. He offered to forward the letter to the local church in Moy. Later I received a letter from the parish priest in Moy who told me that the church records did not go back as far as 1832. He also said that many McKearneys lived in his parish, but there was one, Paul McKearney, who in particular wanted to write to me. The priest offered to provide Paul with my name and address. A year passed with no word from Paul McKearney, so I wrote to him myself; there was still no answer.

Meanwhile, my aunt in Cleveland sent an article from the *Plain Dealer* about a woman named Ellen Mary Margaret McKearney who supposedly belonged to the IRA. Her name appeared first on the list of criminals most wanted by Scotland Yard.

Two years had passed since I was contacted by the priest in Moy when I met a friend's relative who was from, of all places, Moy, County Tyrone. She knew Paul McKearney and told me that a couple of years earlier his parents had been sitting in their living room when two black-masked men came to the door, shot, and killed them both simply because their name was McKearney. The relative of my friend said that the Ulster Defense Regiment (UDR) was responsible and, although you rarely heard of them, they were as bad as the IRA. She related this story to me in the eighties noting how the UDR went to the funerals of anyone whose name was McKearney in search of Ellen Mary Margaret McKearney and her brother. Although this family was from southern Ireland and most likely was not related to me, she cautioned that the UDR shoots first and asks questions later. She advised me not to cross the border. Luckily for me, I discovered this information before I was able to go to Moy where I would have asked about the McKearneys. I might have been jailed or worse: I might have been shot!

Strangely, when this relative of my friend was visiting Columbus and we spoke on the phone, she repeatedly asked: "Are you sure that no one is listening on the phone? Are you sure that your phone isn't tapped?" She was very reluctant to speak of Ellen McKearney and declined to say where she was at that time, although it seemed as though she knew. I later learned through an Irish newspaper that Ellen McKearney's brother had been killed by the Ulster Defense Regiment.

According to my new friend from Moy, Paul McKearney's parents would have been killed shortly after the family had been given my name and address by the priest. No wonder I never heard from Paul.

My Great-grandmother Mary Dalton
Colette M. McKearney

Mary Dalton, my maternal great-grandmother and the paternal great-grandmother to my first cousins Dorothy Modlich and Rosemary Martin, came to New York from Limerick, Ireland, in the early 1850s. She was sixteen years old at the time and came with another young girl who later returned to Ireland. Upon her arrival Mary sought advice from a priest at Old St. Patrick's Church in New York. He helped her to obtain a job as the priests' housekeeper at St. Thomas Aquinas Church in Zanesville, Ohio.

She married Jimmy Downey in 1859. When she was six months pregnant, he was killed on the railroad. In 1864, Mary wed John Loftus, my maternal great-grandfather, at St. Thomas Aquinas Church in Zanesville. He was a widower from County

Mayo with three daughters. Mary and John had five children of their own.

Because of the difficulties they faced finding employment as Irish Catholics, my great-grandparents moved to St. Patrick's parish in Columbus, Ohio. Their daughter, Annie Loftus Bell, was baptized there in 1869 and later attended school at St. Patrick's where she was taught by the Notre Dame nuns. Annie was grandmother to me and my cousins. My mother, Helen Bell McKearney, was also baptized at St. Patrick's in 1897 as was Jerome Emerson Bell, her brother and father of Dorothy and Rosemary, in 1895.

Mary Dalton Loftus's brother remained in Ireland and became Father John Dalton; supposedly, a monument to him exists in Ireland. As both Mary and her son, Jimmy Downey, were members of the Third Order of Saint Francis, I assume that Father John would also have been Franciscan.

Jimmy Downey was killed by a lightning strike in Kansas in 1904. His black hair and moustache were turned red by the lightning. His Franciscan Third Order missal, which was with him at the time, is now in my possession.

In the late 1940s or early 1950s, my grandmother was visiting The Catholic University of America in Washington, DC, where she met Bishop Fulton Sheen. Bishop Sheen had recently returned from a trip to Ireland. Grandma asked whether he was familiar with the monument to her uncle, Father John Dalton, and whether it still was standing. Bishop Sheen said that it still existed and told her that Father Dalton had been his uncle as well. Bishop Sheen and my grandmother thought they were cousins, although I am not certain how far their relationship was removed (first, second, or third).

I have never been able to locate the monument to Father Dalton.

The Extraordinary Death of an Ordinary Irish Housewife

Colette M. McKearney

This story is a true account of the death of my paternal grandmother, who was an ordinary housewife, mother, and grandmother. Although she died before I was born, the manner of her death, which was witnessed by my mother, has been told by my family over and over throughout my life and has always been a great source of inspiration to me.

My grandmother was born and reared in Cleveland, Ohio. Her name was Margaret McKearney. Her husband, my grandfather, worked for the Cleveland Plain Dealer most of his life. They were called Ma and Pa by their family.

Ma and Pa lived on 116th Street in Cleveland, about one-half block from Saint Rose Catholic Church. Here they reared six children, one of whom suffered a developmental disability after having contracted measles as a child. She ultimately had to be institutionalized.

Ma came from a large family. Her mother died when she was still a child, and her father remarried. Unfortunately, there must have been some dissension in the home, because Ma always said that if she ever had a home of her own she would make sure it was a peaceful one. She lived the life of an ordinary housewife, other than when she endured the very difficult and heart-breaking experience of having to institutionalize her developmentally disabled daughter. This decision had to be a heavy cross to carry, one shared by many parents, especially in the days when most childhood diseases could not be prevented.

In her later years Ma developed a heart condition and had been ill for some time. My mother, a persistent novena maker, was helping take care of her. One day my mother said to Ma, "I'm going to make a novena for you to get better." Ma replied, "I'll say it with you." So they started a novena, probably one to Our Lady.

On the ninth day of the novena, Ma's condition worsened; her relatives were notified, and they came from various parts of the

142

city. That evening the family was gathered around her bed at her home. At six o'clock the bells of Saint Rose Church began to toll the Angelus. Ma said, "Oh, I always love to say the Angelus." Mother said to her, "Well, why don't you say it now?" So Ma began to recite the Angelus while her family answered with the responses. According to my mother, who was right beside her at the time, as Ma finished the Angelus, she raised both arms in the air as though she were reaching for something or someone. Her whole body then lifted about a foot off the bed, and she fell back dead.

My mother, who herself died at age ninety-eight, always said that in all her life she never saw such an incredible expression in anyone's eyes as the one she witnessed in Ma's eyes at the time of her death. It seems strange that this unusually beautiful death should have occurred to an ordinary person.

I like to think that what happened to Ma at her death happens to all good living people, only we are not able to see what is happening. For some reason, Almighty God allowed the amazing death of this ordinary housewife to be seen. Surely, there must be a message there for us ordinary people.

My Great-Grandpa was a Bootlegger

Betty Giles Menear

My great great great grandfather (1776 – 1857) Henry Feagans, Sr. (also spelled Feagan or Fagan) came from Gretna, Virginia and settled in what is now Polk County, North Carolina. His grandson Chesterfield M. Feagan had a large farm and plantation house (it burned in 1956). He farmed and ran a distillery when it was legal to do so as long as you paid the taxes on each run. I guess they figured how many gallons you would get on a run. Well Great Grandpa would always run some extra each time that he didn't pay tax on. I guess he could use the income for his 13 children. All were still living when the youngest was 50 years of age.

The corn sheller and some of the jugs Grandpa used are still in the family.

There use to be a lot of bootleggers in the mountains of Polk County. Probably they used recipes brought from Ireland!

The Melletts

Jim Minor, Elaine Minor Hiatt

It is hard to imagine losing all you have and emigrating to another country. I can imagine a mixture of feelings of my grandfather Stephen James Mellett (born 1871) and his father James and his mother Mary (nee Higgins) with sisters Ann, Delia, Mary, and Alice may have experienced as they arrived at the docks somewhere in Ireland to board the ship for the New World. Perhaps feeling despondent at having lost their land in Swinford. County Mayo, Ireland, and leaving their friends and family, as well as their beloved Eire, yet also excitement and anticipation for a new start in the United States, a place that loomed almost mythical to so many poor emigrants in the 1800s. How their land was lost is a tale forgotten in our family history.

The journey of 1885 must have been a challenging one from what viewing a replica of the ships and reading about the conditions of passage. Not being allowed up on deck except to cook a meal and dump the slop jar once a day in such tight, dank quarters must have been an assault on the sensibilities of the courageous passengers.

The arrival in New York Harbor, sharing the common experience of so many of our ancestors viewing the Statue of Liberty, must have given hope to my grandfather, as an impressionable youth. The Melletts did not stay long in New York, however, but traveled on to Chicago to stay with relatives while finding jobs and housing of their own. Chicago was filled with many seeking work, and the growing city of Columbus, Ohio beckoned my great-grandparents with the promise of jobs. Friends and more relatives opened their homes in Columbus, no matter how crowded they were.

James Mellett soon found employment for the Gas Works, allowing him to afford meager living quarters for his family. Their

144

first place was a tenement over an Irish grocery store on Water Street (now Marconi Blvd. where the old police station building still stands). After at time, the family moved to 101 North Front Street, followed by renting on Montgomery Street, which later became a rail yard, and today is an exit off of I-670.

Life was harder in America than perhaps was expected. Although there was no famine, the Melletts were no longer land-owners and depended on low wages and long hours of labor as did so many Irish immigrants to keep a roof over their heads and food on the table. Instead of rolling green pastures and a temperate climate, my grandparents had to acclimate to crowded cities and cold winters. Still, America was perceived as the land of opportunity, where anything could happen, and anyone could raise himself and his family to a better standard of living, and they were grateful to be here.

Time marched on, and Grandpa Stephen grew up and began thinking about a family of his own. One Saturday when he was about 18, he and his buddy were "walking out" as the young people of the day called it, down High Street and two young ladies caught their attention.

The young gents tipped their hats to the young ladies and asked could they call on them. The young women smiled and gave their permission, along with their addresses. Stephen was to call on Brigid Whalen, who with her family lived on Gift Street, in the Bottoms.

Cleaned up and nervous, a few days later young Stephen knocked and a pretty young woman answered the door. He said "I came to call on Brigid Whalen, but who might you be?"

"Well, I might be Mary Whalen," she said tartly with a smile.

"Well, forget Bridget, will you walk out with me?" and the rest, as they say, is the history of my Grandparents. I never met my grandmother Mary, as she was deceased before I was born.

I know from family stories that after my grandfather Stephen started to court my grandmother Mary that his family told him that she came from Shanty Irish and advised him to stop seeing her.

The Melletts and their relatives were Lace Curtain Irish (or so they said) and looked down on the so-called Shantys.

However, Stephen was a determined individual, and not only courted Mary; he took it a step further and married her. Together they started married life renting in the Bottoms. Stephen went to work as a boilermaker to take care of his family and, in fact, retired from the New York Central RR on McKinley Avenue Roundhouse from that job.

As time went by the family grew. In 1897, my Uncle Johnny was born, named for my grandmother Mary's brother, John Whalen. Aunt Margaret came along in 1899, followed by Alice in 1900, who would become my mother.

My Aunt Collette was next in 1903, then two miscarriages before Mary in 1905, Katherine in 1910 and Stephen in 1914. One final pregnancy ended in my Grandmother's death, as well as the child in 1915.

Prior to her death, my grandmother had gone blind, and the girls had to help her around the house. When my grandmother passed, my Aunt Margaret who at 16 was the oldest girl, refused to take responsibility, so my mom, Alice, at 15 became the woman of the house.

In 1916 Uncle Johnny went off to World War I, and Aunt Margaret moved to Chicago to live with relatives. Sometime in 1917 or 18, the Army stationed soldiers at Camp Chase on the far west side of Columbus. My mother and her sisters packed a picnic lunch and went out to the area, as all of the girls were doing, to see the young soldiers before they went off to war. My father was one of the soldiers in camp, awaiting orders to France. It was at one of these outing that he and my mother met.

After conversing for awhile, he asked if was ok for him to write, and she replied affirmatively. She and all of her sisters thought he was handsome. He must have thought well of Alice, as well, because when he came back to the U.S. he did not go home (Kentucky) but to Columbus.

In 1921 my mother took my father to see Father Swartz at St. Aloysius Catholic Church and told him they wanted to marry, but were afraid to ask my Grandpa. Father told them, "Well Alice, you are 21 so you don't need his permission." My mother replied," You do not know Poppa-- he will not allow it even if I am 21!"

My father was not Catholic and the Catholic Church requires a promise to raise any children Catholic, to which he agreed. Father Swartz conducted the ceremony in his house, and they were on the way.

My mom and dad were married about a year and a half when they greeted a new arrival, my sister Cecelia Ann, born on April 27, 1923 in Columbus, Ohio. Fourteen months later on June 14,1924, I entered the world as James Foster Minor, in Lima, Ohio at St. Rita's Hospital where we had moved for my father's work at Lima Locomotive Works. Shirley Alice was born in 1936 in Columbus, Ohio, where we had once again relocated for employment reasons.

While my mother's side of the family (my grandfather, Stephen Mellet and my grandmother, Mary Whalen) arrived about in America in1885 from Ireland, my father's side, the Minors and the Moores, came long before. The Minors were in Virginia before the Revolution.

From family research I know that Mary Whalen descended from Johanna English, born 1844, Ireland (based on census records). Johanna married Timothy Whalen, born 1839, Ireland. Their offspring were: John, born 1863, England; Johanna, born 1872, England; Mary, born 1874, England; Bridget, born 1877, Ohio; and Alice, born 1878, Ohio. Alice Whalen married Patrick Collins in 1905 in Ohio.

Mary Whalen was born in 1874 in Wales and married Stephen Mellet, born 1871 in Swinford County Mayo, and they married in Columbus, Ohio.

Mary and Stephen Mellett's children were: John, born 1896; Margaret, born 1898; Alice, born 1900; Collette, born 1903; Mary, born 1905; Katherine, born 1910; and Stephen, born 1914. Four others died in childbirth.

Alice Gertrude Mellett born in 1900 in Columbus, Ohio married Shirley Guthrie Minor, born in 1900 in Casey City, Kentucky. Alice and Shirley (called Jack, or "Dutch" by his wife) had three children. Cecelia Ann. born in 1923. James Foster (me), born in 1924, and Shirley Alice, born in 1936.

The Ad That Made My Grandpa Mad

Margaret Mooney

"Having watched Mr. Carr's progress through life since the days when he used to drive a grocery wagon..."

Mr. M. L. Carr was my grandfather and my warm and real buddy. He and my grandmother opened their home to my mother and me during the Great Depression when mother's marriage fell apart. It was home. I called him "Daddy Mike". His many friends called him "Mike", but he was "Mr. M. L. Carr" to the business world. He was a very serious business man, a man of determination and a man who sure knew how to sell his coffee!

Mike Carr and his three brothers understood competition in a "dog- eat-dog" world. Born to immigrant parents and raised in the neighborhood of "Irish Broadway" (Naghten Street) and schooled into their early teens at St. Patrick's School, they came of age in the 1890s.

Johnny, the eldest, left home at 14 to make his fortune in Chicago. He first worked in a barbershop shaving necks. Soon he was selling "numbers" for the barbershop's backroom operation, and eventually became a well-known Chicago "bookie". Once, briefly, he was kidnapped by Al Capone's "family", yet he was a businessman: refined, conservatively well-dressed, silver-haired and diamond stick-pinned and quietly successful.

Here in Columbus, brother Joe Carr began as a machinist in the roundhouse of the Panhandle Division of the Pennsylvania Railroad. On the side he became a sportswriter for the Ohio State Journal. He also was founder/manager of the now famous

Panhandle Football Team, a precursor of today's professional football. In 1921 Joe Carr became a founder of the National Football League and from 1922 until his death in 1938 he ran the league as president from the top floor of 16 East Broad Street in Columbus. His firm hand is credited with bringing the infant NFL into national respectability. Joe was a business man and a strict Catholic gentleman.

Eddie, the youngest, was the impeccable accountant for M. L. Carr's "Franklin Coffee Company", founded in 1908 near North Fourth Street, south of Fifth Avenue. He was reserved, respected and another business man through and through. Surely no one could call the Carr boys by that put-down tag, "Shanty Irish"

Reading that 1923 Louis Potter real estate ad for his new homes in Northmoor Place made Mike Carr so angry! What did Potter know of Mike Carr's own struggle to succeed? Sure, nearly twenty-five years earlier Maggie Megahan had been impressed by the new suit, high starched collar, and the livery buggy with the handsome black horse. She always said it had been the big red bow on the buggy whip that caught her eye. But it was at a box social and dance at a farm on the west side of the Olentangy River that Mike wrote "I love you, Maggie" on the cardboard box lunch for which he had bid.

What did Louis Potter, Realtor, know of the year of struggle when Maggie's folks sent her off to her married sister in Oil City, Pennsylvania without a return ticket? They wanted her to meet a well-fixed Protestant fellow and forget Catholic Mike Carr, who was not one of their Scotch-Irish, Pennsylvania, German kind. When she wrote Mike about her situation, he took the train to Oil City and brought her home to her folks, who finally agreed to let Maggie marry Mike.

With his savings and a financial partner, Mike set up his own grocery store at the corner of Mount Vernon Avenue and Seventeenth St., with living quarters upstairs. Maggie Megahan Carr loved Mike and helped him by working in the store and keeping the books. This was a skill she had learned in business school and perfected during her few years of employment in downtown Columbus. She dreaded washdays and putting Mike's bloody butcher aprons to soak in cold water, wringing them out, standing over a tub of hot water, and rubbing them on her scrub board until they were white. She had worked in an office, and now she was a washerwoman.

She couldn't hide her deeper sadness. She was not used to being an outsider. Folks here knew she was raised a Methodist. She didn't even speak the "Catholic language". Living with the Irish was all she feared; she didn't fit in. There was no woman in the Carr family to help her. Mike's mother had died before she met him. His brothers were bachelors, and his father elderly. She sorely missed her lifelong friends in the neighborhood surrounding Third Avenue Methodist Church.

As soon as it could be worked out, Maggie's Mike found a grocery and house on the corner of West Eight Avenue and Worthington Street, not far from the more familiar neighborhood of their courting days. There the family grew to include two beautiful boys, Bob and Jack, and a daughter, sweet curly-haired "Little Margaret".

"Ah", Mike thought, "Louis Potter wasn't there to watch nine-year-old Bob struggle through the scarlet fever that closed his throat so he had to be fed through a rubber tube." Then, so the story goes, someone (I never asked who) gave Bob the bit of cake he asked for, on which he choked and died. He was buried near his Grandpa Megahan and his great grandparents, Jacob and Mary Ann, out at "Protestant" Greenlawn Cemetery. (No stories ever explained that location.)

There came a time when new goals were envisioned and the new idea was COFFEE. Mike studied the coffee trade and learned how to buy, roast, and grind the beans. Over time, he made himself into a coffee-tasting expert. One goal was to develop a market in the restaurant trade; another was to package and deliver to independent grocers in Columbus and in smaller towns around Central Ohio. Both ventures were under the Franklin Coffee

Company trademark. Eventually, Franklin Coffee Company occupied its own two-story warehouse, factory, and office "place of business" on Detroit Avenue, not far from Hamilton Dairy on North Fourth Street. In the 1930s I came to know the building well, with its coffee, peanut butter, and candy-making equipment; its exotic burlap bags of coffee in the bean, delivery trucks, oak paneled offices and the private office for the President, Mr. M. L. Carr. Louis Potter knew about that endeavor, a "successful venture".

After a series of homes, 205 Northmoor Pl. in the "Big New North Side" seemed a perfect place from which to launch young Jack and Margaret into lives of their own. Maybe this home would be the "keeper".

Maybe, Mike thought, he'd better let Maggie see Potter's splashy ad before someone called her. "Kid (he always called her Kid), come see this damn real estate ad! What do you make of that?" She read it through, smiled, and said, "Mike, he glories in your progress. Forget the grocery wagon bit. I did fall in love with this beautiful house. Mr. Potter calls it 'a house with character'. Let it be a topic of conversation. The kids will get a kick out of the ad. Let's save it as a souvenir. We're all so proud to have a progressive, successful man like you to admire."

"Well, then, Kid, don't be surprised if in a couple of years we add some more 'character' to this place. I've been thinking of turning our bedroom and the guest room into a suite, with a walk-in closet/dressing room with shoe-racks and hat cupboards, and a bathroom just for us, like we saw in the movies. And we'll order new furniture from Marshall Field in Chicago. How about that, Maggie?"

And they did! The grocery store ceiling fan in the bedroom was painted pink. I was rocked in front of the gas grate there, and loved to walk among "Daddy Mike's" suits in the closet, and read the Hart, Schaffner and Marx labels.

M. L. Carr died suddenly when I was eleven.

A Brief History of My Morrisseys in America

Patrick M.A. Morrissey

William Morrissey of Lickfinn, County Tipperary, Ireland, had a son, Timothy. Timothy was born in 1792 and married Ellen Bodley from Drangan, a few miles away. Tim and Ellen had 9 children, and immigrated via Liverpool to the United States in June of 1851 aboard the ship Western World.

As happened so often aboard these ships, my GGGgrandfather got ill in route and died shortly after arriving in America. The family continued inland, eventually stopping in Ohio for a brief period before the eldest son, my GGgrandfather James Bodley Morrissey secured jobs for himself and brothers with a railroad building a route in Wisconsin. James, John, Timothy, Patrick and Michael, with their mother Ellen and sisters Nancy, Bridget, Mary and Ellen, eventually settled in a small town in Wisconsin by the name of Waukau. After a few years working on the line, the railroad was going broke, and the family decided that Waukau would be their new home.

After a year or two, one brother, Patrick, moved to Waseca, Minnesota to start a life of his own. The rest of the family settled on about 200 acres divided among the 4 brothers, and began farming the land on what is now Morrissey road just outside of Waukau near Rush Lake.

My GGgrandfather James married Hannah O'Brien and had 13 children, the eldest of whom was named in the Irish tradition after his grandfather, Timothy. All 16 of them (Ellen included) lived together in one house. The other brothers also married and had many children, many of whom had the same names as their cousins. This has made tracking the family a bit challenging, but interesting. The farms remained in the family for generations, with the last Morrissey to live on the original farmstead dying in 1969.

My Ggrandfather, Timothy Bodley Morrissey, married an Irish woman by the name of Nora Joy. Tim was known as "Blackie" around Winnebago and Waushara county Wisconsin because of the black soot on his face from the diesel engine that powered the tractor and wheat threshing machine he used to harvest the wheat that grew on the surrounding farms.

Tim and Nora had only one child, my Grandfather, James Joseph Morrissey. James married Mabel Curran, whose father Tom Curran's family emigrated from Ireland to Canada and joined his brother. Tom and his brothers John and Patrick all played a major part in the virgin logging industry in northern Wisconsin for many years and left their marks on Rhinelander and Wausau, in the case of John and Patrick, and Berlin in Waushara county in the case of my Ggrandfather Thomas Curran.

My Grandfather James Morrissey was one of the first law enforcement officers to be assigned to what became the Wisconsin State Patrol. That would make the Morrisseys a family of Irish immigrants that worked on the railroad, farmed, enforced the law, and with my great uncle Senator Pierce A. Morrissey, were involved in politics as well. Unique? I think not.

Taking a step back, the Morrissey family that started in Lickfinn now has offspring in Wisconsin, Minnesota, North Dakota, South Dakota, Montana, Idaho, Arizona, California, Colorado, Michigan, Ohio, North Carolina, Florida and probably more states. Although the original Morrisseys married and had typically large families, many of the second and third generation did not marry. There may be many more Morrisseys that are not known to me at this point, but thanks to the many years of diligence in tracking the Morrissey name by one of Patrick's descendants, William Michael Morrissey, Fulbright Scholar and accomplished genealogist and current North Dakota resident, I think we know where the clear majority of our lines are now living.

Moving ahead to the 20th century and the 5th and 6th generations, we come to my father William James Morrissey, the eldest of four children born to James and Mabel. After the serving in the Army in WWII and subsequently graduating from the University of Wisconsin, my dad moved to Hortonville Wisconsin where he taught school and eventually started his own business. He married Pauline Samer of Oshkosh, and began what became a family with 6 children; in this order, Timothy, Lynn, Mary, Patrick, Michael and Erin.

I grew up in Wisconsin and after graduating from college moved to Colorado. There I married and began my family. All three of my children are now teenagers, the youngest of which was born here in Ohio.

So here we are, nearly 220 years since the birth of the first of my family to come to America. I recently returned to the gravesite of some of the original family. It is in a cemetery next to a decommissioned Catholic church in rural Wisconsin. The date on Ellen's marker says 1792-1879, 87 years after her birth, and 28 years since leaving Ireland. She is surrounded by Morrisseys, nearly 100 years between her burial and the burial of Nellie, the last Morrissey to live on the original farmstead.

Ours is a story very similar to many other families who came to this great land in search of opportunity, full of hope and looking for a new start. It is not as remarkable as some who have come before and after, but every bit as important.

How German Bratwurst Became a Hit at the Shamrock Club Picnic
Patricia Murnane with children Tim, Colleen, Christine, Shari and Theresa

Agnes and Thomas Murnane met at an Irish Picnic in 1918. Their fourth and final child, Don Murnane, was born in 1931. Don followed in his father's footsteps as General Manager of Westwater Supply Company, a wholesale plumbing supply firm founded in Columbus.

One of Don's good friends, Ed Shafer, represented the major plumbing fixture manufacturer Kohler. Kohler is based in Kohler, Wisconsin. Ed's hometown was nearby Sheboygan Falls, Wisconsin. Ed frequently talked to Don about his beautiful hometown and its Crystal Lake. Ed talked to Don repeatedly about making a trip to Mecca, aka Kohler, and having a family vacation on Crystal Lake.

In 1961, Don Murnane packed his wife and four children (the oldest was eight) into the station wagon and drove from Columbus, Ohio to Sheboygan Falls, Wisconsin. While there the Murnane's enjoyed many local German treats. Bratwurst was the best of the offerings.

Bratwurst is a spicy sausage that most adults know about today. Ball games, picnics and restaurants serve many versions of the porky repast. But in the Ozzie and Harriet Central Ohio of the 50s, brats were just bad kids.

Don loved that bratwurst. He begged Ed Shafer to take him to the butcher shop, Blutz Brothers, where the delectable links were produced. Don wanted to see if this new discovery could be introduced to his friends in Columbus as a neat addition to the traditional hot dogs served at the annual Shamrock Club picnic. The beefy butcher and Don brainstormed. What would be the amount needed? How could the perishable item be shipped? Could the cost be defrayed by the popularity at the picnic?

The arrangements were made. Two orange-crate sized boxes arrived at the Greyhound bus station packed in dry ice. Don took them home and followed the directions for preparation that would guarantee success. Several hundred bratwurst links arrived in a continuous chain so first he employed his children in the task of cutting the links apart. Then the brats had to be re-iced in coolers for transportation to the picnic. In the 1960's, options for large grills were limited. Don contacted his Aquinas High School (Class of 1949) Classmate Jim Williams. Jim's organization, Kirk Williams Co. fabricated by the grill. The grill was stored year to year in Murnane's back yard and loaned to area Catholic Churches for festivals and church picnics.

Once at the picnic, Don fired up the grill with plenty of charcoal briquettes. He then cooked the bratwurst over an open flame. When they were cooked through he moved them to a giant cooking pot filled with a marinade of beer, butter and onions.

Many curious bystanders shied from the greasy pot and the unusual shape of the sausage. But once a few brave souls tried the nouveau cuisine, the line started to form as satisfied Irishmen brought a friend back to share the experience. Don also made sure that the buns were an upgrade from typical wiener wrap using a crisp roll dusted with cornmeal. The bratwursts were a hit!

Don cooked bratwurst at the Shamrock Club picnic for many years and they were always a hit. He purchased the buns from Resch's, a south-side bakery. The buns had to be split by hand to accommodate the brats. Don's children were recruited to clean grates, carry charcoal bags and keep the brats and dogs turning while Don kept the Blarney flowing. It was the epitome of what the Shamrock Club picnic was meant to be: Irish families helping other Irish families enjoy each other.

Tracking the Elusive Past

Margaret Van Ness Nelson

Mike Harden's article caught my eye in this morning's paper so I'm sending you three genealogy articles I've published in Ohio Genealogy publications in 1996 and 2002.

My great-grandmother, Johanna Hynes married John Croke Edmondson in Columbus, as his third wife. They both died here. For a brief time, he was superintendent of the Ohio arsenal. I found his death certificate when I sent to the National Archives for his Civil War pension records.

The "double" where my great-grandmother lived was a funeral home in 1967, and later became a restaurant. When we ate there once, I mentioned this to the person who seated us.

"S-h-h," he said. "We wouldn't want the other patrons to know this had been a funeral home."

My great-grandparents lived on Livingston Avenue near Eddie Rickenbacker, my mother told me. Mother also remembered her Aunt Esther telling about being sent to the bar around the corner for a bucket of beer…not the way beer is sold today.

Following are stories about great-grandmother Johanna Hynes, St. Raphael Cemetery and Recruiting the Irish during the Civil War.

<u>**Johanna Hynes Edmondson and The Ursuline Academy of Brown Co., OH**</u>

<u>An Early Ohio Boarding School</u>

The Report Published Quarterly by The Ohio Genealogical Society, volume 36, Issue 4, Winter 1996, pp. 186-189

A fragile paper in the 1872 Edmondson Family Bible lead me to the Academy of the Ursulines Boarding School, St. Martin's, Brown County, OH where my great-grandmother, Johanna Hynes Edmondson was a student in 1861 and 1862.

Her course load would challenge any high school or college student of today. The Bulletin of Studies, saved all these years in her treasured Bible shows she was in the third class, second section. Her schedule included Christian Doctrine, reading, writing, arithmetic, book-keeping, algebra, orthography, grammar, rhetoric, English Composition, modern geography, astronomy, the use of the globes, philosophy and chemistry, biography, sacred history, modern history, chronology, mythology, antiquities, and plain sewing.

Comments listed by each subject must have served as her "grade card" -- very attentive, improved, good lessons. Her conduct and order were "very good indeed" and her health was good. Numerous premiums were "merited by Miss Hynes" for her studies and good conduct.

Who knows, perhaps this is where she learned to be such a good cook. An 1860 newspaper review said, "Verily! Those Ursulines know how to cook. The sister whose skill produced the 'plum puddin'' is worthy of canonization, and we could almost worship at the shrine of her, who made those good old-fashioned sweet cakes."

How Johanna came to the Ursuline Academy is yet unknown. According to my great-aunt Margaret Edmondson Fitzgibbon of Newark, OH, Johanna and her parents, Margaret (Kiley) and Thomas Hynes, from (Lisnegry, which is near Castleconnel) County Limerick, Ireland. "...arrived in the USA on the 4th of July

1847, after three months at sea, and thought it a fine country and everyday a holiday." Johanna was just a year old then.

The famine immigrant lists do not include this family of three Hynes arriving anytime in 1846 or 1847 -- nor do the passenger arrival records for the port of New York 1820-1846. Hynes was a common name among the more than 1 million Irish who immigrated to the US and Canada between 1846 and 1851. Johanna's granddaughter, Norma Van Ness, says that her grandmother did come as a baby and that Johanna's parents were well to do and brought their furniture with them when they came.

According to the <u>Logan Co (OH) History,</u> Thomas Hynes, (born in Ireland 21 Dec 1810), his wife and one child came to America in 1846. He farmed in Jefferson Co., NY for several years and then moved to Buffalo, NY where he was a merchant. They moved to Iowa and then Ohio.

Census records for 1850 list Thomas Hines (sic), 30, as a farmer in Jefferson Co., Ellisburg Twp., NY with his wife Margaret, 40, and daughter Joanna (sic), 5.

Estate records lead me to (resident) Thomas W. Haynes' (sic) purchase of 160 acres in Washington Twp, Defiance Co., OH, 10 Mar 1864. The cost was $2000. He must not have lived there long because he moved to Bellefontaine, Logan Co., OH in 1865 where he was a grocer. However, upon her father's death, Johanna inherited the Defiance County land and is listed as owner Johanna Edwardson (which should be Edmondson) in an 1890 atlas.

Although no census records have yet been located for the Hynes family for 1860, a Cincinnati directory for 1859 lists a Thos. Hynes at 54 McFarland and Thos. Haynes (sic) of the same address with a coffee house at 146 Vine. There is no Cincinnati directory listing for Thomas Hynes in 1860 or 1861. With Johanna attending school in Brown Co., where were her parents? Her mother died before 1 April 1866 when Thomas Hynes married to Ellen Hartnett Hynes in Logan County.

Thomas Hynes is listed as among the first Catholic settlers in Bellefontaine, Logan Co., OH. and a member St. Patrick's Church of Bellefontaine, which was organized in 1851.

In a brief history of St. Patrick's church, Louise Norris, of the Logan County Historical Society, notes: "There were few Catholics in Bellefontaine during pioneer times and prejudice was strong against them. The Catholics of that time showed courage, perseverance and a love of their church which enabled them to overcome the obstacles placed before them."

In my search for Johanna's parents, I wrote to the Academy of the Ursulines. In reply, Sister Xavier Ladrigan, the school archivist, sent a copy of the school enrollment for 1860-1, which included Johanna Haynes (sic), Cincinnati, along with 28 other girls. In 1862 Johanna, 16, was in the 3rd class. The list of students is as follows:

School Enrollment - 1860

Ball, Kate
Bickett, Henrietta - Fayetteville, O
Black, Helen
Buckner, Kate
Cullinan,---
De la Gauthrie, Clotilde
De Young, Lizzie
Drum, Agnes
Duer, Margo - Cincinnati
Dutton, --
Foster, Mary Jane - Cincinnati
Haynes, Johanna - Cincinnati
Kelly, Nora
Loudon, Lizzie
Magevney, Ellen (Jennie) - Memphis
Magevney, Kate - Memphis
Molyneaux, Frances
Nugent, Jennie
O'Donnell, Amelia
Piatt, Belle - Covington, Ky

Prenalt, Henrietta
Scammon, Mary
Smith, Nellie
Springer, Jennie - Cincinnati
Ward, Mary Ann
Wayland, Anna
West, Libbie
Woodworth, Henrietta
Woodworth, Rosa
Kate and Minnie Anderson from Ironton

(1861)

An ad in <u>The Catholic Telegraph and Advocate</u> of 14 July 1860, said that "(t)he parents or guardians of Young Ladies who reside at a distance are required to designate some correspondent in Cincinnati, who will be charged to liquidate their bills when due." This ad also provided details such as the courses of instruction, the fees, the uniform and the items to bring to school (including "ordinary Table Furniture of two knives, a fork, two spoons, a tumbler, six table napkins and six towels".)

Ursuline Academy was founded, in part, because early real estate promoters, "...wanted a Catholic Church in the wilds to entice settlers." Visitors undoubtedly found its 300 acres a captivating setting. In 1823 two hundred acres were donated by General Lytle, one of the real estate promoters, and 100 acres by the Michael Scott family, the first Catholic family to settle in Cincinnati. Michael Scott was an architect and a carpenter. St. Martin's Church was built there in 1830 and the Ursuline Academy was begun 15 years later.

Mgr. Purcell, the Bishop of Cincinnati, an Irish native, recruited French priests and nuns for the American churches and schools. The Ursuline sisters in France were eager to make the trip to Ohio despite opposition from family and friends. Some had to slip away in the night, disguised as market women, to begin their journey to America.

Eleven nuns under Notré Merè Julia Chatfield, an English woman who joined the French order, set sail from Havre, the 4th of May 1845. They landed in New York on June 2 and after numerous side trips, arrived at St. Martin's July 21 and received their first three pupils in Oct., 1845.

One particularly interesting part of the school history, as described by Sister Monica, was during 1863, a time that was "the darkest of the war", when Southern Colonel John Morgan crossed the Ohio River, against orders. Fortunately, the nuns were warned so they kept a night watch. Shutters were closed. Lights extinguished. Sounds of horses hoofs no doubt terrified them as Morgan and his men rode past their school -- well hidden in a grove of trees.

Johanna Hynes probably missed this historic event, having left the school in June 1862. However, the school continued into the 1900s, providing a fine education for young women and establishing many loyal alumnae. The residence school was closed in 1981 after going through numerous changes. Since 1971 Chatfield College, a liberal arts school has been located there.

St. Raphael's Cemetery, Springfield, Clark County, Ohio:
Margaret Kiley Hynes' Final Resting Place

Published in *The Report* (Ohio Genealogical Society) 42 (Spring 2002), 19-26.

Standing in front of my great-great grandmother's grave on a warm summer day, I looked around St. Raphael's Cemetery and wondered if it looked as neglected in 1865 when Margaret Kiley Hynes was buried there. It took me years to find her resting place because even though my mother had once told me that her great-grandmother, Margaret Hynes, was buried in Springfield, she did not know the date or place. I knew that she must have died before 1 April 1866, when her husband, Thomas Hynes, married Ellen Hartnett in Logan County, Ohio. However, I was unable to pursue that lead because records for only one Clark County township, Mad River, were available at the Ohio Historical Society Archives/Library in Columbus, Ohio.

A surprise phone call in December 1996 alerted me to the cemetery location. Father William Dunn, of Columbus, called to discuss his Coughlin family of Urbana, Champaign County, Ohio. A Springfield native, Father Dunn had obtained a printout of cemetery information from the Springfield Public Library. Somehow he knew that Margaret Hynes was the mother of my great-grandmother, Johanna Hynes Edmondson of Urbana. He told me about St. Raphael's Cemetery and Margaret Hynes' epitaph:

> Erected in memory of
> Margaret
> Wife of
> T.W. Hynes
> Died 15 Sept 1865
> Age 50
> May her soul rest in peace. Amen.

It is a short trip from Columbus to Springfield, yet I did not get there until nearly four years after I finally discovered where Margaret was buried. On Sunday, August 13, 2000, after a special event in nearby Fairborn, I took the opportunity to search for St. Raphael's. I found it on Lagonda Street, seven or eight blocks beyond St. Bernard's Church.

Once I located the grave, I photographed her headstone. Then, as I looked around, I tried to imagine the cemetery 135 years earlier. Who was there to mourn Margaret Hynes? Was hers an unexpected death, such as in childbirth, or had she suffered a long illness? Did St. Raphael's become her final resting-place because there was no Catholic cemetery where they lived in Bellefontaine, Logan County? How long did it take for news of her death to reach her family in Ireland?

I also wondered why so many headstones were off their bases? Were there plans to restore and reset them? Seeking answers, I wrote to the Ohio Genealogical Society (OGS). Lolita Guthrie, statewide cemetery chair, replied:

> *In my work with the Ohio Division of Real Estate, I find that St. Raphael's has a permanent registration number, indicating that it still an active cemetery...the type is "R" indicating religious, so it*

*is owned by either a local church or more likely the
Diocese. Any restoration work would be the
responsibility of the church—or more likely a
"friends of" which could include persons such as
yourself....I do hope this site does not go the way of
the former St. Mary's in Delaware, which was sold
and all markers removed....You are encouraged to
write even a short article for either of the OGS
quarterlies and tell about your family, [including
information about Margaret Kiley Hynes' 1865
burial in St. Raphael's Cemetery].*

More information came from the president of the Clark County
OGS chapter, whose letter noted that hundreds of tombstones may
be missing in St. Raphael's and that for one span of 44 years no
cemetery records were kept. What good fortune for me that
Margaret Hynes' headstone was still standing.

Later, an e-mail (in response to my letter) from Father Dennis
Caylor of St. Raphael's Church confirmed that he shares my
concerns about the cemetery.

*The Cemetery was founded when there was only
one Catholic Church in Springfield. Since then it
has been St. Raphael Parish that owns the cemetery.
We try to keep it up as best we can. As you saw
there has been vandalism at the cemetery. This has
been ongoing. We have talked with the police but
there is little they can do. Given the neighborhood
and the lack of security we do not feel that the
expense of up-righting the tombstones
(approximately ten thousand dollars) can be
justified.*

A paragraph in the Ohio Genealogical Society newsletter
caught the attention of Anne Benston, a member of the Clark
County OGS chapter. She wrote that in the early 1970s, she began
recording information from the headstones in St. Raphael's
Cemetery. These records were put on file cards and a copy of the

163

readings was given to St. Raphael's Church. Anne then moved out of the state. She returned in 1996 and continued the task, adding at least fifty more headstone records, as well as death records from October 1892 to 1910. Thus more than 1,600 names were published in the recent Springfield Township Cemetery Book 2.

During the years Anne was gone, three of her family stones (Biggins) were demolished. She wrote twice about this to Father M. Edmund Hussey, who preceded the current pastor, Father Dennis Cooley. In a letter dated 21 February 1998, Anne Benston wrote:

> *Dear Father Hussey,*
>
> *I had occasion to meet Deacon Norman Horstman at a meeting recently and discussed with him my concerns about the St. Raphael cemetery on Lagonda Avenue.*
>
> *This past month I toured the cemetery and saw first-hand the horrendous destruction of the beautiful monuments of our ancestors. Such sadness and shame came over me I felt I had to speak up. Even the monument for Father Thisse, who laid out and consecrated the ground in 1964, was toppled.*
>
> *Over the last thirty years I've seen the slow deterioration but with the fence removed it has escalated over one hundred fold.*
>
> *My belief is that all Catholics of Clark County have a moral obligation to help in the care of the grounds since it was used at one time by all until St. Bernard cemetery was started in 1878-79. Burials have been taking place until the 1950's.*
>
> *Perhaps the K. of C. Lodge would like to take the initiative and start a campaign for clean up and restoration as a special project.*
>
> *I will appreciate any ideas you may have on preserving what is left of this sacred place.*

A reply from Father Hussey was dated 25 February 1998.

Dear Mrs. Benston,

In regard to your recent letter expressing your concerns about the Lagonda Street Cemetery, it may be helpful for me to give you my understanding of the cemetery's history.

Although I have not done in-depth research into the origins of the deed and the title of the cemetery, it is my understanding that the cemetery did not actually belong to St. Raphael Parish but to a group of Catholics in Springfield and was originally known simply as the Catholic Cemetery. It was organized at a time when St. Raphael's was the only parish in this city, but apparently no fund was ever set up for its maintenance. It seems that individual families acquired plots, which they themselves maintained. As long as the original families remained in Springfield and continued to use their burial sites, this system apparently worked quite well. But inevitably many of these families died off or moved away and some of the other families purchased new plots in Calvary Cemetery or in St. Bernard's Cemetery, after those cemeteries were established. The Lagonda Street Cemetery ceased to be an active cemetery about eighty years ago, although a few burials took place later, the last one a little over fifty years ago.

Once the cemetery became inactive, it was inevitably neglected, at times becoming an overgrown jungle and a dump for discarded furniture and appliances. Occasionally, when the cemetery became an awful eyesore, a group of concerned Catholics, usually under the leadership of St. Raphael Parish, would undertake a clean-up campaign. But, since no structure was established for the on-going care of the cemetery, it eventually became an eyesore again. My predecessor, Father Bramlage, once again tried to clean up the cemetery and used parish funds to have a high school student mow it during the summers. But that was, of course, only a temporary, band-aid-type remedy instead of a cure.

The cemetery's status became somewhat more complicated when someone in the county auditor or treasurer's office discovered an unpaid 1926 assessment against the cemetery for the improvement and initial paving of Lagonda Avenue. This assessment together with their addition of sixty-five years of legal penalties and interest added a heavy debt to the orphaned cemetery's other problems. And, of course, there has been the inevitable vandalism of an abandoned site. In recent years one incident of vandalism was especially destructive, toppling and damaging literally hundreds of stones and monuments, including the beautiful monument for Father Thisse.

I am happy to say that there has been a recent and very significant improvement in the cemetery's condition. Enormous amounts of underbrush and trash have been removed, completely illegible and badly fractured stones have been buried so that mowers can more easily navigate the area, a lawn-care company has been engaged to keep the lawn mowed throughout the growing seasons and the 1926 assessment together with the sixty-five years of legal penalties and interest has been paid. A chain-link fence at the front of the cemetery has also been removed so that the property is more visible from the street, and therefore, more secure, and a night-time mercury light has been installed in the rear of the property. All of this has been accomplished with monies generously contributed by the members of St. Raphael Parish.

If any descendants of those buried in the cemetery or any other interested persons would wish to assume responsibility for the cemetery by forming a non-profit corporation and establishing an endowment for on-going maintenance, I would certainly be happy to put them in contact with the appropriate archdiocesan officials.

Anne Benston's reply to Father Hussy included the following:

Dear Father Hussey,

Your letter of February 25th was well received and greatly appreciated. It gave me more information on the history of the St. Raphael/Lagonda Cemetery.

After incorporating my concerns with your understanding of the cemetery's history, I still came away with a feeling of hopelessness that nothing will be done to preserve the final resting place of the first Catholics of Springfield and Clark County.

Beer's History of Clark County 1881 gives a scattered picture of early Catholics in this area. Prior to 1830 there were no known Catholics, but about 1835 and for the following ten years a number located here namely Lebold, Schutte, Reardon, Spangenberger and Bauer, to name a few. Between 1845 and 1850 came many Irish families including Hennessey, Lynch, Biggins, Cavanaugh and Shea. Most of these early families are buried in this cemetery.

Walking through the cemetery one can see the love and care for these early Catholics by the impressive marble monuments erected for their deceased. These monuments had to have been at great financial sacrifice as many of these early settlers were very poor. To see most of the stones toppled, broken and in decay today gives me little hope for any restoration.

I have taken some slides of the many stones there and will be glad to show them if anyone is interested. Two other people noticed the paragraph in the OGS newsletter. Terry Collis and Virginia Nichols contacted me via e-mail to share their interest in St. Raphael's. They provided the following information.

Terry Collis' great uncle, Charles B. Collis, buried in St. Raphael's next to his son William, was the first Springfield Police officer to die in the line of duty. This event of 7 March 1904 precipitated a riot after the lynching of a black man accused of the murder, bringing the Ohio National Guard to Springfield.

Charles B. Collis' ancestors came to Washington County, Ohio from England in 1818 and are listed as First Families of Hamilton County and Ohio. According to a newspaper article, Charles B. Collis converted to Catholicism on his death bed to please his wife. However, she later remarried and is buried in another Springfield cemetery. She attended a Catholic school in Springfield and may have been Irish.

When Terry visited St. Raphael's three years ago, he found that the Collis stones were intact, probably because they are small and close to the ground. They read as Chas. B. Collis 1859 - 1904 and William, son of Charles and Anna Collis, Feb 20, 1886- Aug 21, 1899. During his cemetery visit, he noticed one toppled tombstone that gave the deceased's immigration date, county and parish. He envied that person's descendants and hoped they benefited from the information about their Irish ancestor.

Terry has a tin box that belonged to William. He described the contents as trinkets that a boy would collect such as tortoise shell buttons, marbles, eyeglasses and schoolwork. He also has some of Anna's school papers from about 1885-90— spelling workbooks, geography (hand drawn maps) and art work.

Virginia Cox Nichols great grandparents, Winifred (Davey) and Michael Cox, are buried in St. Ray's, as their family calls St. Raphael's. In an e-mail message Virginia wrote:

> *Apparently there must have been a tombstone there at one time. No stone is standing for Michael or for Winifred today. Michael and his brothers Luke, John and Peter were listed as some of the actual builders of St. Raphael's Church in a history book that details the beginning of the church....Michael's brother Peter and his wife, Bridget and their sister Mary Cox (who never married) are also buried in St. Ray's. The stones are overturned—face down, but the name COX can be read along the side of the stone. The Cox stones are right next to the road into the cemetery about half way to the back along the right hand side."*

About the Hynes Family

Although the Hynes family had been in America for almost twenty years when Margaret died, they had lived only a few years in central Ohio. Any relatives, neighbors or friends who moved with them from Ireland have yet to be determined.

No other names were mentioned by their granddaughter, Margaret Edmondson Fitzgibbon, whose 1940 letter tells that Margaret and Thomas Hynes, and daughter Johanna, left Ireland in 1847 and "landed on the 4th of July, after three months on the sea and thought it a fine country and everyday a holiday." A well-to-do family, their furniture traveled with them, my mother said. However, ship records have not been located and the famine immigrant lists do not include this family of three. Hynes was a common name among the more than one million Irish who immigrated to the United States and Canada between 1846 and 1851.

Clues about the path they took came from the *Logan County (Ohio) History.*

T.W. Hynes, merchant; Bellefontaine. The subject of this sketch was born in Ireland December

169

21, 1810. In his native country, Mr. Hynes was engaged in farming and after marrying, he with wife and one child, in 1846, came to America, locating in Jefferson County, N.Y. where he was engaged in farming, following this for several years. He then entered the mercantile business in Buffalo, NY. He was a resident of Iowa for some time, and in 1865 came to Bellefontaine, where he has been one of its honored and respected citizens ever since. He is now engaged in the grocery business on Main Street and is recognized as one of Bellefontaine's enterprising citizens.

Census records for 1850 list Thomas Hines [*sic*], 30, a farmer in Ellisburg Township, Jefferson County, New York with his wife Margaret, 40, and daughter Joanna [*sic*], 5. Naturalization papers for Thomas Hines include the following information:

State of New York

Lewis County

Thomas Hines, being duly sworn before Julius A. White, Clerk of the Common Pleas Court of said County, saith he was born in Ireland that he is of the age of thirty years, that he owes allegiance to the Queen of Great Britain that he emigrated from the port of Killarly to the town of Oswego in the County of Oswego in the state of New York about the 15th of September 1837; that he now resides in the town of West Turin in said County of Lewis where he has settled, and intends to reside; and that it is bonafida the intention of this deponent to become a citizen of the United States, and to renounce all allegiance and fidelity to any and every foreign Prince, Potentate, State and Sovereignty whatsoever; and particularly the Queen of Great Britain.

Subscribed and Sworn before me the 18th day of September 1846, Julius A. White

Thomas (x) Hines (his mark)
State of New York
Lewis County Clerk's Office

I hereby certify that I have compared the foregoing and annexed copy of the Intention of Thomas Hines to become a citizen of the United States, with the original copy of such Intention filed in this office September 18, 1846 and still remaining on file in the office and that it is a true transcript therefrom and of the whole of such Original

Witness my hand and the seal of the said County this 5th day of April 1851.

Harrison Barnes, Clerk
State of New York
Jefferson County

Patrick Gilbay and Martin McLaughlin of the county aforesaid being severally sworn, depose and say, that we are citizens of the United States, and have been acquainted with Thomas Hines for more than five years last past; that said Thomas Hines has resided within the United States for more than five years last past, and within the State of New York 5 years; that he has behaved as a man of good moral character, attached to the principles of the Constitution of the United States, and well disposed to the good order and happiness of the same.

Sworn in open Court this 5 day of Sept 1851 Isaac Munson, Clerk: P Gilbay, Martin McLaughlin

Census records for 1860 have not been located in New York or Ohio. However a Cincinnati directory for 1859 lists a Thos. Hynes at 54 McFarland and Thos. Haynes [*sic*] of the same address with a coffeehouse at 146 Vine. There is no 1860 or 1861 listing for Thomas Hynes or Haynes and no Cincinnati church records have been located.

Other records show that Johanna (Hynes/Haynes) studied and boarded at the Academy of the Ursulines, St. Martin's, Brown County, Ohio, in 1861 and 1862. [See Nelson, Margaret Van Ness. "Johanna Hynes Edmondson and The Ursuline Academy of Brown County, Ohio: An Early Ohio Boarding School," *The Report* 36 (Winter 1996): 186-189.] She is listed as Johanna Haynes— Cincinnati, in the 1860 school enrollment list. Nearby Cincinnati seems a logical residence for her parents. An ad in *The Catholic Telegraph and Advocate* of 14 July 1860, said that "(t)he parents or guardians of Young Ladies who reside at a distance are required to designate some correspondent in Cincinnati, who will be charged to liquidate their bills when due."

Although Thomas Hynes did not settle in Bellefontaine until after 1860, he is listed among the first Catholic settlers and a member St. Patrick's Church of Bellefontaine. In a brief history of St. Patrick's church, Louise Norris, of the Logan County Historical Society, wrote: "There were few Catholics in Bellefontaine during pioneer times and prejudice was strong against them. The Catholics of that time showed courage, perseverance and a love of their church which enabled them to overcome the obstacles placed before them."

There were close ties between the early Catholic churches. "It was as a mission from Urbana that St. Patrick's church was organized in 1853 at Bellefontaine, though the band of Catholics of that town had been gathered together in 1849 and had been visited regularly, first from Springfield, and then from Urbana."

Looking for reasons why Thomas Hynes might have settled in Ohio, and then in Bellefontaine, I learned that there were two itinerant priests—brothers J. J. O'Mealy and Patrick O'Mealy, born in Limerick, Ireland—who served in Springfield until 1849. Rev. J. J. O'Mealy was born in 1809 and studied in Rome, France and Cincinnati. Soon after ordination he was made Rector of the Diocesan Seminary in Brown County; Ohio. He died in Springfield, 20 October 1856, and was buried in Dayton.

The O'Mealy family could have known the Hynes or Kiley families in Limerick. Rev. J. J. O'Mealy was about the age of Thomas Hynes and could have met the Hynes family in Cincinnati or he could have known Johanna Hynes at the Ursuline Academy, in Brown County. Johanna was probably withdrawn from school because of the Civil War.

Then, between 1862 and 1865, the Hynes family may have lived in Defiance County, where Thomas bought land in 1864. Estate records led to the deed showing that Thomas W. Haynes [*sic*], resident, bought 160 acres in Washington Township, Defiance County, Ohio, 10 March 1864 for a consideration of $2,000. Although they moved to Bellefontaine in 1865, the Defiance County land was not sold until after Thomas died.

Thomas Hynes died intestate, 6 November 1881, in Lake Township, Logan, County, Ohio. His heirs were Johanna Edmondson and Ellen Hynes. Thomas' estate papers show that Johanna's husband, John Croke Edmondson, borrowed $1,000 on 4 May 1876 and owed $1,273 at Thomas' death. The estate must have sued to get the sum, which Johanna paid, and Thomas' estate was settled in July 1886, totaling about $2,200.

No information has been found about the Hynes or Kiley families in Ireland. According to the Edmondson Bible, Johanna Hynes was born 5 September 1846 in Castleconnell, County Limerick, Ireland and died 7 October 1920 in Columbus, Franklin County, Ohio. She became John Croke Edmondson's third wife on Wednesday, 6 March 1867, married by Reverend J.B. Hemsteger at the Holy Cross Church in Columbus, Ohio.

During a 1994 trip to Ireland, I inquired about the Hynes and Kiley families at the Limerick Heritage Center. There I obtained the local phone number of Michael Hynes, who believed that his family was related to Thomas W. Hynes. Because I was with a group, I was unable to meet him or to visit Kilmurry Cemetery, which he described as located three miles from Limerick City on the left side of Dublin Road about 100 yards behind the Esso Service Petrol Station called Hurlers. He said all the "older" Hynes are buried there, whereas the only ones on record at the Heritage Center were born after 1850—Patrick Hynes, born 1876; Edward Hynes, 1877; Michael Hynes, 1878;William Hynes, 1880; Joseph Hynes, 1882; and Mary Hynes, 1885. Michael said that there were at least two marriages between the Hynes and Kiley families and that the families lived in Lisnagry, which is less than a mile south of Castleconnell.

Conclusion. Three other people who have relatives buried in St. Raphael's have provided poignant stories, creating pictures in our minds of people who were early pioneers in Ohio, or who saved tortoise shell buttons and marbles, or who were policemen protecting the community. The thought that the tombstones of our own parents could ever be plowed under gives us a glimpse into the hearts of those whose ancestor's stones have met this fate. In order to form a "Friends of St. Raphael's Cemetery" group, we would need support from people who live in Clark County, Ohio, in addition to the non-resident people who are interested. An immediate goal might be a compilation of information about the people buried in St. Raphael's. An admirable and more challenging goal would be to fence the cemetery. Suggestions for additional goals are welcomed.

Meanwhile, the search for Hynes and Kiley ancestors continues

"Recruiting Irishmen for the 50th OVI, John Croke Edmondson, 61st OVI, Champaign Co, Ohio."

Ohio Civil War Genealogy Journal VI (September 2002), 24-38.

"In for the War!" proclaims a well-worn notice passed down through the years in the family of John Croke Edmondson, my great-grandfather. John recruited Irish soldiers for the 50th Regiment of Ohio Volunteers. Although Edmondson, a 31-year-old Irish-American with a pregnant wife and five children, served only seven months in the Civil War, he left a colorful and interesting record of his experiences as a soldier and recruiter. His service and pension records, along with relevant histories and official rosters of the Civil War, provide the basic facts of his service and show how the war affected his health. Newspaper articles and military records help clarify the recruiting procedure

John likely followed. Immigration details, naturalization papers, the family Bible, and employment and census records provide a fuller picture of John's life, including his Irish connections and his political appointment.

Recruiting Procedures. According to Whitelaw Reid, every county had a military committee that dealt with recruiting. In a more current book, David Thackery explained:

"Ohio's regiments were organized from military recruiting districts, into which the counties were grouped. The recipient of a commission to raise a regiment would form the majority of his ten companies from his home county, adding three or four companies raised elsewhere in the district."

Those in charge of recruiting no doubt provided John Edmondson with a copy of "Directions for enlisting and organizing volunteer forces in Ohio" and the following form to complete:

Head Quarters, Ohio Militia
ADJUTANT GENERAL'S OFFICE
Columbus, _____, 1861

Sir:

You are hereby notified that the Governor of Ohio has appointed you Second Lieutenant in the _____ Regiment of Ohio Volunteer _____ in the service of the United States.

You will immediately notify this Department of your acceptance or non-acceptance of this appointment. Should you accept, you will report forthwith at these Head Quarters, to be mustered into the service; after which you will repair to your proper station for the purpose of enlisting recruits for a company to be attached to said Regiment. Should you fail to enlist and report, in accordance with the accompanying instructions, at the Head Quarters of the regiment at _____ at least thirty recruits with _____ days from date hereof, this appointment will be liable to be revoked by the Governor of the State.

[Sidebar has the complete recruiting instructions.]

One method John used to encourage men to enlist in the regiment was the recruiting notice now in the possession of his descendents. The notice, which exuded enthusiasm and patriotism, extolled potential adventures complete with a Catholic chaplain, uniforms, food and money. Over the years, the notice was folded, obscuring words and letters in the middle of the page. Someone later attached a small photo of John Edmondson, the only surviving image of him in uniform. [Missing parts indicated by brackets.]

In For The War!
FIFTIETH REGIMENT, O.V.I.
Col. S.J. McGroarty, Com..'ng[ ] P.Nolan, Lt. Col.

The undersigned informs his co[ ] and all others desirous of enlisting in one of the best Regi[   ]sed in Ohio, that he is recruiting a Company for the above [   ] which is composed chiefly of Irishmen and has a Cathol [   ] attached to it. Uniforms and subsistence furnished im [   ] and pay to commence from the date of enlistment.

Now Boys, "Face the Music!"
JOHN C. EDMUNDSON,
Lieutenant 50th Regiment,
Recruiting Officer.
Urbana, O., January 28, 1862.

Lieutenant Colonel Nolan, an Irishman listed on the recruiting notice, lived in Montgomery County, Ohio, in 1870, where he was a lawyer. He served as a Captain in the 11th Regiment O.V.I., Company G, from April to August 1861.

Why Enlist? Although the instructions listed many enticements for recruiters, John's motivation to join, at age 31, remains conjecture. He supposedly left Ireland before July 1850 to avoid conscription, yet 12 years later he volunteered to fight for the Union army. He was probably recruited by Stephen J. McGroarty, who, according to Whitelaw Reid "was a conspicuously gallant and efficient officer; and by reason of his birth, had great influence in securing the support of the war by the masses of Irish citizens in Cincinnati. McGroarty and Edmondson were born in Ireland within a few years of each other.

The *Citizen and Gazette* reported a rally in Urbana, February 13, 1862:

> Col. McGroarty of the 50th regiment, organizing at Hamilton, addressed the people at the CourtHouse on Tuesday evening last [11 February 1862]. Addresses were made by R.C. Fulton and J.A. Corwin, Esqs. This reigment [*sic*], we understand, lacks near 200 men to complete its organization. It is composed chiefly of Irishmen, and has a Catholic Priest for Its Chaplain. What success the gallant Colonel had in getting recruits here, we have not learned.

> J.C. Edmonston [*sic*], who has been recruiting here for some time for this regiment, has had some success in getting recruits. One man, we understand, who enlisted while in an oblivious state, repented of the act when he came to his right mind, and the other day paid a man two hundred dollars cash, to go as a substitute. The substitute was one of the volunteers in the three month's service, and the regiment will gain by the exchange.

Obviously, John did not follow the recruiting directions for assessing a man's "habits of sobriety." During the war, Ohio provided only 8,129 of the 144,221 Irish-born soldiers and officers on the Union side. One wonders how many of Champaign County's 4,112 volunteers (as of 1 October 1862) were Irish. A count of the 1850 census for people born in Ireland showed 196 in Champaign County. According to David Thackery: "In 1860 the foreign born accounted for a little over 6 percent of the population, the largest segment apparently the Irish of Urbana."

Urbana lawyers Robert C. Fulton and John A. Corwin spoke at the Courthouse rally. Corwin, at age 41, served three months as a captain in the 13th Regiment O.V.I. Company K, appointed 20 April 1861, and later served on the Ohio Supreme Court. No service record was found for Fulton, who was 37 in 1860 and lived close to John Edmondson. Fulton was a Common Pleas judge and a state representative.

John Edmondson appears to have been unsuccessful in recruiting enough men for the 50th O.V.I. Thus, on 23 April 1862 his recruits became part of the 61st O.V.I. and he remained a second lieutenant rather than a captain. However, Frederick Stephen Wallace maintains that the 50th, 52nd and 61st were filled quickly, but then depleted to replace troops lost in battle. The 50th O.V.I. was not mustered in until 27 August 1862, at Camp Dennison, near Cincinnati.

The 61st is not one of the nine regiments, completely or at least partly made up of men from Champaign County, listed in *The History of Champaign County*. A comparison of the *Official Roster* with the list of men who served from Urbana shows which men were in John's company.

Name	Rank	Age	Date Entered	Other
Joseph W. Bennett	Priv.	20	24 Sept 1862	Transferred to 52nd O.V.I. 25 May 1862
Edward O'Bryan	Corp.	28	12 Feb 1862	Disc. 28 Feb 1863, scd.
Thomas Fennecy	Corp	28	12 Feb 1862	*Vet.
George S.	Priv.	38	27 Jan 1862	Disc. 17 June 1862

Hoover				at Moorefield, Va., scd.
Farall McCue **	Serg.	22	25 Jan 1862	Mustered as private; appointed sergeant 10 Jan 1863; mustered out 31 Mar 1865 at Goldsboro, N.C. as supernumerary by reason of consolidation.
Dennis McDonald** *	Corp.	34	10 Oct 1862	Died 22 July 1864
Christopher Miles	Priv.	39	14 Feb 1862	Disc. 26 Feb 1863 at Baltimore, MD, scd.
John S. Pearson	Priv.	18	12 Feb 1862	*Vet.
Robert Warnock*** *	Sergt.	20	24 Feb 1862	Disc. 5 May 1863, scd.
Edward White	Priv.	36	1 April 1862	No information.
James Yazel/Yeazel	Priv.	17	24 Feb 1862	*Vet.

(Disc. = discharged; scd. = surgeon's certificate of disability.)
*Veterans transferred to Co. D, 82nd O.V.I, 31 March 1865.
** Terrell McCue is on the Urbana but there is no Terrell McCue in the index of the *Official Roster*. The "T" should have been a "F" in the Urbana list.
*** D. A. McDonald is on the Urbana list so it is unknown if they are the same person.
**** Robert Warnock from the Urbana list was a major so probably was not the same person who served in Company B.

Middleton's 1917 *History of Champaign County* lists the 61st as a regiment that included men from the county and notes the death of two Champaign County men from Company B.

Patrick Madigan	Pvt.	28	3 April 1862	Died 17 Jan 1864 Covington, Ky. Buried there in National Cemetery.
Ephraim Obenour	Pvt.	18	18 Feb 1862	Wounded 1 July 1863 in battle of Gettysburg; died in the hands of the enemy, 5 July 1863. Buried in Gettysburg National Cemetery.

It is not surprising that Champaign County recruits, particularly Irishmen, were scarce in January 1862. Almost 600 men, including Irishmen from Saint Paris, had already joined the 66th O.V.I. in December 1861. Apparently, men in all-Irish companies or regiments fared better than those with native-born soldiers or those of other nationalities. "An Irishman, particularly a Catholic, has a devilish hard road to travel when not in an Irish regiment," testified an Irish-born captain in Tennessee.

Also, according to Kerby A. Miller "anti-Irish Catholic prejudice remained blatant even in wartime, manifested in the military draft's inequitable application to working-class Irish wards, in the mistreatment of Irish-American conscripts and soldiers, and—some Irishmen felt—in the unnecessary, if not intentional, waste of Irish regiments in hopeless combat situations. As a result, suspicion and resentment were prominent themes in the letters of Irish soldiers in the Union Armies."

David Thackery noted that men in regiments from their own county tended to receive better treatment and have more opportunity for promotion and advancement. In Champaign

County, the 66th was raised by a Republican organization and advertised in a Republican paper, another drawback for John Edmondson, a Democrat.

It was not uncommon for recruiters to be unable to fill their unit, Whitelaw Reid observed: "Efforts by Captain O'Dowd to raise an Irish Catholic regiment proved futile, and excited the wrath of the State Adjutant-General to such a pitch that he reported: If the intention had been to enlist men to stay at home and be exempt from the draft, no change of proceedings would have been required to effect these objects."

Wallace noted that Colonel McGroarty's 61st regiment seemed to be mostly Irishmen, or men of Irish descent while Robert G. Carron described the 61st as some immigrants from Ireland, Scotland, and Germany but also recruits from Ohio, Indiana and Kentucky.

<u>Service and Pension Records</u>. Although his family believed him to be a captain, John C. Edmondson is listed in the *Official Roster* as a second lieutenant in Company B, 61st Regiment, Ohio Volunteer Infantry, who enrolled 23 January 1862, at age 31, and resigned 30 June 1862. The dates in the pension vary slightly from those in the *Official Roster*. Interestingly, the records contain no personal description.

John's resignation letter from Moorefield, Hardy County (now in West Virginia) reads:

> *Moorefield, Va.*
> *Head Quarters 61st Regt. O.V.I.*
> *June 18, 1862*

To
N. Schleich
Col. 61st Regt. O.V.I.
Sir
  I have the honor hereby to tender you my resignation as 2nd Lieutenant Co. B. 61st Regt O.V.I.
> *Respectfully yours*
> *J.C. Edmondson*

This Resignation is approved and I beg that it may be accepted.

Lt. E's PO is Urbana, O.   *N. Schleich*
                                             Co. 61st Regt

A return in his service record notes that John: "Tendered his resignation on June 17/62 and had leave of absence for 30 days for the Governor to accept his resignation." On the back of the Officers' Casualty Sheet, which gives 30 July 1862 as the date of his discharge, is written: "Head Quarters III Division, Strasburg, June 22, 1862. Approved and respectfully submitted to Major Gen. Fremont, Comdy. Department C. Schurz Brig General Comdy. Division."

John first requested a pension on 11 May 1886, 24 years after his discharge was approved at Rapidan River, Virginia on 18 August 1862. His stated reason for needing a pension was that while serving in Company 50, he was disabled by acute pleurisy March 1862, at Camp Chase, Ohio, where he was treated by the regimental surgeon of the 50th and 60th Ohio Volunteers. The company roll reported him present until 30 April 1862, and then absent May, June and July 1862. He resigned on 17 June 1862, when he received a 30-day leave of absence, and was discharged 30 July 1862 in orders from War Department, based on a letter from his commanding officer.

It is obvious that he never reached Rapidan River, Virginia. Apparently, he traveled as far as western Virginia because Thomas Fenacy, also with Company B, 61st O.V. I., testified that Edmondson had another pleurisy attack at Petersburg, Hardy County, Virginia. The regiment, ordered to Virginia May 27, joined Major General John Charles Fremont's army at Strasburg, Virginia, 23 June 1862.

In response to his pension request, the War Department confirmed John's service even through his resignation papers had been lost at Fremont's Headquarters. Confusion may have resulted in transition when Fremont refused to serve under Major General John Pope, who was his junior in rank, and Franz Sigel assumed command 10 June 1862. Interestingly, George S. Hoover, 38, from Company B, and a neighbor of John's in Urbana, also resigned 17 June 1862 at Moorefield, Virginia, on a Surgeon's certificate of disability. Perhaps they traveled home together.

Pension record affidavits attesting to John Edmondson's condition were given:

- 15 August 1888, by <u>Elizabeth Maurer</u>, 45, of Urbana, Ohio, who affirmed that she was "well and intimately acquainted" with John C. Edmondson, as his next door neighbor from September 1879 to February 1882. She often heard Edmondson "complain of pains or trouble in his chest from pleurisy and she knew him to be sick in bed of said disease." She believed that Edmondson "was wholly unable to perform manual labor on account of his chest trouble."

- 29 May 1889, by <u>Thomas Fennessy</u>, 55, of Urbana, Ohio who said he had known Edmondson since 1859. They shared quarters at Camp Chase in Columbus. He observed Edmondson's repeated attacks of pleurisy and his treatment, by the surgeon L [T?] Bonnet [Bounet?] of the 50th Regiment, who applied blisters and mustard plasters to the chest. Fennessy helped the surgeon make these "appliances." Fennessy said Edmondson was "of sound bodily health and free from disease before the service" and that the pleurisy was contracted at Camp Chase "as a result of the cold, muddy, inclement, damp weather, exceptional duty, and cold, open and insufficient quarters." Edmondson had a recurrence of the attack of the same disease while at Petersburg, Hardy County, Virginia with the 61st Regiment, June 1862.

- In January 1891, Edmondson, 60, now in Franklin County, Ohio, applied for an increase in his pension of $12 month "by reason of his disabilities, which were disease of lung and heart, and auchylosis of left elbow joint, wrist and fingers." He believed that his present rate was too low and disproportionate to his disability. T.D. McElroy and H.M. Crow of Columbus affirmed his identify. However, at John's death in 1905, his pension was still $12 a month.

Dates of Johanna Edmondson's applications for a widow's pension, and the witnesses, were:

- 22 February 1906, by <u>Mary Moynihan</u>, 68, of 111 East Ward Street, Urbana who said:

    I became acquainted with the soldier John C. Edmondson in the summer of 1852; I learned as a matter of general information in this community that said John C. Edmondson had been married in the month of May, 1852 to Julia Pierce who died about six or seven weeks after her marriage to him; at the time I became acquainted with him she had been dead about two weeks; from personal knowledge I know that the said John C. Edmondson and Ellen Hickey were married in the month April, 1853 at Dayton, Ohio; Mrs. Ellen Edmondson died at Urbana, Ohio August 2, 1865; the said John C. Edmondson married Johanna Hynes, of Bellefontaine, Ohio at Columbus, Ohio on or about March 6th, 1867.

- 12 March 1906, by <u>John T. Ryan</u>, 39, also well acquainted with John Edmondson, was the Urbana undertaker who received the dead body of Edmondson 6 November 1905 from the Pennsylvania Railroad Company in Urbana, identified and prepared it for burial in Oak Dale Cemetery, Urbana, Tuesday, 7 November 1905.

- A certified copy of the Columbus coroner's finding, dated 13 March 1906, stated that the coroner, Joseph A. Murphy, M.D., was called to 393 Lexington to inquire how the deceased came to his death. He examined the body, heard the evidence, and found the cause to be organic heart disease. No postmortem was held.

- 14 March 1906, by <u>Griffith Ellis</u>, 75, of 472 Scioto Street, Urbana. He affirmed that Johanna was the widow of John C. Edmondson, whom he had known since 1851.
- 2 May1908, by <u>Worthington Kautzman</u> and <u>J.P. Brennan</u>, both of Columbus.
- 4 April 1916, by <u>Mary Pratt</u> and <u>William Hartnett</u>, both of Bellefontaine. William, 76, was the brother of Johanna's stepmother, Ellen Hartnett Hynes, who died in 1904.
- 14 September 1916, the last declaration for a widow's pension, noted Johanna's Irish birth on 5 September 1846 and current address: 1430 E. Long Street, Columbus. When she died on 7 October 1920, her residence was 2331 North High Street, Columbus.

<u>Becoming A Citizen</u>. Research supports the family's story that John Edmondson took his mother's maiden name after he left Ireland. He arrived as John Croke, shown by his application for citizenship—now in the archives at Paul Laurence Dunbar Library at Wright State University in Dayton, Ohio—4 April 1851, "John Croke Jr., an alien and native of Ireland...came into open court and declared upon his solemn oath that he first arrived in the United States on the [ink spilled here] of July 1850, and that it is his bonafide intention to become a citizen of the United States of America..."

He supposedly entered in Canada, to escape arrest and deportation although the records do not tell his port of arrival. Then as John Croke Edmondson, he became a citizen on 21 August 1855 at Urbana, Ohio. His original certificate of naturalization from the State of Ohio, Champaign County, belonged to Thomas Edmondson III of Columbus, Ohio but is now lost.

<u>Family Background</u>. In the 1840s and 1850s, Irish railroad workers, possibly illiterate, were the first Catholics in Urbana. In contrast, John, an educated man, quickly acquired a job, a wife, land, and children. The 1860 census documents that John C. Edmondson, Urbana, Ohio, age 30, was a bookkeeper with real estate valued at $2,500 and a personal estate valued at $200. He

lived with his wife Ellen, 26, and children Augustine, 6, John, 4, James B., 3, and George, 1.

In 1940, John's daughter, Margaret Edmondson Fitzgibbon, wrote to her niece, Norma Thorp Van Ness:

> Your grandfather Edmondson enlisted in the Civil War as Leutenant [*sic*]—very patriotic—he left a wife and six children to go— he must have had an itchy foot. He got a pension for rheumatism contracted while sleeping on damp battlefields—Ma used to say he never saw a fight only what he made himself. He was raised to the rank of captain— however he got it, he got it—Your uncle Harry fit [*sic*] and bled at the bloodless battlefield of Chickamauga Park in the Spanish American war, 1898...Your great-grandfather, the English Gentleman, was in the Franco Prussian war, I believe, maybe it was an earlier war.

Actually, John had only five children when he enlisted, but the sixth was born 13 March 1862. The family Bible, begun in 1872 by Johanna (Hynes) and John Edmondson, gives the following information: [Death dates of the children added by author.]

John C. Edmondson: b. 7/22/1831 Mooncoin, Cnty Kilkenny Ire.
d. 11/5/1905 Columbus, Franklin, OH

(Wives)

Julia Pierce   b. Knuckawn, Cnty Kerry, Ire.
       d. 7/8/1852 Urbana, Champaign, OH

Ellen Hickey   b. Duagh, Cnty Kerry, Ire.
       d. 8/2/1865 Urbana, Champaign, OH

Johanna Hynes   b. 9/5/1846 Castle Connell, Cnty Limerick,
Ire.   d. 10/7/1920 Columbus, Franklin, OH

Marriages

John C. Edmondson and Julia Pierce   Mon., 17 May 1852
       by Rev. James Meagher at Urbana, OH

John C. Edmondson and Ellen Hickey   Sat., 2 April 1853
       by Rev. Joseph O'Malley at Dayton, OH

John C. Edmondson and Johanna Hynes   Wed., 6 March 1867
    by Rev. J.B. Hemsteger at Columbus, OH
        Children of John C. and Ellen Edmondson
            All born in Urbana, OH

Augustine Edmondson	2 Mar 1854	1 Sep 1932
John Edmondson	16 Jun 1855	28 Mar 1931
James Edmondson	9 Dec 1856	28 Mar 1929
George Patrick Edmondson	18 Mar 1859	11 Oct 1870
William C. Edmondson	7 Sep 1860	18 Dec 1934
Patrick Joseph Edmondson	13 Mar 1862	1 Apr 1862
Mary Eliza Edmondson	1 Jan 1865	27 Jun 1952

Children of John C. and Johanna Edmondson:
            All born in Urbana, OH.

Margaret Edmondson	24 Dec 1867	30 Apr 1953
Thomas Augusta Edmondson	3 May 1870	22 Sep 1938
Esther Maria Edmondson	4 July 1872	30 May 1951
Frances Anne Edmondson	7 Nov 1874	13 Dec 1945
Patrick Edward Edmondson	4 Oct 1876	12 Oct 1876
Harry Andrew Edmondson	12 Dec 1877	14 May 1914
Johanna Gertrude Edmondson	2 Dec 1880	1 Aug 1967

Post Civil War. After the war, John Edmondson led a busy life, with the war's effect on his health being more evident in his later years. In 1870, John Edmondson, age 40, lived in Urbana with his (new) wife, Johanna, 24, his mother Eliza Edmondson, 65, born in England, and his children Augustine, 16; John, 15; James B., 13; George P., 11; William, 9; Mary E., 6; and Margaret, 2. All the children except Margaret were in school. Still a bookkeeper, his real estate was valued at $3000 and his personal estate at $500.

In 1880, the census recorded that John C. Edmondson, 49, born in Ireland to parents born in Ireland, was a grain merchant in Urbana. His wife Johanna, 43 (actually 33), was born in Ireland to Irish parents. His mother Eliza, 80, a widow, was born in England to Irish parents. All except the youngest child were attending school—William, 20; Mary E., 16; Margaret, 12; Thomas, 10; Esther, 8; Frances, 6; and Harry, 3.

In 1882, the family moved to nearby Bellefontaine, Logan County, Ohio, and in 1890 to Columbus, Franklin County. The Veteran's Census of 1890 showed John C. Edmondson at 448 East Gay Street in Columbus; temporary housing while looking for a family home, no doubt.

His appointment as superintendent of the arsenal was short-lived due to the election of a new governor in 1892. In 1900, John C. Edmondson, age 65, a grocer, lived at 519 Mound Street in Columbus. Married for 33 years, he and his father were born in Ireland and his mother in England. He immigrated in 1850 and had been in the United States for 50 years. John died on 5 November 1905 and his missing death certificate was found in his pension papers by the author.

Political Appointment. John's experience made him a natural to keep records at the State Arsenal as "Superintendent of Arsenal and Book-keeper." Perhaps he gained the appointment through his wartime experience or through contacts, such Champaign County's Colonel Frank Chance, an aide-de-camp to Governor Campbell in 1890. Governor Campbell assumed his duties 14 January 1890, so John's job probably began then, too. He earned $1,200 in 1890 and $1,500 in 1891. John's daughter Esther Marie, called "Babe," also appears to have profited. One item on record for 29 November 1891 was $15.00 paid to E.M. Edmondson for making 250 powder bags.

In his annual report of 1890, Adjutant General Thomas Dill wrote: "To Captain John Edmondson who, in addition to his charge as Superintendent of the State Arsenal, is also the book-keeper and paymaster of the department…[other names here are omitted by author] …my sincere thanks are due for prompt and intelligent co-operation in every request made upon them looking to a creditable administration of the affairs of the department." No wonder his family thought he was a captain! The 1890 report gave John's name as Edmondson, and the 1891 report as Edmundson.

Obituaries and Funeral Article.

UNANNOUNCED CAME THE DEATH
MESSENGER
TO HOME OF A FORMER RESIDENT OF THIS CITY AT
COLUMBUS

John C. Edmondson Dies Suddenly and
Unexpectedly—News a Shock to His children

W. C., T. A. and Harry Edmondson and
Mrs. James F. Hearn were called to Columbus
Sunday morning, the distressing news of the sudden
death of their father at his home in that city having
been received by them. The body will be brought to
this city Monday evening at 6:24 and will be taken
direct to the home of Mrs. Hearn in West Ward
street. The funeral will be held from St. Mary's
church Tuesday morning at eight o'clock.

The news of Mr. Edmondson's death came as a
great shock to his children in this city as it was not
even known by them that he was in poor health
although he had suffered a stroke of apoplexy some
time ago. His lifeless form was found in the bath
room in his home in the Capitol City at three
o'clock Sunday morning.

The decedent was formerly a resident of this city,
having at one time conducted a grain elevator here.
He was born in Ireland and was 76 years of age at
the time of his death. Several years ago he left this
city and went to Columbus and has since made that
city his home. In addition to the children above
named he is survived by A.C. Edmondson, of
Marion, and Miss Fannie Edmondson, of
Columbus.

Mr. Edmondson will be well remembered by
many of the older citizens of this city all of whom
will be pained to hear of his tragic death.

Life in This City

189

Mr. Edmondson during his life in this city was one of Urbana's most prominent men. He was a book-keeper in the hardware store of Lemuel Weaver and afterwards clerked in one of the banks of the city. Then for years he kept books for Winslow, Wiley & Mosgrove, later engaging in the grain business under the firm name of Blose & Edmondson. He moved from this city to Bellefontaine and at the time of the election of James E. Campbell as governor he was appointed superintendent of the state arsenal in Columbus and since that time has made his home in the Capitol City.

During the civil war he organized Company B, of the 61st Ohio and was elected its captain. When the regiment moved on to Columbus the 50th, 52nd and 61st were consolidated. Capt. Edmondson going to the front as a lieutenant in his company.

He is survived by his wife, he having been married three times, and eleven children. The latter are: John C. Edmondson, Jr. of Titusville, Penn; Dr. J. J. Edmondson of New York; A. C. Edmondson, of Marion; Will Edmondson and Mrs. James F. Hearn, of this city; Mrs. Frank Fitzgibbon of Newark; T. A. and Harry Edmondson, of this city; Esther, Frances and Gertrude of Columbus.

FOREVER LAID
In Quiet, Beautiful, Oak Dale Are
Remains of John C. Edmondson

The remains of the late John C. Edmondson arrived in this city Monday evening at 6:24 from Columbus and were taken direct to the home of Mrs. James F. Hearn. Tuesday morning the body was removed to St. Mary's church from where the funeral was held at eight o'clock. The requiem high mass was sung by Rev. George F. Hickey. Following the services the body was taken to Oak Dale where it was laid to rest in the family plot. The pallbearers were David Powers, James McGuninness, Martin Ryan, Michael McGroe, James Ryan and Timothy Graney, all old time friends of the decedent. The services were attended by a number of the relatives from a distance.

DIED SUDDENLY

Remains of John C. Edmondson Laid to Rest in Oak Dale

John C. Edmondson, formerly of this city, was found dead in the bath room of his residence in Columbus Sunday morning at 3 o'clock. The remains were brought to this city Monday evening and were taken to the home of the deceased's daughter, Mrs. James F. Hearn. The funeral was held Tuesday morning from St. Mary's church.

The death of Mr. Edmondson was sudden. He suffered a stroke of appoplexy [*sic*] some time ago and had been in ill health lately. He was born in Ireland and was 76 years of age. He was a former resident of this city and during his residence here he was one of the prominent business men. He was clerk in one of the banks and was bookkeeper for several firms and later was in the grain business under the firm name of Blose & Edmondson. He was appointed superintendent of the state arsenal in Columbus by Governor James E. Campbell and since then has lived in Columbus. He served in the civil war as lieutenant in his company.

He is survived by his wife, he having been married three times, and eleven children. The latter are: John C. Edmondson, Jr., of Titusville, Penn; Dr. J. J. Edmondson, of New York; A.C. Edmondson, of Marion; Will Edmondson and Mrs.

James F. Hearn of this [the word city omitted] Mrs. Frank Fitzgibbon, of Newark; T. A. and Harry Edmondson, of this city; Esther, Frances and Gertrude, of Columbus.

Conclusion. Although John Edmondson was an educated man, he left no personal writings for his descendants. However, his Civil War records attest that John did not fit the description of the Irish soldier courageously charging into battle. Even so, he played a small part in history because "[t]he Civil War was America's first conflict in which the Catholic Irish were significant participants." Although in military uniform for less than four months, he was credited with seven months service and probably never drew his sword.

John's photo shows a handsome man who no doubt was attracted to the glamour of the uniform and the sword (now owned by a grandson of Margaret Fitzgibbon, whose letter hinted that her father had an Irish temper). The fact that he received a pension impressed his family.

Literate men, such as John, directed the Civil War—a necessity considering all the forms that needed to be completed. John may have been motivated by war reports he read in the newspaper, such as one in *The Citizen & Gazette* (Urbana) of 10 October 1861, about Colonel James A. Mulligan, of the Irish Brigade in Chicago, who was ordered to Lexington to aid General Peabody. All Irishmen surely discussed the Irish Brigade of New York, too.

It is questionable whether John knew much about the 61st Regiment's assignments, except perhaps that he did not want to participate, even in good health. Still, his service was sufficient to obtain his appointment as superintendent of the Ohio arsenal in Columbus, a job where he used his bookkeeping skills. The most significant consequence of John's resignation from military service is that he did not die in battle. If he had, my grandmother, Johanna Gertrude Edmondson, would not have been born, and this article would never have been written.

SIDEBAR: The 61st's daily routine at Camp Chase devised by Colonel Newton Schleich for training and indoctrination, 23 April to 27 May 1962, while the men served as prison camp guards.

Time	Activity
5 a.m.	Reveille and Roll Call
6 a.m.	Breakfast
6:30 a.m.	Morning Reports
7 a.m.	Surgeon's Call
7-8 a.m.	Officers' Call
8 a.m.	Guard Mounting
9 –10 a.m.	Squad Drill
10:30-12 p.m.	Company Drill
12 Noon	Dinner
2–4 p.m.	Battalion Drill (first call for same 1:30 p.m.)
5:30 p.m.	Dress Parade
6 p.m.	Supper
7 p.m.	Retreat
9 p.m.	Tattoo
9:30 p.m.	Taps

The Three Noon Brothers of County Donegal

Monsignor Robert L. Noon

My ancestors on the Irish side of my family came from County Donegal but from what area I have never been able to find out. On my third trip to Ireland in 2007 I finally got to Donegal City and some of the coastland in that neighborhood. But where my ancestor lived I do not know, at least, I could now say that I had been in the area of their homesteads.

It seems that three brothers came to the United States in the late 1820s. One settled in Johnstown, Pennsylvania, one went "west' to Wisconsin, and one settled in Perry County, Ohio. Now for what little I know of any of these:

1) The Pennsylvania Noons settled around Cambria County. The only one of these folks I ever knew anything about is a Dominican priest, Father Dominic Hyacinth Noon born in the

village of Munster, Cambria County in 1819 and was baptized by the famous missionary of the Pennsylvania territory around the central part of the State, Father D.A. Gallitzin. Father Dominic H. Noon was pastor of Holy Trinity Church in Somerset, Ohio, for twenty years dying there on September 18, 1894.[1] One story of him says that he kept no horse or livery and was known to walk from Somerset to Lancaster when the train could not get him there the same night.[2]

One history records that on the ashes of the burned Saint Mary Academy in Somerset and after the Sisters moved to Columbus Father Noon built a building "of greater magnitude and elegant style"[3] This history written in 1882 says that the building is to be three stories high and describes it in part as, "a cistern is to be erected on the third floor to supply drinking water to the rooms, the baths and the water closets below; the baths are to be hot and cold and so connected with the sewerage as to insure the utmost riddance of the premises from miasmatic effects, the entire cost reaching nearly $20,000 even under the utmost economic and sagacity of Father Noon."[3] This building served the Somerset parish into the 1960s. Its third floor served as the Holy Trinity School, the second floor was the priest's residence and some classrooms while the first floor was the printing office of the then famous Catholic printing house, the Rosary Press.

In the middle 1980s I stayed over night in Johnstown, P A, and looking in the telephone directory I found the Noons listed 41 times and the only one I ever heard about was the Father Dominic H. Noon and he was not listed in that phone book.

2) The Wisconsin Noons. I didn't even know of any Noons in Wisconsin until one day at a Catholic Record Society luncheon in Columbus (circa 1999) the speaker was a Dominican Sister from Sinsinawa, Wisconsin, who related stories about their founder, a Dominican priest from Somerset, OH. I talked with the Sister afterwards and she told me that they had a Noon in their Community who was 100 years old, Sister Roseann Noon. I wrote to her and answering she said she was of the Wisconsin Noons. I

planned to visit Dubuque, Iowa, where she lived and arrived one day at the Villa of Saint Dominic and asked for Sister Roseann as she knew I was coming. She was now 101 and left word that she would see me "as soon as I finish this bridge game!" Well she soon came to the parlor and we visited for a couple hours. We talked about our various origins from the three brothers from Ireland and their ancestry. She told me about her younger brother who was then in his eighties. I later corresponded with him for a couple years but no new information came out of this letter writing. Sister died two years later at the age of 104 and is buried at Sinsinawa, Wisconsin.

3) The Ohio Noons and their stories; Very few. Since my grandmother was the only grandparent I knew and she had married into the Noon family, our contacts as I was growing up were primarily with her relatives, the Bennetts from Perry County. At the time my father was born in 1884 his parents lived in Rendville, outside Corning, OH. The village still exists but there are few houses left. My grandfather, Philip Noon, operated a store in the first floor of their house as they lived upstairs. He also was a sort of traveling salesman for the territory selling tobacco. About 1885 they moved to Zanesville, OH. My Dad used to say that Rendville was noted for two reasons: 1) Adam Clayton Powell was born there and 2) so was my Dad! On traveling through Rendville in 2009 their home was one of the few houses still standing in the village.

I am always amazed when I think of what our ancestors had to live with and live by. I once heard that the two greatest changes in life styles of the home came about with 1) central heating and its opposite, air-conditioning, and 2) indoor plumbing. I am now 86 and can well remember visiting relatives, especially in Perry County on Sunday afternoon rides in the late 1920s and throughout the 1930s and being confronted with outdoor plumbing. On these Sunday rides around the Zanesville and into Perry County to visit relatives we always had to be back home by 4:00 as Dad had to listen to the radio and the Father Coughlin program from Detroit.

(As some will recall Father Coughlin broadcast from the Shrine of the Little Flower in Royal Oak, MI. and eventually in the late 1930s became somewhat radical in his dislike for FDR and the Russians but we never missed his program.)

References:

1. Coffey, J. R., OP, Pictorial History of the Dominican Province of Saint Joseph, New York, NY, 1946, page 57.

2. found in a newsletter of the Perry County Genealogy Society, New Lexington, OH.

3. Unknown author and title. I have only a couple pages copied from the book, but I have references to a couple books from which the material might have been taken:

1. Mills, History of Perry County, 1880,

2. (author unknown to me) A History of Perry County, circa 1882, Pages 495 & 496. These two books may be the same book.

The O'Connor's from Kerry

Jim O'Connor

My father was the oldest child in a family of 7 children living on a farm in Ventry, Co. Kerry. The old familiar story of the Irish immigrants, there was no work or promise of work, so he immigrated by himself to Springfield, Massachusetts when he was a young man. In Springfield there was already a relative there to live with, and he helped him to secure work eventually at Westinghouse Electric, later transferring my father to Lima, Ohio, where there was another Westinghouse plant. This is where we, all of the O'Connor children were all raised and schooled as youth.

My great-great grandfather in Kerry was Timothy O'Connor, who married Margaret Dunleih (Dhuinnshleibhe) in 1830. Margaret was a kinswoman of the great Irish poet Sean Dhuinnshleibhe. One of their 5 children, born 1837 was Tomas Eoghain Bhain O Conchubhair (O'Connor), who became the only weaver on the Blasket Islands, and lived in the Protestant school on the Blaskets. He was referred to many times in the classic books of the Blaskets; The autobiography of Peig Sayers of the Great Blasket Island by Peig Sayers, Twenty Years A-Growing by Maurice O'Sullivan, and The Islandman by Tomas O Criomhthain (Crohan). In MacMahon's preface for Peig he mentions Cait and Eoghan O'Connor; he was the weaver on the Blaskets and was my great-great uncle on my father's side.

One of my great regrets in life was not being able to go to Ireland with my father. He was born and raised in Ventry, County Kerry, and came to America by himself. Since he was the oldest of several children, my father never really was able to grow up together with the rest of his siblings. When my wife and I finally felt financially able to make our first trip to Ireland in 1985, our 25th anniversary, my father was already deceased, but we were able to stay with his brother Bob in the family farmhouse where my father was born. It was eerie to see Bob's mannerisms mirroring my father's, particularly how he interacted with the grandchildren! Even though they grew up continents apart, they displayed the same habits of speech, behavior, humor, etc. On that trip, we were able to share an evening with an old pal of my father's, by that time age 77. He told tale after tale of what he and dad did to fill their days in Ventry, climbing down the cliff walls to fish for cod and lobster! A magical evening it was, with the cold rain falling outside his little cottage, we sitting near the turf fire, and drinking what had to be poteen as we remained transfixed in our evening of listening!

"About the O'Connor Family – Cork, (Kerry?)"
John C O'Connor

Born in 1864, John Francis O'Connor set sail from Passage West, Cork, Ireland at the age of 19. This was the year 1883. He landed in Boston and became a teamster. He joined a Massachusetts Infantry Regiment and was posted to a fort in the Dakotas during the Blackfoot Indian Wars. He was a recruiting sergeant during the Spanish-American War. While stationed at Ft.

Hayes in Columbus, Ohio he met and married Mary Lyons. He mustered out of the army and joined the Columbus Police force. Rising from the rank of patrolman, he became Chief in 1904. With the next change in city administrations he was demoted back to patrolman. He climbed through civil service to Chief Inspector of Police. He acted as Interim Chief again between appointments. He was a Roman Catholic and member of the Ancient Order of Hibernians. He died, after a heart attack, in 1950 at the age of 86. Most of his family are interred in the Mt. Calvary section of St. Joseph's Cemetery, south of Columbus.

Grandfather Washington Montgomery

John C O'Connor

This story is about mother's grandfather, Washington Montgomery. His father, Anthony Washington Montgomery, was born in Virginia the day Cornwallis surrendered at Yorktown. "Wash" was born 48 years later (1829) and eventually moved to Shepard, Ohio (now part of Columbus) to receive the water treatments from a spa on the northeast corner of 5th and Nelson.

In his youth, he went to California in 1949. Instead of mining for gold, he wound up managing a stage line between Marysville, California and Columbus, Ohio. During this time he luckily avoided a murder plot when a female passenger (she suddenly started to cry leading to an inquiry by Washington) admitted that she was supposed to persuade him to divert his stage to a spot where he was to be ambushed. He said that their plan would have worked if she had not had that attack of conscience. The stage line went out of business after the rail lines expanded to Marysville.

He then made a living by running a livery stable and trading horses. When he settled down in Shepard, he happened to live next to Stonewall Jackson's sister. She had moved there after the Civil War, upon marrying a Union Army officer from Ohio.

When Wash died, he still had a twenty dollar gold coin which his father had given him to teethe with. It still had the marks of his early teeth on it.

My mother's father, Frank, ran a general store in Shepard, in the same building that is now a lumber store, north of the old spa (no longer existing), off Nelson Road.

My Irish Ancestors

Pat O'Dell

In 1991 I moved to Columbus from my birthplace of Chicago not realizing that I had any ties here until my Chicago cousin, Jim Gormley, wrote me and asked me to look up in newspaper archives articles concerning President Lincoln's funeral train. I found my great grandfather's name listed as the engineer on that train between Columbus and Piqua.

Years ago someone in my family, had a genealogy done. It states that James Gormley was born 9, Jan 1839 in Mullingar, County of West Meath, Ireland. He came to America with his parents and lived with them until their deaths. Both parents, James and Bridget were buried in the Old Catholic Cemetery on Mount Vernon Avenue. On May 15, 1873 they were moved to Mount Calvary cemetery in Chicago.

Family tradition states that during the night of his birth, they had what is known as the "Big Wind", one of the greatest storms ever known in the country. Other sources date the "Big Wind" as having occurred January 6 and 7.

At about 12 years of age he was employed as an engine wiper for the Pennsylvania. Railway Company in Columbus, Ohio and at age 21 was a locomotive engineer driving fast passenger trains between Columbus and Piqua and while in this service drove the funeral train of President Lincoln between these two cities.

In 1868 he was promoted to foreman of the Railway Shops in Chicago and occupied that position until his death 8 April, 1891 in Chicago.

In recognition of his long and faithful service the Pennsylvania. Railway Company closed the shops a day and furnished a complete funeral train of engine and cars for the convenience of family and friends and sent them over the Chicago & North Western Railway tracks to Calvary cemetery where he was buried.

He was married 21 December, 1859 in Columbus, Ohio to Ellen Corbett born in 1840 in Ireland. Their first three children were born in Columbus including my grandfather, John Falls Gormley born 19 June, 1861. He was baptized in St. Patrick's Church by Father Fitzgerald. His Godparents were John Hannon and Mary Reilly. He accompanied his parents to Piqua, Ohio and in 1870 settled with them in Chicago. He married Rose Reilly on 28 December, 1886.

The same cousin Jim Gormley, mentioned in my first sentence, was contacted by a former Northwestern law school classmate from Columbus, Tom O'Keefe, because Tom found the Gormley name in his wife, Sally's genealogy. We already knew each other when Tom started his search and were stunned to learn that Sally's grandmother and my grandmother, Rose Reilly, were sisters. Sally and I are both from Chicago and now live in Upper Arlington.

John O'Grady's Family Recollections

John O'Grady

John O'Grady rose to speak saying that he felt it intimidating after hearing the long history that both the Dorrians and O'Shaughnessys have in local politics to speak of his family's history in politics. He sounded a little rueful when commenting that he had no family with him but that if his eleven brothers and sisters had known he was going to speak that day they surely would've come and that would have filled up the room.

He followed Maryellen's and Julia's comments about their families' political involvement saying that he too had been raised in a political atmosphere...it was just something that the whole family did. John showed a bit of Irish sentimentality when he said that talking about his parents who are now deceased is difficult for him to do. He said that he gets a bit misty-eyed when he remembers his parents.

John said that the O'Grady Family is different from the Dorrians and the O'Shaughnessys in that the O'Grady Family is much newer to the United States as well as Columbus. John's grandfather Michael O'Grady came to the United States in 1916 after the Easter Uprising in Dublin, Ireland. Michael O'Grady was a reporter for a newspaper in County Mayo, Ireland. After the Uprising Michael O'Grady was pursued by British Troops for writing items that the British considered inflammatory. Michael jumped on a boat and came to Cleveland, Ohio where he had connections; family and friends. Something that many an immigrant tended to do when coming to a new land and a new life; settling in where you know there's a friendly face to help you. He noted that many Mayo folks at that time headed for Cleveland.

Right after his grandfather, Michael came to Cleveland, Ohio he was conscripted into the United States Army and fought in World War I. When he got back from the war he married Anna Sweeney in 1918. John's father was born in 1920 and they named him Eugene Pearse "Pete" O'Grady. The Pearse is in memory of Patrick Pearse of the 1916 Fame, a friend of John's grandfather. The O'Grady Clan has continued to remember Patrick Pearse in the naming of family members; Michael Pearse O'Grady, Pete's oldest son, Pearse Joseph O'Grady, brother Mike's oldest son and William Pearse Wemlinger, another nephew, as well as John's two sons: Patrick Pearse O'Grady and John (Jack) Pearse O'Grady. Continuing the Irish tradition of naming a child after family members or people close to the family, his son Jack is named after John "Jack" McGing his uncle and godfather who was a Cleveland firefighter whose family was also from Achill Island, County Mayo and son, Patrick is named after Patricia Feller O'Grady, his grandmother who passed away just before he was born. As for all those Pearse's they don't forget they were in memory of Patrick Pearse the Irish revolutionary.

John's Grandfather Michael became active in Cleveland's political organizations. He also became the director of the ODOT Garage in Northeast Ohio. During the Depression years of the

1930's there were pictures of John's grandfather who became somewhat of a celebrity because of the innovative way he ran his garage enabling more men to retain their jobs. He got permission from his supervisors to ask the men to voluntarily give up one work day a week. The reduced four day work week allowed for more men to work a shortened week than a reduced work force would have worked a five day work week. Everybody got less money but more workers got some money so that those people could continue to feed their families in those difficult times.

John's father, Pete O'Grady served in World War II and upon returning home he also became politically involved by working in the Ray T. Miller organization of the Cuyahoga Democratic party's day-to-day politics of Cleveland making it somewhat like a Cleveland version of Tammany Hall. That's where his Dad really got started in Democratic Party politics even though he'd been around similar experiences with his Dad, John's grandfather. In the 1950's Pete O'Grady was the President of the Cuyahoga Young Democrats; he was the bailiff of the Cuyahoga Court System and he became involved in Cuyahoga political campaigns. In 1960 he became the state chairman of the Kennedy for President Campaign becoming very involved with Jack Kennedy.

During the time period, 1950-1964, the O'Grady family grew rapidly for they had 12 children in 14 years. During this period local newspaper pictures of the family often showed the O'Grady children wearing political placards for different political campaigns. The family pictures are memories that record the O'Grady family attending Democratic Party functions. Family vacations consisted of John's Dad attending a conference and taking the family along. In the early 1960's Pete O'Grady served under Governor Michael DiSalle as the Director of the State Commerce Department and from 1967-1970 he served as the Chairman of the State Democratic Party and in the early 1970's Pete O'Grady was the Director of Highway Safety under Governor John Gilligan. All of the O'Grady Family pictures taken during those years are those taken at State Parks during family attendance at conferences relating to Pete O'Grady's current position. With 12 children is made financial sense to combine business and family vacations. John then commented that in looking over the pictures of those days it almost made him anticipate a return to the wearing of red polyester slacks as a male fashion statement.

Retiring from state government Pete O'Grady became a lobbyist, one of the original independent large lobbyists in Central Ohio with many clients. At this time there are pictures of him playing golf which he seemed to be doing pretty often? Pete didn't start playing until his young son; John was old enough to accompany him. Whatever else was going on in that family politics was a constant factor in the family whether playing on the lawn of the Governor's Mansion or hanging out with Senator Glenn and Mrs. Glenn.

The O'Grady family grew up in a modest house on the West Side of Columbus near Briggs Road. All 12 of the O'Grady children attended Bishop Ready High School. The young O'Gradys were just like everyday kids from the West Side with nothing different about us unless you'd notice that they talked about politics all of the time.

John remembered that as a kid he wanted to be anything but a politician. Now that he is older he feels that to be a politician is a great calling, to be involved in public service. While John is the only one of his family to run for public office other family members have worked in the political arena. John's sister, Betsy was a delegate in the 1980 convention for President Jimmy Carter and worked for Anthony Celebrezze for most of his public service career. His brother, Mike also worked for Anthony Celebrezze as well as Lee Fisher. Mike has been a legal consul for the Ohio Democratic Party and is active in political affairs. In 1984 John's sister, Tina was a campaign staffer for the short-lived presidential campaign of John Glenn in New Hampshire and she currently works in the administration of Governor Strickland.

Returning to his own political career John said that he became involved in politics in 1985 at the age of 21 working for Mary

Ellen Withrow both in her state office and political campaigns. While working for Mary Ellen Withrow he met Mark Dempsey and the two young Democrats have been friends ever since. John said that he enjoyed following the family tradition of working as a staffer and working for instead of being a political official. He never had any idea of running for public office; his family just didn't do that until the summer of 2000. That summer his friend, Mark Dempsey encouraged him to run for the political office of the Clerk of Courts. John won that election and became the first Democratic Clerk of Courts in many years and he was reelected to that office in 2004. In 2008 John was elected to the Franklin County Board of Commissioners thereby continuing his family's tradition of public service.

Don't Mess with a Determined Woman

Michael Stephen O'Keefe

In 1978, Mom decided to leave her home and move to Nazareth Towers, 300 Rich Street. We started the moving process in January of the year of the great blizzard of 1978. We only had her halfway moved in when the blizzard hit, and it took us a whole month to complete the moving in process.

Among several requirements for securing an apartment at Nazareth Towers was that you must make out a card and post it on the inside of your front closet with information on the next of kin, with their contact information; your funeral arrangements; church you were to be buried out of; etc.

Now Mom lived at Nazareth Towers for about 12 years and, in her early years at the Towers, Mom had thought she would let Egan-Ryan handle her funeral arrangements. George Ryan, of Egan-Ryan, was building good relations with the senior citizens around town and often stopped by Nazareth Towers to be helpful, to both the residents and Dominican Sisters who managed the building. Mom was appreciative of his efforts.

Mom lived at Nazareth Towers for quite a while and, in due time, George Ryan had died. John Quint of Maeder-Quint started coming by Nazareth Towers and establishing friendly relations with the occupants of the Towers. Mom also started going to more funerals down at Maeder-Quint, as that establishment had begun getting more business from the occupants of Nazareth Towers. Being from the south end, Mom was familiar with them and the area. So, eventually, Mom said to me she wanted to be buried by Maeder-Quint because they do such nice work down there. Maeder-Quint has now become known as Maeder-Quint-Tiberi.

Mom was doubtful that I would approve of this change in plans. She seemed to think I was in with those Ryans and I wanted her to be buried by them, but I told her it was up to her to choose. They were both fine establishments and either one would be fine with me, but she didn't seem to believe me. So one day, Mom and Veronica Maclean hopped on a bus and went down to Meader-Quint to put money down for their prearranged funeral arrangements. Mom came back home, and later told me what she had done, saying, "I've made up my mind. I'm going to be buried by Maeder-Quint." She showed me the paperwork and we posted the changed funeral information on the card posted in the closet.

About three years went by. I had forgotten all about the changed plans and one day she told me that she had gotten an envelope in the mail. She told me, "It was from the Franklin Bank on High Street and I've never dealt with that bank. The letter informed me that I have an account, a Certificate of Deposit, that's going to turn over." Well, I looked at it, and I told her that it was to pay for her funeral arrangements. Mom said thoughtfully, that they must have made interest on it. Interest rates were high at the time and the certificate had paid a pretty high interest rate. I told her to go down to the bank to check on it

Mom did go to the bank and they said that, yes, they did have money there, the certificate was ready to turn over, but the bank couldn't turn it over to them. The people at the bank went on to tell Mom and Veronica that the bank had to have the original, not a copy, when they came in. If they could give them the original, then the account money would be theirs.

So Mom and Veronica went down to Maeder-Quint. On that day, the red-headed Mrs. Quint was manning the office and wouldn't give them the original certificate. Mom, Veronica and Mrs. Quint were dickering back and forth. I think Mom was doing most of the talking. Although I wasn't there, I got the information second hand later. The ladies were at a rather tense stand-off when Mr. Quint came in, and immediately, being the good business man that he was, said if they wanted their certificate, of course, there would be no problem. If they needed them, they could have them back, so the ladies took the certificates and left. It was a very warm day and they were standing on the sidewalk waiting for a bus. In the meantime, Mr. Quint, being very smart, got out his car, turned on the air conditioning, and drove around up to the ladies, offering them a ride. He drove them to the Franklin Bank, where they got their money, and then he took them back to Nazareth Towers. They left the car and Mr. Quint wished them a good day and went back to work. To Mom's satisfaction, the funeral certificate of deposit made about 1,000 dollars and she gave 500 dollars to each of her children, who were glad to get the money.

In about a week, Mom said that, as she thought about the whole affair, Mr. Quint was such a nice man, that she thought she'd go back to Maeder-Quint and sign up again for her funeral, which she did. Only this time, however, Mr. Quint was smarter and he put the certificate of deposit in both their names. Veronica went back down and she signed up too.

That was the story of Louise, Veronica and John Quint. In the years after, when I've had dealings with the Tiberis, during the funerals of my Aunt Margaret and Aunt Helen, I like to tell the Tiberis the story of how Mom put one over on them. They are always very polite and they smile, but you can tell it hurts…it is an affair they'd like to forget.

"The best laid plans oft' go awry"
Michael S. O'Keefe

In 1903 Michael O'Keefe died and that same year his grandson, my father, Michael was born. The grandson was named Michael, after his grandfather. In 1918 young Michael went to work at Foersters Restaurant, when he was around 15 years of age, to pay for his high school education. He had graduated from Holy Family Grade School and wanted to attend Aquinas College High School. My grandparents, John and Bertha O'Keefe, did not have the funds to pay for his schooling. I think he only went to school for a couple of years, working part time, before he left school. He later returned and finished high school in 1925.

Michael worked at Foersters for over 40 years. During that time he was a member of many downtown organizations. Some of them were: The Friendly Sons of St. Patrick, the Germania Club, the Swiss Club and the Knights of Columbus Council 400 which met at State and 6th Street. He was a great joiner of fraternal groups and became friends with many people.

A good friend of Dad's was Jerry O'Shaughnessy. Jerry and Dad knew each other as students together at Aquinas; another good friend was Mike Ryan. Both the O'Shaughnessy and the Ryan families conducted well known funeral establishments in Columbus.

In the autumn of 1958 Dad became ill. Later that year, while a patient in Grant Hospital, the doctor had made it pretty clear he wasn't going to make it. So he and Mom talked about his final wishes. Dad told Mom, "Louise, because several of the family had been buried by the Ryan's, I owe Jerry O'Shaughnessy a funeral, so when I go, make sure that O'Shaughnessy gets me."

On the day Dad died, I went down to the hospital with Uncle John, Dad's brother. Uncle John wanted to give mom some alone time with dad because it was clear that Dad was dying. So, Uncle John and I ate at the Garden Restaurant on State Street. When we came back up we found that Dad had passed and we all felt very bad. I went with Mom to talk to the doctor and Uncle John disappeared. Uncle John went to call the Ryan Funeral Home and they promptly came and took Dad away to their establishment. When Mom came back she went to call O'Shaughnessy's to make arrangements for Dad's funeral. When she found what Uncle John had done, she was livid.

However, we had dealt with the Ryans through other family funerals and they, as well as the O'Shaughnessys, were customers of the store, so she let Uncle John's arrangement go on through. Mom gave him a thorough dressing down, although I never knew exactly what she said.

I always thought the reason Uncle John called the Ryans after Dad's death was because he had worked for them as a paid pallbearer during the depression years. As a matter of fact, that's how Uncle John had been involved in the founding of the Shamrock Club. He was with the group in the back room of Ryan's in 1936.

At fifteen years of age, I had never been involved in the planning of a funeral and I didn't remember Mom arranging any funeral either. Anyway, Mom and I went over to Ryan's to pick out a casket for Dad. When he knew he was dying, Dad had told Mom that, because he had often been a pallbearer, he knew how hard it was to lift and carry a heavy casket. So, he had asked Mom to make it easy on the "boys" (pallbearers) and to be sure to pick a light casket for him. However, Dad didn't explain what he meant by "light", so Mom picked his casket for its beauty and I heartily seconded her choice, a beautiful cherry wood casket. We didn't know that the solid wood casket she and I chose, while beautiful, was one of the heaviest kind made at that time.

After the funeral and burial, both Uncle Declan and Charlie Mitchell, two good-sized fellows, who were among the pallbearers, came up to Mom and complained that it was the heaviest casket they had ever carried. I don't know what Charlie said but Uncle Declan said, "Jesus Christ, Louise, I know Mike wanted a light casket but that was the heaviest casket I've ever carried." So much for Dad's final wishes but we tried.

The Story of Richard O'Keefe and his Brothers

Terry and Judy O'Keefe

Maurice Francis O'Keefe and Elizabeth Catherine Nugent O'Keefe had a large family of eleven children and here are stories of three of their sons as written by their grandson, Terry.

My uncle Richard O'Keefe was in the Battle of the Bulge. Afterwards he wrote his company's history. After the war, he returned to Columbus and going to NYC for a weekend never returning to live in Columbus. Richard enrolled in The American Academy of Arts, where he studied theatre. His friends included Grace Kelly, Peter Falk, Don Murray, Tom Poston and Helen Hayes. Jason Robards remained his friend for many years. During this same time, he fell in love with Greenwich Village and he lived there until his death in 1986. His courtyard was used to film the movie "Serpico". Rick as he was called eventually became known as the 'mayor' of Greenwich Village.

Rick began his career in the restaurant business while attending the Academy of Arts. He was a maitre'd at many fine establishments, including The Four Seasons. He was familiar with many celebrities; including Lana Turner and Barbra Streisand. Rick first met Barbra while judging a talent contest and he was instrumental in her career. She remained friends for years; even inviting him to one of her birthday parties.

Well known as 'a man about town'. Rick was especially known for his dancing prowess. The image we have of 'Rickie O'Keefe', as he was known in the Village, is bigger than life. He always entertained the O'Keefe family with his storytelling when he would return to visit.

Jimmy O'Keefe moved to Las Vegas in the late forties. He went to work in the gambling business. He worked his way up to being the pit boss at the Desert Inn and continued there until the mid sixties. Upon leaving the Desert Inn, he oversaw the gambling floor at the Tropicana. His last establishment was the Fremont Hotel. Jimmy, as most of the O'Keefe's, loved golf. A tournament, The Jimmy O'Keefe Open, was established for the dealers in Las Vegas.

Maurice O'Keefe, a brother of Jimmy and Rick, worked his way from being a bartender in Chicago to the manager of the Medinah Country Club. Two Western Opens were held at the club under his tenure. Medinah was then and continues to be one of the premiere golf course/country clubs in the United States.

All three brothers stayed in contact with their Central Ohio family contingent during their interesting lives.

Reminiscences of a Political Family
Maryellen O'Shaughnessy

Speaking to the Catholic Record Society Maryellen began by talking a bit about her recognition of those she knew in the audience; family members, community friends and acquaintances.

Continuing with her comments Maryellen stated that many traits shared by the Irish tend to steer them towards public life. Irish-Americans tend to be patriotic, out-going and gregarious, and competitive all traits that are necessary for one engage in the public arena.

Maryellen noted that the Irish roles in political activism largely stemmed the influence of Daniel O'Connell in his political activities in Ireland prior to the "Potato Famine" or the Great Hunger in the 1840's which swelled the tide of Irish immigration to the United States.

Maryellen's great-grandfather Jerry O'Shaughnessy born in 1853 in Delaware County to Irish immigrants began the family's participation in Columbus, Ohio's public affairs. His career was often documented in the Columbus newspapers. Maryellen made note of another early Irish-American politician, Billy Naghten, whose career was tragically cut short by a railroad accident, and who became Columbus' first Irish-Catholic president of City Council.

In 2010, the O'Shaughnessy family will celebrate 100 years of involvement in the political life of Central Ohio for it was in 1910 her great grandfather Jerry O'Shaughnessy ran for State Representative from Franklin County. It was a countywide election at that time. He lost that 1910 election but it was a start. She mentioned several important items from that election 1. He used the phrase "he is a man who will wear no man's collar" referring to his independence from papal dictates a position later taken by John F. Kennedy in his presidential campaign of 1960, fifty years later. She feels that this issue has tended to be an issue that has not been fully settled for Irish-American politicians in the practice of their political activities.

Another Ohio political issues that were connected to the O'Shaughnessy clan was the Right to Work law in 1958. Governor O'Neil was behind this issue but the Ohio Labor Movement rose up and defeated it.

At this time Thomas Francis O'Shaughnessy became a state senator, he died soon after what would have been his first term for he died soon after beginning a second term. He was the first of three brothers to serve in the same 15th state senate district in the General Assembly the only family to have that distinction. The other two were Jeremiah Patrick (Uncle Jerry) O'Shaughnessy, he was elected in the 1965 and 1966 to the Ohio House of Representatives after being defeated he later served two years in Columbus City Council. Jerry O'Shaughnessy later was elected to the Ohio Senate he died in office in 1972. Robert Emmet O'Shaughnessy (Maryellen's father) was appointed to fill his brother's place in1972. When it was time to run for re-election He was not endorsed by the Democratic Party Robert E. O'Shaughnessy had built up a program that was approved of by coalition the Irish Community's political leaders and they broke from the party to endorse Robert Emmet O'Shaughnessy. This action was tagged by the Columbus Dispatch as "The Irish Mafia"; the family was not pleased with that title because they felt they were being depicted as thugs.

In response to the "Irish Mafia" tag the O'Shaughnessy family defiantly answered "Yes, we are!" On the next St. Patrick's Day there were a lot of people wearing buttons that proclaimed; **CHARTER MEMBERS IRISH MAFIA.** Her father did win that primary and there is a picture of Maryellen with her father at that time (1974). Her father served in the 15th State Senatorial District until 1978. He was defeated by John Kasich, who is still active in politics today.

Fourteen years later Maryellen was approached to run for office and she decided to do that because at that time in 1992 with one day to go before the election the Democrats had no one to oppose Dorothy Teeter and the voters of Franklin County had no choices. So with three hours to go they had put her name up we had the fifty signatures and by the end of the day she had packed her bag and left her job at Business First, needless to say she did not win that election.

But that election laid the groundwork for running for Columbus City Council with now Mayor Mike Coleman in 1997. Maryellen served on Columbus City Council for 11 years and she is now Clerk of Courts for Franklin County.

Proffitt's Fairy Ring

Dorothy Proffitt

My son Joe Proffitt and his wife honeymooned in England and in Ireland. While visiting in Ireland, they spent a few days with a cousin in rural County Mayo.

On our cousin's property there is a field which holds a fairy ring. This property is owned by our cousin, on our maternal side, and his cousin, on his paternal side. The two of them separated each one's piece of land with a wire fence. The fairy ring is located on both parts of the land. Our cousin turned his part of this field into a pasture for his cattle. This fairy ring encompassed a circle of small trees with a fence built right through the center of the ring. The other cousin built a fence around his part of the ring and nothing has penetrated this part of the fairy ring. Through the years some of the trees on our cousin's land have been trampled and a few trees are missing. The last time I visited our cousin in 2000 and checked the fairy ring, the other side of the ring was still untouched. I guess through superstitions and old beliefs the one part of the ring should remain as it was many, many years ago. At the far end of the pasture, lore has it that it was a famine burial plot.

Joe and his wife were visiting at the time of All Hallows Eve and they both swear that upon going to the fairy ring that night they saw a ghost sitting on a huge rock back at the burial site. They participated in some of the games played during this occasion. Joe carved a Jack-O-Lantern from a turnip. They both played the game of searching for a ring, a coin, and a piece of paper with the word "Journey" baked into a Barmbrack (cake). Upon eating the cake, the person finding the coin meant (finding your fortune), finding the ring meant (marriage) and the paper saying "Journey" meant you would immigrate. These stories are often told when families get together for holidays, weddings and wakes.

Father Patrick Quinlan

Tim Quinlan

The Quinlan's are an old Irish family but I have yet to identify their origins in Ireland. I do know that my great-great Grandfather, Dennis Quinlan, immigrated to Athens County, Ohio in the 1860's and was a railroader. My grandfather was also named Dennis Quinlan as was my father (I carry Dennis as my middle name). My Grandfather and his three brothers (John, Patrick and Joseph were orphaned in the late 1890's as their parents both died at a young age. The four boys stayed in St. Vincent's orphanage downtown and then were split up and adopted by various families in Columbus and the Athens area in the early 1900's. Three of the brothers were even raised by a Catholic Priest for Awhile.

The latter obviously had an influence on the third brother, Patrick. He grew up to become a multilingual scholar, and a graduate of the prestigious American College of Louvain, Belgium. Patrick was ordained as a Catholic Priest in 1922 at age 28 in Louvain. He was a founding Pastor of a large parish in a Hartford, Connecticut suburb as well as a faculty member at the Diocesan seminary. My four siblings and I never got to meet great-

Uncle Patrick. He was still serving his last parish in Kingstree, South Carolina upon his death in 1971 while we were small children. My father and two Aunts used to speak highly of Father Pat and I know he was revered by his three brothers. I do know the Quinlan families visited Father Pat often at the parishes he served in Connecticut and South Carolina.

In February 2008 I was contacted by a gentleman from the Charleston Diocese in South Carolina. He was commissioned by the local Bishop to research and write a biography on Father Pat's life. "Why?" I asked. "Because the Bishop believes your "Great-Uncle" is a candidate for Sainthood!" Over the past two years, the Author has provided me with many details about Father Pat's life and mission. Additionally, we have helped each other fill in some of the missing gaps in the lives of the four original brothers. What we have learned about our Great Uncle does fill us with gratitude and family pride. More importantly, ne is a shining example of a family member who overcame tough obstacles early in life to pursue his calling in leading a life of service to God and others.

The stories I have read about Father Pat's ministry have left a lasting impression. At age 53, he requested a transfer to South Carolina in 1947, where he served in Williamsburg County, the states poorest and largest (900 square miles) county. He was attracted to mission work and to the problems of the Church in rural areas. He wanted to bring the Good News of the Church to those who would not otherwise hear it and actually used a Motor Chapel to tour the large county. He saw his duty as reaching out to the uninformed and misinformed not just the unbelievers. I could go on and on but rest assured this man had found his calling.

Our Great Uncle and his three brothers did not have an easy life growing up. Two of the brothers even served in World War I. Some of their vocations included Railroader, Painter, Grocer and Priest. Over the years these four brothers chose their own paths and preserved in their own way. Thankfully, they remained close through the years...a "band of brothers!" This is a lesson worth repeating not only for the Quinlan's but for all families and future generations.

William "Billy" Naghten

Tim Quinlan

The first time I recall hearing the name William "Billy" Naghten was in late June, 1989 at St. Patrick's Church in downtown Columbus. The Quinlan family was gathered for the funeral of our Great-Uncle, Thomas Paul Coady. "Uncle Paul" was the brother of my late Grandmother Katherine Quinlan (who died in 1951 before I was born). Katherine and Paul happened to be the grandchildren of Billy Naghten, whose family name along with the Coady's were carved into the pews of St. Patrick's. Many stories about the Coady's and Naghten's were relayed that day to my four siblings and me. While I'm sure our Irish ancestry was discussed many times when we were younger, it took a funeral for us to start connecting the family dots...Naghten Street used to be called "Old Irish Broadway" and it was named after our great-great Grandfather, William Naghten!

The second time I remember hearing about Billy was from a phone call from my Aunt, Jane Quinlan, in the early 1990's. She was distressed that the City of Columbus was considering renaming Naghten Street! Jane urged me to join her in contacting the local Irish leaders and historians to preserve the Irish heritage of our family name as well as that of Columbus. My Aunt explained that Billy came to America from County Westmeath, Ireland, that he was the first Irish President of Columbus City Council in the 1850's; a Railroader by trade: a founding member of St. Patrick's Church and also on the building committee (Secretary) for St. Joseph's Cathedral. The Quinlan's were tied to Billy through our Grandmother Katherine and her mother, Jennie Coady, youngest daughter of Billy and Kate Naghten.

After my Aunt's passing in 2002, we discovered a literal treasure chest of family history on the Coady's, Quinlan's, Blackwood's and Naghten's. Jane had Billy's original naturalization certificate from 1854; articles on Billy's wife and son, John; a photograph of Kate; and lastly, a newspaper "The Ohio Statesman" dated January 10, 1870. There in black and white, was a front page story on the funeral of Billy Naghten. The article was impressive and clearly showed that he was a well-respected and loved man by his community. I've made a few visits to Billy and Kate's resting place in Mt. Calvary cemetery and often wondered what they must have endured to immigrate to this country.

Since 2002, I have immersed myself in learning more about our family's Irish heritage. I know that someday soon I must travel to Ireland to do intensive research on the Quinlan's, Coady's and Naghten's as we all originated from the homeland. I wish that some of my relatives and Father were still alive today so that I could quiz them some more about our origins. Consequently, I have made it a point to share each new discovery with my siblings: Tom, Terry, Kathy and Bob. They now know that there lineage traces back to their great-great Grandfather William "Billy" Naghten, an inspiring Irish-American who got involved with his Church, his Community and his City.

Addendum to Quinlan/Naghten Stories

Further information about Father Patrick Quinlan's activities in South Carolina can be found: The Origin of the Church in a Rural County and Father Patrick Quinlan-the Apostle of Kingstree by Jim McLaughlin. Both articles appeared in The New Miscellany, a newspaper published by the Diocese of Charleston, South Carolina.

http://themiscellany.org

Further information about William "Billy" Naghten can be found in an article of that title written by Donald Schlegel for the Barquilla de la Santa Maria, the newsletter of the Catholic Record Society of the Columbus Diocese. Vol. XIII, Number 3, pg. 23-25

http://catholic.org

Ann's Family Recollections

Ann Bennett Rader

It was a chilly afternoon just before Christmas 2008 when Ann and Julie met to discuss Ann's Irish heritage. Ann has long been active in the Daughters of Erin, a Columbus, Ohio organization of Irish-American women. So several years ago Ann and her family were excited when Ann's granddaughter, Natalie Mercuri went to Ireland as an Irish Way recipient from the Daughters of Erin, enabling Natalie to reconnect with her Irish heritage in the country of her ancestors.

Ann's great-grandparents, the Calls, settled in Pennsylvania where her grandfather, Charles Call was born in Philadelphia. Later the family moved to Ohio settling in Shawnee. Shawnee is in Southern Ohio where Charles Call lost his eyesight in a mining accident. The family later moved to Columbus where they attended St. Francis Church.

As a youngster Ann was a close friend of the pastor's niece and when help was needed to collect money for offerings to be used for masses said at St. Francis for recently deceased parishioners. Ann remembered that if the deceased person was popular there might be enough money for flowers.

Wake and funeral traditions were important to many families in the 19th century. The ceremonies surrounding the final rites were to be carefully observed and that was true in Ann's family. Ann remembered the wake or death watch tradition which dictated that someone would be assigned the duty of staying with the corpse overnight before the funeral would take place. In Shawnee, a young adult had died and the friends of the deceased arranged for two of their acquaintances to be the designated "overnighters". The two designated "watchers" were a couple that had not been acquainted with each other. However after conversing and getting to know each other during the long watching hours they became attracted to each other and later married. Ann's parents, Lester and Mary Ann Call Bennett, found love while serving as the designated watchers during an Irish Wake.

Ann has passed on the family tradition of showing respect and caring for deceased family members by continuing to bring flowers to the cemetery on Memorial Day. Her daughter, Beth Shelley, shares an anecdote of a family cemetery visit in the story, "Karen".

Ann also passed on a saying she remembered used by her family that she thought might be of Irish origin: "Just because you were born in a barn doesn't make you a horse." Could this refer to the upward climb our Irish immigrant ancestors faced?

Abby's Irish Family

Abagail Moran Robinson

In the very early 1900's my grandmother's uncle, Mike, from Ireland, came to visit her and her 7 sons, of which my father was the youngest (and the only one born after 1900). Mike came by sea and the trip over was long, arduous, and apparently none too hygienic. After a good visit, and washing, he went back to Ireland.

That winter while the boys were studying their catechism and learning about the saints. John, the oldest proudly proclaimed that St. Patrick had taken all the snakes out of Ireland. My father got in trouble for countering that Uncle Mike had done the same with the lice.

As far as immigration information is concerned, that part of my family emigrated from County Kerry at various times between 1830 and 1860 and settled in Augusta County (Staunton) Virginia. They apparently didn't all come at once but my paternal great grandfather came between 1850 and 1860 and my paternal great great grandmother arrived after the Civil War. These were Morans and Donohos (or Danaghys/Donohue/Donoghe)

The other part came around the same time but settled in Lewis County (Weston) Virginia. That area is now West Virginia. These were the Downeys and probably hailed from County Cork.

Dad, like myself, was the youngest in the family. He had six brothers, his mother had 7 sisters, and his father had 7 brothers and sisters.

Both sides eventually came to Huntington, WV when Collis P. Huntington brought in the railroad. The Downey's came with the Baltimore and Ohio, The Morans with the Chesapeake and Ohio. Apparently, many Irish families came to Huntington at that time. My father was always telling tells about several of his cousins. Alas, his brothers never procreated, leaving me virtually cousin-less; but the tales of parties and celebrations as well as what Huntington was like then (Dad, the youngest, was born in 1901 – all his brothers in the 1800's) sounded like great fun.

I have done some genealogy work and have records that anyone who has any interest in these areas may access. Just call me.

Grandmother Rose and her Sister
Fr. J. Patrick Rodenfels

Jerome Patrick Rodenfels, was born August 13, 1946, son of Frank W. Rodenfels and Mary Frances Hanratty. Mary Frances was the daughter of Hugh Bernard Hanraty and Rose Ann Henratty, both born in the village of Crossmaglen, County Armagh, Ireland.

The author of the letter/story Rose Hanratty Callahan was an Aunt to my maternal grandmother, Rose Henratty, a sister to my grandmother's mother. My guess is that since this Aunt settled in the Ohio area, my grandmother, two of her sisters, and one brother ended up here because of her. They came over about 1912. Other siblings to my grandmother remained in Ireland.

Rose Henratty, Daughter of Felix Henratty and Ellen McShane was baptized according to the rite of the Catholic church on the 14th of January, 1858 as appears from the Parish register in Upper Creggan, June 26,1879 sign by J. Rafferty, P. P.

The story/letter below was found by my mother in an old desk belonging to her mother.

A Plucky New Lexington Girl
(Three times she crosses the briny ocean alone)

Eight years ago, Rosetta Henratta, now a resident of New Lexington was quietly living with her mother in dear old Ireland. She was but fifteen years of age and had heard and read enough of America to have a desire to go there. She had distant relatives in New York and also in Perry County, Ohio. She said she could do nothing in Ireland and resolved to cross the ocean which she did, taking steerage passage and after a search of a few days through the City found her New York relatives. There she remained a few months and then came to the neighborhood of New Lexington, living a few years with the family of her Uncle Thomas McShane and eventually decided to learn the tailoring trade which she did in a merchant tutoring establishment of this place.

Miss Henratta was very industrious and economical and though earning rather scanty wages managed to lay up money. After eight years of American life our heroine concluded that she must see her Mother and sisters and prepared to cross the broad Atlantic on a visit to her old home. Procuring something like a Saratoga trunk and a ward robe befitting an industrious and plucky American girl, she went to New York and took cabin passage on a steamer for her native land.

The ocean journey and afterwards two hundred and fifty miles by rail were pleasantly made without accident or hindrance and she started to walk a few miles from the railway station to her mother's house. Here, for the first time on her long trip, she became bewildered and lost the way. At last belated and unexpected she reached her Mother's door when no doubt there was a family commotion. The brave and dutiful girl spent three months very pleasantly among friends and acquaintances who were however, amazed at her big trunk and to them – marvelous wardrobe. One very pleasant incident occurred while at her mother's house. Rosetta caught a glimpse of a well dressed man as he passed the window, and soon there was a rap at the door. She supposed it was a land agent who had business with her mother, but this lady directly said Rosetta, the gentleman wishes to see you. Rosetta walked out and there stood Dr. McKenna of Junction City, Ohio, who had learned that a Perry County, Ohio girl was there and called to see her.

Miss Rosetta has recently returned to her home in New Lexington, Ohio. The ocean journey back was not pleasant, there was a rough sea and the huge vessel rolled and pitched for three days in a terrible equinoctial storm during which time the passengers could neither eat or sleep. The spray and fog was dense and nothing could be seen in the darkness. The ship had a fearful collision with another vessel and at first all on board thought they were going down. Many of the passengers were on their knees in prayer and even the sailors looked as pale and frightful as ghosts.

However, the ship, though badly damaged did not spring a leak, but outrode the storm in safely and brought all securely into port. Neither the name or the fate of the other colliding vessel was discovered. Miss Rosetta Henratta left home in the first place with her Mother's consent to escape a slavery and thralldom almost worse than death, and with the hope of bettering her condition in this land of the free and home of the brave.

Well, she has bettered her condition certainly, and that she is brave enough to live in this free land, no reasonable person will dispute.

This simple story of a plucky girl may be a useful lesson to many of both sexes who think they have extraordinary hardships and that they are enthroned by insurmountable difficulties. The young lady herself will probably be about the last person to realize that she has accomplished anything remarkable.

By Rose Hanratty Callahan

Rose Hanratty Callahan died Jan 14, 1892
John Callahan, 13 May 1858 to 6 Nov 1907

My Sheridan Family

Donald M Schlegel

Mike Sheridan was orphaned in *An Gorta Mór* (the great famine). The living tradition that has come down to us is that his parents were a Sheridan who married a Sheridan. The parents died in the famine and Mike and his siblings went to live with their grandfather. Then the grandfather also went to his reward, so the children came to Columbus when Mike was thirteen, because their uncle lived here. Research has put names and dates to the story: the parents were Mike and Mary; the siblings were Mary, John, Phil, and Kate; and they arrived in New York City in 1849. Mary and Kate lived in Columbus, but we still do not know what became of John and Phil. The uncle was James.

Hard-working Mike got a job and married Mary Burns (or Byrne) before Father Fitzgerald at St. Patrick's Church. Mary had migrated with her family from County Kilkenny a few years before the famine and arrived in Columbus on the canal. Mike and Mary lived for a time with one of his cousins on East Gay Street, but soon moved west across the Scioto to Mitchell Street, a small residential area surrounded by industrial works. Mitchell Street now is represented by the tree lined drive behind COSI. Mike found work at Emrich and Carrols' soap factory, on West Mound Street at the Scioto. One sad story remains of those days: their daughter Emmy died at the age of six, after finding and drinking some hair coloring fluid. We suppose she is still buried in the old Catholic cemetery that now is the heart of the Columbus State campus. There were seven children. Mike died suddenly during a heat wave in the summer of 1881, while walking home from work to dinner one July afternoon. He suffered a sunstroke near the "gravel bank" (on the west side of the river between Mound and Sullivant) and died almost at once. He was only 47. The family struggled on.

Mike's youngest daughter Elizabeth was close to her second cousins, the granddaughters of Mike's Uncle James. The photograph, a tintype, shows the two Lizzie and two Katie Sheridans; Mike's daughter is wearing the darker dress. Elizabeth married Phil McDonald, a supervisor at Doddington's lumber mill on West Broad Street, and they built a house next to her mother's on Mitchell Street. In time, Elizabeth's brother and Phil tore down Mrs. Sheridan's little frame house and replaced it with a brick double. The family were all members of Holy Family Parish during this era. Elizabeth's brothers were blacksmiths with their own shop on West State Street.

In the next generation, contact with the family of Uncle James was lost, but my mother, Elizabeth's daughter, remembered the few family stories and passed them on. My sister and I would often pester her to tell us who the people were in the tintypes and carte de visites in her aunt Mary Sheridan's photo album. I never thought to ask how that album survived the 1913 flood. You can imagine my joy when, in researching the branches of the family, I found that a great-great-great granddaughter of Uncle James Sheridan lives just four houses from me! She looks as if she came straight from old Erin. Her youngest son has some Irish looks about him and, at least at his present age, is not tall. Since I always imagined my great grandfather being of small stature, I can't help thinking when I drive by and see him playing basketball, there goes Mike Sheridan!

Final Memories

Joan Shanahan

In 1996, Peter Shanahan was diagnosed with cancer. I think, because of his Irish background and Catholic Faith, he prepared himself and his family for this event.

His family came from County Mayo and Sligo originally. He spent five years in St. Meinrad Seminary along with two of his brothers, Father James and Brother Bob. He was born and raised in Rushville, Indiana.

When he realized that his life here on earth was limited, he started making his plans. He was at peace with God and enjoyed his visits from Father Missimi. He prepared his obituary and got the specifications from the funeral director about preparing his own casket. His son, Timothy, built the casket in our garage while Pete watched most days. Kevin, Sherri and Bridgid painted and lined it. It wasn't exactly like those of the Monks of Saint Meinrad, but it was beautiful: white with "green" handles. When May of 1998 came, he was totally prepared spiritually and physically. Before he was buried and the casket closed, those who wanted, signed the lid with messages and signatures. Also in the casket was his favorite shirt, put in by Joan, and a beer and a Twix candy bar supplied by the sons!

He made it very easy for the survivors, but it was a bittersweet day!

The Letters of Michael Toolen

Peter F. Shanahan family

Peter's mother's maiden name was Toolen. The following letters tell the story of her grandfather, Michael Toolen and his quest in finding and courting his beloved Maria. This account came to our attention in 1958 from a cousin, Sister Marion S.N., the Holy Names Convent in Maryhurst, Oregon. Sister Marion sent copies of Michael's letters to their cousin, John R. Shanahan.

The following notes and explanations are from Sister Marion and Joan Shanahan regarding Michael's life and his letters: The first letter, dated May 12, is from Gascote Hall Brick Works, England. He had gone to England to find work. On a return to Ireland he found out that Maria had left Ireland six years before and had gone to America. Maria's sister, Celia gave him her address and so the pleas began to her that she replies to his letters. In July of 1862 another letter to Maria was sent after he had received one from her. He immediately starts planning his trip to America. On October 2, 1862 he sends another letter to Maria, this one he tells of talking to his employer about leaving. On October 3, 1862 he sends another letter to Maria. By December 14, 1862, Michael is in New York at Sweeny's Hotel on the corner of Chambers and Chatham Streets, after a stormy sixteen days across the Atlantic. He tells of some experiences in New York. The next letter is dated December 17, 1862 from Carr House in Rushville, Indiana.. He is delivering it to Maria, hoping that she will meet. The next letter is dated January 8, 1863; he has gone to Cincinnati to see about work and is very discouraged. He meets several people that try to help him. He talks of everything being very dear there: wood is six and seven dollars a cord and a Mrs. Geraghty's sister is paying five dollars a month for two rooms barely fit to live in. Michael and Maria must have gotten married sometime between Cincinnati and Rushville. In another letter, dated January 14, 1863 he is still in Cincinnati looking for work and regretting the hardships Maria must be going through while he is gone. He said that when he does come home he would bring gifts and so inquires about colors and materials. He is very aware of prices and merchandise. In a letter dated January 23, 1863 he is still in Cincinnati, three days had passed and he had not received a letter from Maria. He is still hoping work will show up. He signed this letter 'Your disconsolate husband!' On March 23, 1863 in Cincinnati, a letter to Michael Toolen from Mr. Losty refers to a business meeting with a Mr. Abercombie. He talks about tea prices and thanks Mr. Mel for helping him get exempted from the conscription. This was a short letter having to do with business. Michael Toolen became a successful merchant.

One is not surprised to learn that Michael became a successful merchant. The signs are evident in his correspondence, his noting the differences in prices in England and in Cincinnati, his plan to sell the extra trunk, his good taste in selecting the trimming for the ladies' bonnets, and the offer to make purchases for the boys and girls in Rushville. The store he opened soon after his return to Rushville prospered. Michael moved into a comfortable home and also built a small brick building. The old timers say that he would have become a millionaire had he lived. The little old building still stands where he conducted his business affairs.

Grandfather Toolen was a leader in the parish and influential is getting the first resident pastor for Rushville. He donated the property for the first Catholic cemetery and there is a window in the church with their name on it. When the cemetery's land was consecrated the people asked among them the natural question, "Who will be the first to be buried here?" This turned out to be Celia, the infant daughter of Michael and Maria. Two weeks later Grandfather himself died after a baffling illness of two days, and in the spring Maria lost her eldest son, Michael Owen.

It was the books that Michael bought with him from England that young Jim Geraghty used to borrow when he came to town for Sunday mass. Was his taste in reading influenced by that of Grandfather Toolen? This seems quite probable.

The good friends in Cincinnati that Michael mentions in his letters were Anthony Geraghty and his wife. Anthony, the first of Grandpa's brothers to come to America, also died at a comparatively early age.

[First Letter]
Gascote Hall Brick Works
May 12, 1862

My dear Maria,
It is many years now since I heard from you and

I am almost in despair of hearing from you this time. Nevertheless I shall write this once more and see what the result may be. May it be more favorable than I dare to hope it will. It is now about six years since you left Ireland, if I remember rightly. You were gone from that country some time before I knew that you had ever left home. Oh! that I had known then; it would have spared me many hours of wretchedness and misery, for I would, if human exertions could accomplish such an event, have prevented you going to America. Since then I have frequently written for your address but never could obtain it until I went home to Ireland a short time ago when I got it from your sister Celia whom I asked repeatedly if you were married but she never would tell me

Oh! Maria it is your fault that I should have been separated from you so long when from a false delicacy you. forbid me writing to you to Ireland because you were afraid of giving the tongue of the slanderer any pretext to exercise its hatefull functions at your expense and alas I foolishly complied with that request, and had I not done so but kept up a regular correspondence with you I would have known of what was taking place and the result would be that in all probability you and I would be living in happiness together. Ah! will this ever come to pass? May God in his goodness to me grant that it may. But I am afraid that the lying tongues of those who ought and who professed to be my friends have done a great deal to bring about the present state of things as existing between you and me. If so may God forgive them for they do not know the amount of injury they have done me.

Maria you cannot be ignorant of the fact that I loved you dearer than any one else in this world. This you know and now I must tell you that that love which I confessed to you in my youth is still the same and under all circumstances and all time will be the same. Such love as mine for you knows no change. It is immutable and if circumstances are such that you can no longer return that love you will at least write to me. This you can do without any impropriety and explain how you are situated. If single do not give up the place which I flatter myself I once held in your affections. If you are married then adieu to all happiness for me on this side the grave.

Remember that these professions are not made by a thoughtless and rash youth but by one whose love has stood the test of ten years and is more intense at the present than it ever was in my youngest days. If you answer this -- which I conjure you by the memory of your sainted Mother to do -- and if things are as I should wish them to be then I shall suggest a way to you by which we may both be happy yet. Dear Maria I never can nor ever will love a stranger who can have no sympathy with me or whom I cannot have any sympathy with. I have never been out of employment one single hour since I came to this country. I have been most fortunate in this respect. I am now engaged for two years at a good salary but nothing will prevent me from seeing you if the answer to this be as I dare hope it will. My brother John was here with me about three weeks ago and staid with me a fortnight. He gives a sad account of G_____. About the people being all dispersed, scarcely any of the old inhabitants to be seen there and children who were scarcely able to walk when I left home are now married. This sounds so strange to me as I always think of people and things as I left them. Dear Maria in conclusion I must again beg the answer to this and if you are married may you be happy shall be my constant prayer.

Your Affectionate friend,
Michael Toolen

[Second Letter]

July 21, 1862

My dear Maria,

Your letter has just been handed to me and to say that I received it with pleasure would convey but a very faint idea indeed of what I feel and I am sure I am so excited that I shall say, I fear something that will make you think me nothing but an old goose. I am glad that you have written yourself. You ask me to excuse your writing. Why it is beautiful and I would rather have it as it is now than if every letter was of diamond on a golden tablet, because I feel that it contains your own simple and unaffected expressions of love and kindness to me, and this I could not depend on if another had written for you. Maria I must congratulate you on your very nice style of composition. It is long since I have read anything so beautiful. Who could write anything that could give me so much pleasure as you have in the following three sentences- "I have always loved you. I shall never love any but you, and I have been continually thinking of you." I shall never love any but you, I can depend on these being your own sentiments, they have been committed to paper by your own pen and I have sufficient faith in you to think that they are the outpourings of your own heart. May I never find out that I am mistaken and may you always be true, as I hope you will, to these expressions that have given me so much unbounded joy.

Dear Maria for the last four or five years I have never been so happy as at this moment. During all this I have been hoping, fearing, and doubting about you but thank God, all is now cleared up and my patience is rewarded more than I ever expected it would be. Truly the ways of Providence are unsearchable. Who could have ever thought for the last years that you and I should ever see each other again? as we now have every reason to hope and when this comes to pass! Ah! how I anticipate the sweet delight that must follow our meeting, never to part again in this world, to continue forever to share in each other's joys and sorrows, talk over the past, of the many pleasant winter nights we spent together with our young friends in the dear old land, of the many little adventures that each have gone through since our separation. Dearest Maria who could ever marry a stranger? Not I. No stranger could ever understand me. How could I talk to her of the past? and how could a strange woman sympathize with me? Ah no! Such a thought would be worse than death to me.

Dear Maria you ask if I can make up my mind to leave this place to go to you? I do not hesitate to answer this question and most emphatically I can. That I could leave any place to and live with you. This land has been a desert to me. I have mixed little with society ever since I cam here though from my position here there has been a great temptation for me to do so, but as I have before stated, I never lost hope of seeing you again some day and this thought has been my guiding star. I think I told you in my last that I had been at home in Ireland about a year since. I never shall forget what a friend there told me about you. Ah Maria , you ought to have written to me when you were in trouble, and should not I only be too happy to smoothen all your difficulties. When I heard, dear Maria, that an awkward looking country fellow wanted you to marry him, and that your poor Father was willing to give him everything he himself had got to depend on for the future sooner than see you go to a strange land, where perhaps he should never again see you in this world. I say when I heard this my heart was filled to bursting with indignation at the thought of your becoming a partner forever of such a fellow. But dear Maria when I was told of the choice you made under such trying circumstances, divided as you must be between your love for your poor Father and the dislike to become the mate of this man, I could scarcely refrain from falling down on my knees to bless you. Yes I thought I must drop on my knees and nothing less.

Dear Maria if I had not a little experience myself in those matters I should not be surprised how you managed to free yourself from all your Sisters. I am not ignorant of the scene at Jas. Kearns' on the night of your leaving home and I am also aware with what zeal a friend has pressed his suit in America. Again I must ask why you never wrote to me on these occasions? Surely my sympathy would have been worth something.

Now dear Maria I want to ask you if there is plenty of work out there and if I can be able to keep you respectably with my labour or could a few pounds be turned to my advantage so that one could do something without working at day labour. I do not fear this thought I know it will be very strange to me for a time but you are aware I have been used to work when at home, and consequently I know I shall not feel it like one that had never done any. I should wish for you to come here but I could not think of asking you to lave your brother and sister. Does Annie live with you and Michael? I would much rather you had been living out, for I would like you to learn a different style of housekeeping to that practiced in Ireland. Something more than to know how to boil the praties and sweep the house up. O course Annie is a big girl, in this country they would call her a straping wench. Ask her if she remembers "phullen Dugnan". You can tell her that I am not a bit like that now,

Dear Maria I want to ask you if I may tell your Father that I have heard from you. I think he would be glad to know that I have, and that you have intrusted your happiness to my keeping. Of course I shall not do so until I hear from you. Did I tell you in my last that I was carrying on a business in a small way on my own account? I have had a brick yard where we make bricks for building but because of the war in your country I have been obliged to give it up. I have got a small quantity of brick unsold, but I hope they will be sold before I hear from you again. I can leave my present situation at a month's notice, when, if you wish, I shall at once, thatis when I hear from you, leave here for your place. You must send me directions what route to take.

How did you get my letter without any one knowing of it? Let me know if any one knows about it and remember your promise to "let me know everything in your next." I shall only give you 3 days from the time you get this till you post me again, and mind the example I have et you in writing me a long one. Please tell me if any of Thos. Burns family are in that part of the country and how they are doing. I suppose they are all married. You and I are the only two of our crowd that are not married. I hope we shall not be long an exception to the rule.

When my brother John was over here he staid with me a fortnight. I told him then of my determination to write to you. I know he would be glad to know that I heard from you but your wish shall be sacred to me. I shall tell no one of your letter without your consent. Dear Maria I don't think you would know me if you were to see me. I have grown much stouter and wear whiskers and moustache enough to stuff a pillow with. I know I shall very much surprise you when you see me. Should you wish before you have read all this that I had not written so much? Well, you will never tire me with reading yours.

Well, I shall wish you goodby for the present and I hope soon to hear from you again.

Yours true till death,
M. Toolen

Mind I am to have all particulars in your next.
[Third Letter]

October 2, 1862

My dear Maria,
I never wrote a letter more against my will than this. I received yours on Monday last and have been in hopes ever since that I would be able to leave here immediately. I have not been able to see the gentleman that I am doing business for since I got your letter till today. He was furious when I talked of leaving him, and he now insists on me giving him a months notice from the next pay-day which is a fortnight from now. I must tell you that this is a most bitter disappointment to me and I fear that is will be to you also and yet I cannot be sorry that you shall feel it as then I may think that you are

wishing for me to be with you as sincerely as I am myself. Dearest be sure that I shall not wait one moment more than is necessary. Perhaps I may get off sooner than I expect. My master may not, after a few days, insist on so long a notice. But I may tell you that the law is with him if he thinks proper to do so. I do not blame him much for he knows that it is very difficult to meet with one that he can place confidence in for the situation which I hold. This country is so very wicked that it is rare to meet with a trustworthy person.

Dear Maria it was cruel to hint a doubt of my constancy to you and I beg once more to assure you that nothing this side of the grave can end my fervent and pure love for you and all I ask in return is that you love me with the same sincerity and never again let a doubtfull thought enter your mind concerning me. Ah! I would not doubt you for a whole world. I should never be happy again if ever you were to give me cause for doubting. No, welcome death sooner than such a thought.

Dear Maria

I know my poor Mother will feel my going away but am I not the same here as if in America? I am lost to her for ever whether I stay or go and as she knows this is so. I feel sure that in time when she comes to know that I have given my happiness into your keeping I am certain she will be pleased. I do not know the sort of shawl that you want but I shall try and get one. There has not been any of these things such as you want worn here for years. What shawls are worn are black. I want you to tell me what sort of dress you should like from here and what sort of cloth I should buy for my own clothes. I do not know what I shall do about an overcoat. I am wanting one but I think of waiting to have it made in America. Yet I do not think there can be much difference in the style in either of the countries but I must ask you to advise me in all these little things. You must not make many shirts for me as I have got a stack of these things that will last me for years. You will have plenty of little things to do that will fill up your spare time untill I go out. There is one thing that I must tell you and that is that I shall want to be married before I am many hours in Rushville and I shall also want some employment directly after I get there. Could you not come to me to the next town to Rushville and get married before I went there at all? You could come in the morning and I could go back with you the same day. You must write to me the day you get this as I fear that I shall not be able to go till I may have an answer.

Yours now and for ever,
Michael Toolen

[Fourth Letter]

October 3, 1862

Dear Maria,

I have seen my employer today and have come to a final arrangement with him. I shall have to continue in his service till the 8th of November, with diligence I shall have the answer of this from you within a day or two of that time. When I shall have nothing to wait for only to execute your little commissions. Do not forget to let me know about your dress, what sort it should be and the sort of cloth for my own suit. The day after I get yours I shall be on the road for your place. So do not delay an hour. When I get to you I shall be a good lad and try to make out by my attention to you for this little disappointment. I shall take about eighty pounds with me. Can I have it exchanged in Rushville? Or should I exchange it in New York? I have one very good trunk that I had made in Birmingham but I have got a great many books and thought that I might take these in any sort of a box, but if you think a trunk say so and I shall buy a trunk to take them in. If there are any other little things that you think I should take with me from here do not hesitate in letting me know. It will not be any trouble and if there is anything that could be bought cheaper here it would be right for me to take it out with me. If you have not got a black silk dress I should like to bring you one but if you have one of this sort you may rely on my taste in choosing a coloured dress. What shall I bring Annie? You must tell me this. I shall be waiting for your letter

Yours ever and yours <u>alone</u>,
Michael Toolen

[Fifth Letter]

Sweeney's Hotel
Cor. Chambers and Chathem St.New York
December 14, 1862

My dear M.

Here I am after a stormy passage of 16 days across the Atlantic. I shall leave here on the express this evening for Cambridge where I shall hope to meet you. Do not forget this. I think I have earned this much for I question if ever knight, even in the ancient days of chivalry, has done more to prove his devotion to his Lady love than what I have done. If I can find Bernard Leonard's house, I shall go there but if not I shall be at the principal hotel so that Mr. Leonard will soon be able to find me. Now pray let no false modesty prevent you coming. If you fail I shall certainly come to the conclusion that you have brought me out here under false pretences. I have been staying here ever since Friday evening. I found that I could not get to Rushville without having to stop Sunday on the road and so I considered it better to stay here till this evening when I can go right through without stopping.

I must tell you that I have not seen any nice girls in this city. I hope that the country will be able to show some prettier ones. Remember--Wednesday morning I shall expect you. Get to Cambridge on Tuesday night. No person at Rushville need know what you are going to Cambridge for and if they should I cannot for the life of me see now that should influence you. So remember and come Wednesday.

Yours ever,
M. T.

[Sixth Letter]

Carr House
Rushville
December 17, 1862

Dear M.

I am staying at this place but I shall walk up toward your house and try to get this conveyed to you. I shall then wait for you in the street or come to me here. I feel dreadful lonesome. Do come and dont wait to be particular about your dress. Put the quilt about you and put shoes on your feet as the ground is cold. Oh! I cannot joke, I feel so lost in this place.

Yours

M. Toolen

[Seventh Letter]

Cincinnati, Ohio

January 8, 1863

My dear Maria,

If I had not promised you that I should write I should not do so for some time, at least for a few days. I took down my writing case last night but felt so down that I feared I should write something in the mood in which I was in that would give you pain. I am sorry that I must say that I am not at all favorably impressed with the city, but perhaps I may, in time become accustomed to those things that seem so very disgusting now. I had to wait 5 hours at Shelbyville for the train from Indiana. This made it late before I got here, 1 1/2 o'clock. No bed so I lay wrapped up in my coat till morning. For this and my breakfast they asked 1 1/2 dollar. I gave him a 3 dollar bill and in giving my change he returned 3 1/2 dollars and I never told him of his mistake, for I considered that his charge was most extortionate.

I seen W. Laughton's nephew yesterday morning, and he was very kind. He invited me to stop at his house till I got a situation and at the same time he would be continually on the lookout for me. I, of course, refused to stay at his house but promised to call everyday to see what he might make out for my advantage. I have seen Mr. and Mrs. Geraghty and they treated me in the kindest way possible. Mrs. G. would have me stay for dinner and G. walked with me about town all *afternoon. She never got your letter till late last night and you know you told her to look after me and acting up to your instructions, she was after me pretty soon this morning. I asked her what was the matter and she said that she received your letter and that you asked her to take care of me, "and she would." They both went to a ball last night. They asked me to go with them, but of course I felt too low in spirits to do anything of the kind.*

I have not heard, as yet, of anything to do that would suit me but Mr. Duffy and his friend say that if nothing better offers I can have a job in the depot with them. The work here is rather hard but I shall not care about this (if I can get it). It will suit me till something better turns up.

Everything here is very dear. Wood is now from 6 to 7 dollars a cord, and house rent is equally dear. Mrs. Geraghty's sister is paying 5 dollars a month for two rooms that are scarcely fit to live in. I am much afraid of bringing you here, when I see what the little village of Rushville has done to you. I fear what the dirty, foetid air of this city may do to you. Just fancy me looking at you penned up here, looking ill and sad!!! The very thought would kill me. And then again, when I think of the healthy, rosy hue that the country would naturally give you cheeks, the contrast makes me feel uneasy. Oh! I only wish that I could get something to do in the country. I will write to you again when I am employed, if employed at all, and if not you may expect me in Rushville next week.

I have been speaking to Mrs. Geraghty about Annie and she thinks that you had better leave her in Rushville till you get settled here. I have thought much about her this last day or two. I wish you never let her go to a party, and if you come here without her, as I fear you must do, you must get her to promise before her Mrs. that she will not go to any parties till she comes out here, nor to keep company at all. She could stay sometimes with Biddy Burnes so long as Biddy staid in her own house but on any account I would not allow her to run about. You may think that I am out of place in saying so much about Annie as I have done but I must tell you that if I was never married to you I feel that she is entitled to my care and advice as far as possible. In fact the same thing that made me fond of you makes me take an interest in Annie--the loss of a good Mother. I have often wondered, though I have said nothing about it till now, that Michael allowed her ever to go to a party at all. I will just ask him this question, does he not despise, or would he have any girl for his wife that goes to parties? I can answer this question for him, I feel sure that he would not, well then in the name of all that is good, let us not hear of her going to any more parties while she stays there, and if you come here as soon as we get settled we shall have her come out and stay with us till she can get a place that we know will suit her.

But do not say to any person that I am going to stay here for fear that I might be disappointed but at the same time hold yourself in readiness to come at a moment's notice. Have everything packed and ready to turn out. I hope that Michael will come with you. He could say in Rushville that he was only coming to see you safe here, then if he got a job here he could stay with us. Surely now that we are so far from home, and so few, we ought not to be separated if possible. I hope that he will take this into consideration, and wishing this I must bid you good by for the present.

Your affectionate
Husband.

[Eighth Letter]

174 East Pearl St.
Cincinnati, Ohio
January 14, 1863

My dear Maria,

Your letters have made me very happy this morning I am sorry to have to tell you that I have not done any good since I came here, nor do I see any prospect of doing any. There is not an Irishman nor Englishman in town of any influence that I have

238

not solicited and all to no purpose. There is only one hope remaining for me now, and this I have not much faith in. Mrs. Geraghty went with me to Father Edward Purcell, the Bishop's brother. He told me to call and see him in a day or two. I shall do so today but I fear it will not be much use. I am willing to labour at anything, but from appearance employers think I am not. I have shaved all my beard off and tried to make myself look as much like a working man as possible. Still no use. I think I told you that there is a priest in Rochester that I knew in England. I have a good mind to go from here to that place and if not successful there to go on to Canada. I should like for you to go with me. Can I think of subjecting you to the hardship of traveling in this severe season of the year? Do you think I had better leave from here or go to Rushville before I go? If you post on Friday morning I shall have your letter on Sunday at latest. I shall wait here till then.

I am afraid, dear Maria, that I was too selfish in inviting you to become my partner. My passionate love prevented me from studying your interest properly. Many a time this week have I reproached myself for this. I ought, if I only had common sense seen my way clear to support you comfortable before doing what I have done. I am fully conscious of what a wretch I am, the selfish cause of making you miserable at a time that should be the happiest of your life, but I must trust to your generous nature to forgive me and let us both hope that a brighter side may before long present itself. I know that it is sinfull to feel so despairingly, and take such a dark view of things as I do, but really I cannot help it. It is entirely on your account that I do so. I so much fear that you may have to undergo hardships that you have not been used to, and on my account too!-- that would sacrifice every happiness for your sake.

If you wish me to go back to Rushville before I leave here for the places I have mentioned I should like for you to tell me what I must bring to Mrs. Burns. Dresses are very expensive. If I bring you

*and Annie your bonnets they must be green or
p____ coloured for there are no white bonnets nor
any light coloured one at all that you would like. If
you like two of these I shall endeavor to get them as
nicely trimmed as I possibly can. If I buy all these
things I shall have to buy a trunk to put them in. Do
you think it could be sold to any of the boys or girls
in Rushville? You ought to ask the girls if they want
anything and say what a good opportunity it would
be for them to get one. In fact if any of them are
wanting anything from here you may say that I shall
be glad to bring it to them. Certainly everything
here is much cheaper than at Rushville with the
exception of house rent, firing, and provisions. Now
do not delay in answering this as you did the last
one. If you knew what a relief it has been to me to
hear from you, you would not delay a minute. At all
events remember I do not stop here longer than
Monday. If I can get no work, and I fear I shant, I
shall want your letter before then or not at all. Mind
it wont reach me if it dont come before that. I am
glad that Michael stays much with you and the girls
too. Remember me to Mr. and Mrs. Fagan and Amy
Feely.*

*Write in a minute and answer all questions and
please your loving and affectionate*

Husband
M. Toolen

[Ninth Letter]

Cincinnati, Ohio
January 23, 1863

My dear M.

*Three more mornings and never a letter from
you yet, this is too bad. I am fearing that there is
something the matter with you, or that some of you
must be ill at Rushville. Be sure I would not stop
here so long were it not that I am promised from
day to day that something will turn up in my favour
and too, I do not wish to leave as long as there is a
hope remaining. There is only one thing that I
regret and that is that I did not take you along with
me. I wish with all my heart that you were here at*

this moment, however inconvenient it would be for you.

I go to see Father Edward Purcell every day. I have seen him this morning and have got to see him tomorrow again. If it were not for that I would go home in the morning and be with you on Sunday. I have never spent a time so wretched in all my life. What with being away from you and alone here, and not being able to succeed in my expectations. I never have been tried so before and I hope never shall again. I do not often go to see Mrs. Geraghty, not more than about twice a week.

Only think, to be so near you for a whole 3 weeks and not be able to see you. There is only one train leaves here for Rushville every day, and leaves at 5 o'clock in the morning, so that I shall not be able to see you to-morrow night after seeing Father Edward, and I am afraid after all my waiting that he will not be able to do anything for me. Is not this desheartening? Did any two persons ever spend such a honey-moon as you and I have spent? But we will make out for all this when we meet which I trust we shall be able to do before long.

I shall write to-morrow morning if I am not to go home on Monday. I shall certainly know in the morning what my prospects here will be. The two bonnets that I have looked out for you and Annie will cost 12 dollars each. They are both white-- uncut velvet, nicely trimmed, that is according to my ideas. Perhaps my letter to-morrow will be for you to come here, if so you be ready to leave home as soon as ever you get it. That, or I shall be home with you on Monday. Feathers are worth 40 cents per lb. here, do not mind buying any till you come here if you are to come at all.

Your disconsolate Husband

[Tenth Letter]

Cincinnati, Ohio
March 23, 1863

My dear friend Toolen,
I received your letter of the 18th inst. I am happy you are all well also that business has

improved since I left. I have had the pleasure of meeting with Mr. Abercrombie down here last week. I would have gone back with him but work with him was not very busy therefore I concluded to stay a few weeks longer. There was a fine turn of the Catholic associations here on Patrick's day. Tell Mr. MeL. that I am ten thousand times obliged to him for his kindness to have me exempt from the conscription. Tell his at the same time that I feel no way put about because of that affair neither would I have any man think that it was on that account I left Rushville.

On receipt of your letter I went and ordered those brooms. They are the cheapest that can be procured in this city. They have raised considerably since you were down here. I forgot too, to tell you the tea I sent you has raised from what you paid for it to what I had to pay. I have seen your letter to Minor and Andrews telling them to correct the mistake which was in fact (at least they told me so) a rise in the tea. However Minor said they would make it all satisfactory.

Give my respects to all inquiring friends and acquaintances and my wishes to Maria and Annie.

Yours truly
A. Losty

Karen

Beth Shelley

Each year on the Saturday before Memorial Day, I take my Mom to St. Joseph's cemetery, some years one of my sisters, nephews or nieces will join us. This particular year my niece, Karen, who was five decided to join Mom and me. So I picked up Mom and we loaded up flats of flowers, jugs of water, clippers and gloves then headed off to pick up Karen. On the way over I remembered that we had forgotten a hand shovel, not to worry we could borrow my sister's.

When we got to my sister's house Karen seemed a little apprehensive but ready to go. I remembered we needed a shovel so

I turned to Lue and asked to borrow one; Karen looked up with real big eyes and asked, "Why are you going to dig them up?"

I am still taking my Mom to St. Joseph's each year, Karen is now in her twenties and I will always remember her words, it brings a smile to Mom's and my face.

My Grandfather Stephen James Mellett

Shirley Minor Spellmire

My grandfather was Stephen James Mellett. He was born in Swinford, County Mayo, Ireland in 1871 (my brother Jim has more precise records in his possession). Stephen came to this country in, I believe, 1888. He married Mary Whalen in Columbus, Ohio and they had several children, including my mother, Alice Mellett Minor. I believe she was the third child, at least of the ones who lived to adulthood. Her brother John and sister Margaret were older. The others, who achieved adulthood, were in order: Collette, Catherine, Mary and Stephen Jr. Stephen was a two year old when Mary Whalen Mellett died. There is a long story of my grandfather's single parenthood, and my mother raising the other children. John and Margaret were not involved in that. The Mellett "girls" were forever a unit after that, with Alice and Catherine as buddies and Collette and Mary also best friends. The four of them were formidable, indeed! I have many tales, both from my childhood and related to me by my mother. Remarkably, my brother has many others different from mine! The gap in our ages seems to have given rise to rather different experiences. My mother was such an influence on all members of the family that today, 26 years after her death, she is still quoted, and known as "She who must be obeyed"!

My grandmother's parents came here, as well as Grandpa Mellett's parents. I believe there were some class distinctions, of the lace-curtain and shanty variety, but I am not clear which is which. Ask Jim for that clarification, since he told me it involved one set of parents not approving of the "walking out" of their child with the other.

243

Grandpa never told me much at all about Ireland, only some stories about taking the barn doors off and dancing on them. I am sorry I missed so much. He was a younger man with my brother and sister, and may have told them more. I will get more information together for you, but just wanted to acknowledge your first request.

The Family I Found

Patricia Wright Stover

I cannot remember a time when I wasn't aware of my Irish heritage. I was told that my maternal great-grandmother, Annie Kelley, had lived on a horse farm just outside Dublin, Ireland. She lived with her father, John Kelley, who managed the farm for the owners who lived elsewhere. After John and Annie immigrated to America and settled in Licking County, Ohio, John drove the stagecoach between Columbus and Newark. There was a deep ravine on Route 40 just east of Reynoldsburg, Ohio, that the locals called Robber's Glen. Family lore said that John's coach was robbed there twice by bandits.

Several years after both my parents were deceased, I was going through a box from their home that contained papers and pictures having to do with the families. I found a term paper for a course at Ohio State University that my mother had written about her family. She mentioned how her mother's family, the Smiths who came from Virginia and Maryland, had looked down upon the marriage of her mother, Lucie, to her father, Tom Besse. They considered Tom, whose mother was Annie Kelley, to be less than worthy of Lucie. My mother adored her father and resented the Smiths' behavior.

My father didn't want my mother to speak of her family. He said that she was too busy putting on airs. He was the seventh child of an Appalachian family of tenant farmers in Johnstown, Ohio. He was very proud of German ancestors who had served in the Prussian Army. It was all that he would speak about.

While I was going through that previously mentioned box full of papers and pictures, I discovered a multi-paged letter written to my father by a distant cousin. The letter traced his family of origin and mine back to the Wrights who were from Northern Ireland. This revelation was something that I had never heard before reading that letter. My mother treated her knowledge of our being Irish by rebelling against anyone who looked down upon her heritage; my father treated his knowledge of being Irish by keeping it a secret. Such were the various ways of being Irish in my family of origin. When I turned twenty-one years old and left home, I immediately began to learn as much as I could as fast as I could about everything Irish. I'm still learning today.

A Special Relationship

Mary Grady Strickland

My Grandfather Michael Grady came to the United States in 1907 from Shawree, County Mayo, Ireland. After getting settled he sent for his bride Mary who arrived in Cleveland, Ohio on Halloween. When she got off the boat and began looking around unaware of the American custom of dressing up on Halloween she was appalled at what she saw and told Michael if this is how they dress in America she was going back.

My grandparents Michael Grady and Mary McGregor were married in 1906 and came to America in 1907. They returned to Ireland for a visit in 1913-14. They still had no children so when they arrived home, they made the pilgrimage to Croagh Patrick. Their prayer on the top of that beautiful place was to have a child. When they arrived back to America my Grandmother Mary was pregnant with my father Austin who was born October 12, 1914.

In 1996 three grandchildren and three great-grandchildren of Michael and Mary made the pilgrimage to Croagh Patrick. It was a wonderful feeling to be able to walk and pray where your ancestors asked for the most beautiful gift of all.

The entire Grady clan has a special relationship with this mountain and St. Patrick

"The Reek"

Catherine E. Sullivan

Have you ever heard of "The Reek"? Have you ever climbed "The Reek"?

On our 2008 trip to Ireland, Jim Fath and I challenged "The Reek", urged and accompanied by our good friend Glenn Hagan. Not knowing what we were getting into, we rented walking sticks for one euro, which would be returned upon our return (of the stick)!

Mount Croagh Patrick, locally known as "The Reek", is located near Westport in County Mayo, Ireland. It was on top of that mountain that St. Patrick fasted for 40 days and nights in 441 A.D. Each year, nearly one million people make the 2,510 foot hike to the top where there is a small church, built in St. Patrick's honor. Some people make the journey to pray, do penance (in which they climb the very rocky mountain barefooted), or just enjoy the magnificent view of the area.

The climb was very treacherous, especially when you got near the top, with slippery, loose rock and narrow paths. We climbed through fog the entire time, but when we finally reached the top, suddenly all of the fog blew away. The sky opened up, the sun came out, and there was a breath-taking view of the surrounding countryside and Clew Bay, where the locals claim that there are 365 islands, one for each day of the year! We made it! What a feeling of accomplishment for us (although some of the locals practically run up the mountain)!

The trip down was even more treacherous. Because of all the loose rocks and stones, I lost my footing and fell three times. When we told the story to some of the local Irish ladies, each and every one of them would gasp and say that "Jesus fell three times"!

As we reached the bottom of the mountain, we ran into a group of young people who were all dressed up. The girls had on mini-skirts and extremely high-heels, and, believe it or not, were going to attempt to climb "The Reek"! We were in total disbelief! We shook our heads, and after that long and difficult hike, were very thirsty and tired. At the bottom of the mountain was an oasis ... an old rustic pub! The girl in charge was beside herself with worry. The group, that we had just passed, were gypsies, who had just come from a wedding, and she was frantic that they were going to steal her blind. We tried to comfort her as she waited for the owner of the pub to rescue her. The gypsies didn't get far up "The Reek", and were back at the pub before long...for whatever purpose!

A Marriage Made in Heaven

Sister Mary Elaine Tarpy, SND

This is the story of one of the grandsons of John Tarpy, who emigrated from Sligo, County Sligo, in 1863. He settled in Columbus, Ohio and married Bridget Roush. They had five children. Their son David Joseph married Amelia Buehler in 1907. They had 15 children and named their 12th child, David Joseph.

This David Joseph was born July 9, 1922. He developed a magnificent tenor voice and could sing every stanza of every popular song ever written. As a member of the Shamrock Club, he often sang solos. In 1975 he toured Ireland, then flew to Rome to visit his sister Elaine, a Sisters of Notre Dame de Namur. From there, he made a weekend pilgrimage to the Shrine of Our Lady of Lourdes in France, to pray to meet a woman to marry. There he met Mary Elizabeth King from Clifden, County Galway. She went to Lourdes to pray to meet a man to marry. They exchanged addresses, corresponded, and the following summer, Mai spent a month in the States visiting Dave. They became engaged and married a year later, May 18, 1979 at the Shrine of Our Lady of Knock, in County Mayo.

Mai was the manager of St. Mary's B & B in Clifden, so together they continued the business until 1984, when they closed it and retired. As devotees of Our Lady, together they prayed the rosary every night. Dave belonged to Our Lady's Rosary Makers, headquartered in Brook Park, Ohio and made rosaries on the side. Thousands of these were sent to the missions in Africa and Latin America. Mai died on the Feast of Our Lady of Mount Carmel,

247

July 16, 2008. Dave passed away on March 11, 2010. They are buried side by side in Ardbear Cemetery, Clifden, County Galway, by the sea.

My Irish Family's Story

Mary Kelly Tisdale

Our family moved to the east side of Columbus in August 1963 because dad, Sidney John Kelly accepted the position of Dean of the Engineering and Technology Department of Franklin University. Mom and dad spent one weekend in Columbus deciding on a home and school for us four daughters. At that time, there was a waiting list for the elementary Catholic grades, no tuition and no kindergarten. So it was another year before all four of us were at St. Philip the Apostle School, which was an easy walk through the neighbors' back yards. Mom, Mary Louise Kelly took a job teaching math and English at Bishop Hartley and remained there throughout all the girls' high school years.

Traditionally we celebrated March 17 by wearing something green and eating corned beef and cabbage. Except for my parents becoming engaged on that day in 1951, there was no major fanfare at that time of the year.

A well-known story told in the family is that my maternal great-grandmother, Katherine Sweeney, took off work at her Ligonier PA. boarding house only twice a year; St. Patrick's Day and Independence Day. My grandma, Agnes Sweeney Kenney remembers having the boarders lift the cooking pots for her; because at ten years of age she could cook but not lift the heavy hot water pots. By the time we four girls were on the scene, our family had mellowed the annual celebration.

I married Paul George Tisdale, 100% Irish-American Catholic from Boston, MA. Paul was an associate engineer and I was a county special education teacher. When our oldest of two daughters expressed an interest in dance, someone suggested Irish dance; after seeing the dancers, our five-year old Megan was hooked. It became a way of life in the Tisdale household, especially when her sister Erin followed in her footsteps four years later, both continuing to take group and private lessons simultaneously for over 13 years. Both Paul and I were very active with the dance school, feisana, and oireachtas; planning and implementing many facets of the dance world including performances in the Soviet Union and competitions in Ireland, Canada and all over the United States for our own as well as other dancers.

Although I am only 50% Irish with some Slavic and Swiss mixed in, my husband is 100% Irish; in a way this makes our children more Irish than I am! Joining the Daughters of Erin a few months after its inception and giving memberships to both daughters strengthened our Irish ties in the community with knowledge of our heritage and especially meeting so many other families who shared our desire to practice our strong family ties together.

Suddenly, no one in our immediate family worked or went to school on March 17 due to participation in the mass, parade, reunion and dance performances. The festive air was contagious, my three sisters, Patricia Thomas, Eileen Baesmann and Katherine Kelly were also members of the DOE. Not only did we have something to celebrate, we had a whole day of planned activities with over 5000 of our closest friends!

Throughout the years our family participated in Irish picnics, fundraisers, elections, installations, charities and cultural events. Neither Megan nor Erin ever went to school on March 17 until they went to college. Megan taught Irish dance with Lauren O'Neill James in Washington DC for a few years while working fulltime in college admissions. She recently relocated to Chapel Hill, NC and Duke University. Currently Megan is an advisor and founder of the Irish Dance Student Group at Duke University. Erin instructed the first Irish dance classes at The Ohio State University Dance Department while working on her MFA degree. She worked closely with Peggy Shanahan Roach's O'TIS School for part of her thesis. Erin now resides in Chicago IL and is the Video and

Technology Consultant for the Dance Department at Columbia College. She and Gary Feiler are planning a summer 2008 wedding.

The Irish community has been very good to our family; Megan was the Irish Way representative for the DOE in 1992 and then served as an Irish Way chaperone in 1998; Erin received the Daughters of Erin Vivian Lermonde Scholarship Fund towards college in 2002. My mom received Irish Woman of the Year in 1985 and my sister Eileen received the honor in 1995.

My Irish heritage and the trials of my ancestors vividly came to mind on a Friday in March 2007. I thought of those people coming to a new country, attempting to establish homes, families and jobs in the New York City and Pittsburgh areas, and wanting to give their children better opportunities to obtain more than their parents had. And I thought of the communities that now salute diversity where prejudice was once the rule. On that day, I, Mary Kelly Tisdale personally received commendations from Mayor Coleman and Columbus City Council, the Franklin County Commissioners, and State Representatives broadcast on television from City Council Chambers on Proclamation Day for receiving the honor of Irishwoman of the Year 2007. Yes, my family has continued to be an active part of the Irish community because it has given so much to us.

Foley Family Railroad History

Jim Underwood

My late mom was a Foley from early Columbus Flytown. Her name was Mary Margaret Foley Underwood. Mom was a DOE and Shamrock Club member. She died in 2004. My Aunt Ann Foley Kollasch who lives in Phoenix wrote the following story.

My Great-grandfather John Foley, an immigrant from Ireland, landed in St. John's Newfoundland in 1846. He worked on the building of the Cleveland and Pittsburgh Railroad out of Bedford, then a suburb of Cleveland.

He then went to work building the Cleveland, Mt. Vernon, and Delaware Railroad, now the Akron branch of the Pennsylvania

Railroad. When the track was finished to Marshallville, he was made First Section Boss. Sometime he moved to Columbus and was section boss laying track in western Pennsylvania.

In those days there were no pensions or Social Security, so when too old or worn out to do the hard heavy work, they just had to quit or get an easier job. My Great Grandfather started a grocery store in Columbus, Ohio called "Foley's Market" (Red and White chain).

When the youngest son, Edward, was old enough to go to work, his brothers decided he wasn't big and strong enough to work on the railroad, so they put him in charge of the family grocery store in Columbus. He eventually did better and made more money than they did on the railroad.

In the early days, whenever anyone in family wanted to go downtown, they would just go to the rail line and hop on a car and off again downtown. One of the great aunts (Anna) misstepped and fell under a railroad car and had her left leg cut off. I remember her. She had an actual "peg leg". It looked something like a piano leg but smaller.

My Dad, Tom Foley, worked as a blacksmith in the railroad shops in Columbus, repairing engine parts. He got the flu real bad during an epidemic about 1920s and got Parkinson's Disease as a complication of the flu. He lived to be 72.

When I was a kid, we only traveled to places where we could get a "pass" to and had relatives or friends to stay with. My mother took me to Philadelphia and Chicago where we saw the sights. I also went to Washington D. C. while in nurses training. I stayed and visited with girl friends, who showed me all the sights; i.e. the White House, Dolly Madison's House etc.

So due to the railroad I saw some pretty interesting parts of the country. My Grandfather had three other brothers who also worked for the railroad.

The James Michael and Julia Kerrigan Varley Family

Erin Michael Varley

My name is Erin Michael Varley a 1990 Graduate of Columbus St. Francis DeSales. I was recently made aware about your compilation of Irish Families in the area. I currently reside in Roland, IA. Below is my information

James Michael Varley and Julia Kerrigan Varley came over to United States from County Mayo Ireland in approximately 1850 – 1855. They settled in the Wellston, Ohio area. My family stayed there until the early 1900's when my Great Grandfather Bill Varley moved to the Columbus area. My father Michael Kevin Varley and Mother Barbara Ann Varley both attended DeSales and graduated in 1967. They both live in Columbus. I have a sister, Meghan Eileen Varley who graduated in 1993 from DeSales and lives in Galena, Ohio. We have begun researching the family. We have not found any other Varley relations in central Ohio at this time. Out here in Iowa there are actually a few Varley's in the western part of the state, but as far as we can tell no relations.

My father was a member of the Shamrock club in the 80's. We attended several St. Patrick's Day parades and spent a lot of time at the family reunions at Vet's Memorial.

THE CONNOR FAMILY

Nancy Connor Walter

My great-grandparents, Michael and Catherine Hogan Connor came to this country from Ireland before 1860. I don't know what Irish county they came from, or if Catherine's (Katie's) maiden name was Hogan, Hoban, or another variation. My brother found a notice of a marriage in 1854 in Syracuse, New York, of Michael Connor and Catherine Grogan. The Marysville, Ohio, Journal-Tribune published a notice of Mr. and Mrs. Michael Connor of Union Twp. celebrating their golden wedding anniversary on November 4, 1903. I received a letter from their granddaughter, Isabel Connor, in 1989 (after I had located her in California) in which she told about "Michael and his brother James arriving in

America on the same ship (name and date unknown); and when they landed, there was a fire on the ship, they waded ashore and got lost and never saw each other for years." She also recalled that when she was a child and heard about the Irish potato famine she "was always worrying about the why? Why? Why did they have a famine? I wanted to send them potatoes!"

Michael and Catherine came to Milford Center, Union County, Ohio, and lived on a 40-acre farm. They were listed in the Union Twp., Union Co. census of 1860; Michael was listed as a farmhand, they had three children. By the 1870 census, seven children were listed: James age15, Mary age 11, Ann age 9, Alice age 8, Michael age 6, John age 3 and Thomas age 1. Thomas was my grandfather. Another census record of 1870 lists a James Connor and his family of Rush Twp., Champaign County.

My father, Larry Connor, described his grandfather Michael as "short, round, had a broad brogue, wore an Irish peaked hat, and smoked a pipe." When Larry and his family visited the farm, Grandmother Katie would give him a dollar "to buy insurance".

Michael (Sr.) and Catherine have a large monument where they are buried in Milford Center Cemetery, with a nearby stone for son Michael M. and Anna Connor, and smaller stones for James, John and Alice.

Mary, the oldest daughter, married a man named Austin Cheney and lived in Springfield, Ohio. She was described as "beautiful and Spanish-looking". Alice was a school teacher in Union County for 38 years. She never married. James and John also remained single. As children we were taken to visit Great-Aunt "Allie" and Uncle John and Uncle Jim, who lived together on the family farm. One of the uncles was very reclusive and shy and often didn't appear when we visited. Daughter Annie married a man named Miller, had no children that I know of.

Son Michael married Anna Phillips. They had three children. He was elected mayor of Milford Center but died before he could take office. He died when the oldest child, Leila, was about 16. His widow Anna and the children moved to Marion, Ohio so the children could go to better schools. Isabel, mentioned above, in her long, rambling letter to me, told about the good background she received in art and that she eventually went to college and became head of art in the public schools in Long Beach, California. Leila's daughter Isabel also wrote in her 1989 letter to me, my only contact with her before she died at over 90 years old: "When I was old enough to remember we had a reunion and a whole family of Connors came from Michigan. There was a boy my age and grown-ups all dressed up. They lived in a city. We liked them but no one had time to write letters".

My grandfather, Thomas, bought a livery stable in North Lewisburg, Champaign County, where he met and courted my grandmother, Grace Hunter. I heard about their courtship, when he would call for her, driving an unbroken horse and often the horse would run away, taking out across the fields before being reined in. They married on January 10, 1901.

Thomas first earned his living breaking horses, then as a streetcar conductor in Dayton, and as builder and operator of the second drive-in filling station in the United States at First Avenue and North High Street, Columbus in 1913 or 1914.

Thomas and Grace had three sons; my father Laurence (Larry) was the only one who had descendants, with two wives: Nancy Grace (me), William Michael, Jonathan James, Laurence Davis and Elizabeth Virginia.

Larry became a newspaperman, working in college and after at the old Ohio State Journal, then as chief editorial writer for the Columbus Dispatch from 1932 to 1960. He covered many important events and went to San Francisco in 1945 for the opening of the United Nations. I have enclosed some copies of newspaper clippings about him. We five children are all still alive: Elizabeth and I in Grandview, '"Mike",retired engineer, in Marysville, Jon ,retired geologist, in Denver, Larry ,attorney in Detroit. There are also twelve grandchildren and 28 (?) great-grandchildren.

My 100% Irish grandfather Thomas was ill with tuberculosis for almost all of the time that I knew him and so I remember an old, sick man. He died in 1940 and his funeral service was held in our house, which soon after was bought by Mr. Deyo and became the Deyo-Davis Funeral Home still doing business in Grandview Heights. Because Thomas married Grace Hunter, a Methodist, our family did not follow the Roman Catholic faith. I am not aware of any connection to the other Connors in Columbus, although there may very well be. On our two trips to Ireland, my husband and I saw the name "Connor" and "Michael Connor" in many, many places.

Catherine Caulins

Anne Downey Wohlfrom

Catherine (Kate) Caulins was born in the Balbriggan/Balrothery area, Co. Dublin, Ireland and was baptized on September 5, 1829. The Caulins and the Coyle families were friends and Kate was a special friend of Peter Coyle. As a result, she was very familiar with the Coyle home.

In the fall of 1851, the Coyle family decided to immigrate to America. Kate's brother made arrangements to travel with them. Kate would have liked to go, but she and Peter were not married. Also, it is likely that her family could not afford to send more than one child, and they decided to send her brother Matthew. Kate had to wait for three years until she could leave. She may have come on a work agreement because she and Peter did not get married until two years later.

Kate and Peter lived in Loveland, Ohio. During the Civil War, Confederate General John Morgan led 2,460 mounted raiders into Ohio. They entered the state at a point just north of Cincinnati and then proceeded in an easterly direction which took them to Kate and Peter's farm. Morgan and a group of his men stopped at the farm and demanded that the Coyles provide food for them. It was a frightening time for Kate as she was especially concerned about the safety of the children. Sally was six years old, Katie was five and Willie was a year and a half. She also had to worry about herself; she was almost seven months pregnant at the time. As frightening as the experience must have been, it could have been worse. After Morgan and his men had eaten, they left and took many of the farm animals with them. Only one cow was left. Kate was relieved that no one was hurt.

Years later, when her grandchildren would ask her about her life in Ireland, she would usually tell them that she was an American now and was not thinking about Ireland. The one time she talked to her grandson Ed Coyle about Ireland, she reminisced about the Coyle property in Balbriggan and how she could look out the kitchen window and see the lake below. Apparently she was happy that she was happy that she was given the opportunity to make a new life in America and thought it was best not to look back. Another eighty years would pass before her great granddaughter would go to Ireland. Anne met the Coyle family who farmed that same land, but they weren't sure that they were really related until they heard the story about looking

out the window and seeing the lake. The Coyles in Ireland said that they had no idea that anybody in their family had gone to America.

Louis A. Downey

Anne Downey Wohlfrom

Louis Downey was a first generation Irish-American. He was born in Urbana on July 2, 1878, the youngest of twelve children. He moved to Columbus around 1904. On July 12, 1905, he married Rose Walsh. In 1913, Louis was living with his wife and his two sons, William and Francis, at 63 Richards Avenue. This was in the area of the West Side called "The Bottoms."

In March, 1913, a flood hit the West Side of Columbus where Louis and his family were living. On the morning that the floods hit, the rains had actually stopped. Louis had breakfast and left for work. As he walked to work, he noticed that the river was rising. He realized that in all probability the river would continue to rise because of all the ice in it as well as all the rain of the past few days. Louis knew that "The Bottoms" was particularly vulnerable to floods. He owned The Great Western Storage Co. and had bought the warehouse at 768 West Broad Street because that site was high enough to escape any foreseeable flood.

Louis was determined to move his family before the floodwaters hit. He returned home where he found William and Francis taking turns pushing one another in their red wooden wagon. Louis quickly walked up the steps and yelled to Rose that they must leave the house as quickly as possible. Rose and Louis carried most of the furniture from the first floor to the upper level of the house. By the time they were ready to leave, the only furniture that remained downstairs was the large dining room table, which was too cumbersome to move. After they had done as much as they could with the house, Louis loaded William and Francis in their wagon. He also put some food and blankets in the wagon and the family began their move to higher ground.

As the family moved toward the warehouse, Louis warned many people about the danger of flooding. Most of the people refused to believe that there was any danger. Some people actually ridiculed Louis and his family for being scared. Louis was secure in his evaluation of the situation and was not bothered by his neighbors' comments. He stopped by a grocery store to get some more food so that the family would not go hungry. The flood did strike about an hour after the family had left their home.

The Great American Storage warehouse was a large structure made of paving bricks and sometimes described as being as strong as "The Rock of Gibraltar." Despite what was happening outside, the family felt safe in the building. They turned on the radio to keep informed of the flood's progress. At one point during the news broadcast, there was an announcement that the Griggs Dam had possibly broken. This meant that much more water could come in a matter of minutes. Louis put on his boots and ventured into the flooded streets to lead his friends and neighbors to the top of the building. Luckily the dam had not broken. However, even so some of the West Side was covered with twenty-six feet of water and ninety-three people died. The warehouse survived the strong currents, and the family remained there until the water went down enough to travel.

When Louis and the rest of the family returned home, they looked in the windows and saw that the water was still up to the ceiling and the dining room table was floating on top. As he was draining the house, Louis saw his brother-in-law, John Dailey, drive up in his horse and wagon. John offered to take the boys back to his farm in Urbana so that Louis and Rose could clean up the house. As difficult as the flood was for everyone on the West Side, it was good for Louis's business. Since the warehouse proved to be so watertight, every time there was a threat of flood, people would arrange to have their pianos stored at the Downey warehouse.

William Joseph Coyle

Anne Downey Wohlfrom

William Coyle and Anna Bradley were both first generation Irish Americans. They were married in Cincinnati, Ohio on August 10, 1892. They lived in Loveland, Ohio during the early years of their marriage until Willie, who was working for the Pennsylvania Railroad, was transferred to Columbus, Ohio in 1902.

While the family was living in Loveland, Nick, their oldest son, loved to play with his cousin, Cornelius Conway. The families were close and the boys were able to see one another almost every day. One morning when Nick was about five, he was sitting at the kitchen table having breakfast and occasionally adding to the family conversation. When his mother asked him if he had a good night's sleep, he said, "Yes, but Cornelius woke me up during the night."

His mother asked him what he meant. "How could he wake you up?" The family lived in a two-story house and the bedrooms were on the second floor.

Nick replied saying, "Cornelius was banging on the window and it woke me up. I looked at the window and he started waving at me and then he went away. Then I went back to sleep."

Nick's mother just smiled and said, "That's nice. Well, finish your breakfast and you can go play."

A little while later, one of their relatives came to the house and told the family that Cornelius had died during the night.

Tommy Madden's Exploits

Heather O'Leary Ziccardi

Here are the stories about my grandfather Tommy Madden, as written by E. S. Wenis in "Quaint Tales of Old Chillicothe". The stories happen in the place that he settled, Chillicothe, Ohio. In 1845 Tommy was born in Dublin, Ireland and immigrated to the United States in 1865. Tommy and his wife, Mary Jane, had a total of eleven children, all boys but two. He reared a big family and was a character. Tommy passed away on January 4, 1907 in Ross County, Ohio.

"Old Erin's sons come to Chillicothe in rather large numbers following the disasterous famine in Ireland back in the late forties. The new land across the sea brought letters of the more adventurous back to the 'ould sod' and the young men and women were eager to get away from the hardships and the tyranny of the British over lords, who owned the land which they cultivated with most meager returns, and to come to America.

Among those adventurous spirits was one Thomas Madden. He was a true son of Erin. He had red, curly hair, a pair of scintillating blue eyes and he never knew anything but hard work. Somehow he landed in New York and made his way out to Chillicothe, and finally by saving and scraping he managed to get a hill farm out beyond Mt. Logan on the Marietta Pike.

Madden was a bibulous gentleman when he visited the city. He reared a rather large family and was a little king out on the hill farm. He usually made his visits to the city riding on the running gears of a farm wagon and driving a team of wiry sorrel horses.

259

While his entrance to the city was always made quietly, his departure was always something to wonder at. When one heard something like a whirlwind coming east on Second Street, over the bridge at the canal, one could always make certain it was Madden, homeward bound. These horses were tearing and Madden was slashing them, giving vent to rousing cheers as he rode like the wind.

Madden continued his farming career until he was a man perhaps of 50 or more, when he decided that his family had grown up and his wife had died and he wanted to go back to visit Ireland. So, he sold the farm, had a big farewell party and told everyone he was going to spend his day over on the soil of Erin.

He went to New York, where he was to board his vessel and he liked New York so well that he put on another party, and as a result, he was skinned of all his money and when he came to sober consciousness, he found he had just about enough money to get back to Chillicothe by 'bumming' his way on the trains.

At any rate, he landed here a crestfallen man, but with undampened ardor as to his ability to make a living.

The Jardine Plumbing Co. was then only recently organized by the late Graham Jardine and Robert G. Tomlinson, and Madden got a job with the firm digging ditches in which to lay water and sewer pipes. Of course with his reduced monetary resources his resorts to bachelor entertainment were rare, but he certainly relished them.

On occasion, when his spirit did rise as a result of over stimulation, he was wont to give expression to a true 'Maddenism'. He would jump up from the floor and twirl his feet like a youngster and shout, 'Kick a hole in the flure.' Asked about the cause of the celebration, he would answer; 'I'm workin' for Jardine & Co.' Jardine incidentally, was a very abstemious and temperate man, who did not countenance drinking at all. Tomlinson was more liberal in his views. So Madden would explain about those two in this wise. 'Jardine, he buys me the soda water and Bobby buys me the beer. Hooray for Bobby.'

The local Hennessey Club, a subsidiary band within the local Elks' Lodge, adopted Madden's slogan of 'Kick a hole in the flure' as theirs, to put on a green silk ribbon headed with a champagne cork and tailed with a buckeye on the occasion of the Elks Grand Lodge meeting in Cincinnati back in 1904. They sold for as high as $3.50 apiece as novelties, for the club not only adopted Madden's slogan, but many of his other qualifications, and that made the badge a desirable quantity.

Madden is dead now these many years, but if one has true Celtic blood in his veins, he can still hear Tommy shout and driving his team down Second Street on nights when the moon is gibbous and everything is eerie.

Pictures

Charlie Madden

Bessie Madden and son,
Chillicothe, Ohio

John Canty, Margaret Ford, Mary Ford Canty, Bill (Willy) Ford
taken in 1950's

Charles Call with grandsons

Pictures

Mary R O'Keefe
and son, Declan

John Cronin with visitors

Ellen Monica Moriarty
1856 - 1938

Michael O'Keefe
1839 - 1903

Michael and Anastasia Powers Cody 50th Wedding Anniversary; Feb. 1909

Pat & Maggie Moran's 50th.

Son of William "Billie" Naghten

Katherine, wife of William "Billie" Naghten

This barn was used as the first church structure prior to construction of   St. Michael's Church in Carlisle, Ohio. This church society began in 1803.

The farm cottage on the Stack family farm in County Cork, Ireland.

John and Anne Gallagher
Malloy Wedding Picture

Jack Anderson visiting the grave of
John J. O'Keeffe in County
Tipperary, Ireland

Prayer Card for Cecil Toolen

Pictures

James O'Brien
1839-1914

Mary Mangan O'Brien
1835-1909

Frank McNulty and Granddaughter Jennifer Brockmeyer

Tackney Home, Bailieborough, County Cavan, Ireland

Terence Sexton (Tackney) with
daughter Mary Ellen

The Sheridan Cousins; two
Lizzies, two Katies.

Pictures

Thomas and Jennie Naghten
Coady with younger adult

Rev. Patrick Quinlan

L. to R. Joseph Quinlan, Fr. Patrick Quinlan, John Quinlan, and
Dennis Quinlan

Family Histories

and

Genealogies

Stack Family Irish Roots

Kory de Oliveira

The following is a history of the Irish family roots of two long time DOE members, Patti Ardrey and Eileen Douglass. Patricia "Patti" JoAnn Clark Ardrey is the daughter of Eileen Patricia Stack Clark Douglass, who was both born in Brooklyn, New York. Eileen's father, John Joseph Stack, was born in Manhattan to William Joseph Stack, an immigrant from County Cork, Ireland. William Stack was the son of Florence Stack, the owner of the Stack Family farm in Schull, County Cork, Ireland.

The Stack Family farm is located in the extreme west of County Cork. The farm, which still exists today, is found on the side of a mountain named Mt. Gabriel in Schull. Florence Stack owned this 73 acre farm, which is believed to have been inherited from an elder Florence Stack, who was born in 1765 and lived to be an impressive age of 100! The younger Florence Stack married Hanorah Sullivan, born in County Kerry and the daughter of Dennis and Mary O'Sullivan, and together they had 10 children. When Florence died at the age of 60 in April 1874, the farm was left to Hanorah. However, in 1881 she passed the farm onto her daughter Anne's husband, Matthew Coughlan. The Stack sons had already left the area, many of whom crossed the ocean to start a new life in New York. Anne and Matthew lived their entire lives on the farm. This land stayed in the Coughlan family until the 1970's, when William "Bird" Coughlan died. The land was left to Myra Shannahan and later transferred to Eileen Cleverly. She is still the owner today.

Hanorah Stack made the voyage to New York with her daughter, Nora, in 1887. She lived with her son, William, who had been in NY since 1870. Nora married Richard Coughlan, who was already living in NY and was the younger brother of Matthew. William was married to Hannah "Annie" Marie O'Neill and had 4 children. Hannah arrived in New York in 1879, but it is unknown if she came alone. Only one son survived, John Joseph Stack. He was born on June 29, 1893 in Manhattan. William's mother, Hanorah, passed away from pneumonia on March 29, 1895. The following year his brother, Florence Robert Stack, died of Bright's disease in January. William died at 52 on July 8, 1902 from unknown causes, leaving young son John alone with his mother.

John Stack married Lillian Rose Nevlin a few years after his mother, Annie, died in 1916. They had 6 children: Anna Marie, John Robert, Lillian, Eileen, Gerard and Mary, but lost Lillian at a young age to diphtheria. Eileen Stack and her siblings were born in Brooklyn, New York, and helped their mother take care of their tenement at 110 Lynch St. Eileen met Cody Clark while he was on leave from the Navy during WWII and they married shortly thereafter. Patti was born in Brooklyn, but her siblings were born in West Virginia and Ohio, where the family eventually settled.

Hugh Henry Harper

W. Patrick Graham

Hugh Henry Harper was born about 1840 in Carroll County, Ohio. His two older sisters, Jane and Mary E. were born in 1833 and 1835 in Rockcorry, County Monaghan, Ireland. We haven't been able to prove his parents although we think his father was also named Hugh.

Hugh enlisted in the Civil War and ended up in the cavalry with the rank of Sergeant. After the war, Hugh was a tailor. On February 6, 1865 in Preble County, Ohio he was married to Sarah A. Show. They had a daughter Lyda who died in infancy. Sarah divorced Hugh in 1871 stating that he had left her and was also guilty of "habitual intoxication". On Christmas Eve 1874 in London, Madison County, Ohio, he married again to Mary Elizabeth Green. From this union were: Charles Henry, Florence June (my grandmother), Mary Ellen, Jessie Fremont, and William Harrison. Upon receiving Hugh's Civil War Pension papers, we learned he had left his wife and children and they had assumed he died. When his wife Mary had applied for his pension, she was shocked to find out he was living in the Veteran's Home in Dayton, Ohio and was already drawing his pension. When Hugh died, January 16, 1897, he was buried in the Dayton National

Cemetery and he had instructed that his personal effects be sent to his sister Mary E. Moore in Ottumwa, Iowa.

The Dublin Connection

Robert J. Gueth

In the early 1990's, my business partners in Dublin, Ireland and myself in Dublin, Ohio started a company known as Aldiscon. We invented the computer software that the cell phone companies use all over the world to do text messaging on your cell phone.

My family connection to Ireland traces back through my maternal line. My father Clarence Gueth, Jr. married Jacqueline Cummins, daughter of Katherine Keenan of Clogheen, County Tipperary and John Cummins. Katherine was a descendant of the Meehan's.

The Corbett Family

Mary Alice Ryan Kerns

The six sons of James Corbett who immigrated are John, Patrick, Michael, William, James and Thomas. Patrick, Michael, William, James and Thomas and Kate (John's wife and two babies William and James) arrived August 30, 1852 on the ship Lord Ashburton. John had arrived earlier and his naturalization application was filed early August 1852, five days before the Ship Lord Ashburton landed.

My family is descended from Patrick and Mary (McGrath) Corbett who had five children; John, James Patrick, Katherine, Patrick, Jr. and Elizabeth. Michael married Honora (Hannah) McGrath and William married Catherine McGrath. Three sisters married three brothers. Michael Corbett is credited with bringing the railroad to Groveport by donating land and raising money for the effort. He also built the abutment for a bridge at Canal Winchester and there was a Corbett Hotel at one time.

James Patrick Corbett was born in Groveport in 1864 and married Mary Lou Irwin and they had four children; Mary Pauline (my grandmother), Lawrence, James and Eugene. Mary Anne Corbett descendent of William and Catherine became Sister Mary

Angelica and was a Dominican nun for 62 years serving at St. Mary of the Springs for part of these years. Paul G. (Gerry) Corbett is a descendant of William S. and Elizabeth (Clifford) Corbett and was a Dominican priest at St. Patrick's and taught history at Aquinas and counseled prisoners at the Ohio Penitentiary. Mary Jane Corbett who descended from Thomas became Sister Thomas Albert. My grandmother Pauline and her husband were vaudevillians and returned to Columbus where they had a dance studio and she was also a noted singer.

My Story
Kathleen Marie O'Brien Krutsch

My parents were both O'Briens when they married; my father, Thomas Francis O'Brien and my mother, Martha Louise O'Brien. Using some Civil War discharge papers, I was able to follow my mother's side back to Licking County, Ohio and before that, where they came from in Ireland.

My family came over in the 1840's but did not come in at Ellis Island. They settled in Newark, Ohio. My great, great grandmother, Ann McCarty, applied for a pension after her son Henry died from a heart ailment, directly related to being in several Confederate prisoner of war camps during the Civil War. Her husband left her a few years after settling in Newark and eventually died out west somewhere. Her daughter Martha married Michael O'Brien and their youngest child was my grandfather. According to my mother, my great grandfather had the first hothouse tomatoes in Ohio.

Following is what I found on the web under the History of Licking County, Ohio:

"O'BRIEN, MICHAEL, son of Clark and Ellen O'Brien, was born on February 7, 1841, Clare county, Ireland. He came with his parents to America in 1849 and first settled in Hillsboro, Ohio, remaining about one year, when they removed to Lancaster for another year, after which they located in Newark, where they have resided, principally, ever since. Mr. O'Brien lives about one mile north of the public square of Newark, on the Mt. Vernon road, where he is engaged in the gardening business. He was married to Martha McCarthy, November 5, 1861; she is the daughter of Edward and Ann McCarthy (note: it's spelled McCarthy here, but I don't think that's correct), and was born March 4, 1846, in Ireland. Her parents emigrated to America when she was quite young, and settled in York State. Mr. and Mrs. O'Brien have six children: Ella, born August 26, 1865; Elizabeth, born February 11, 1869; Anna, born November 9, 1871; Maggie, born June 28, 1874; Mary, born February 14, 1877; Edward (my grandfather), born June 17, 1879."

A few years ago, I took my daughter and my niece to find my great Uncle Henry McCarty's grave. He was the Civil War veteran mentioned before. We knew that he was buried in Mt. Calvary Cemetery in Newark, Ohio. When we arrived, we couldn't believe our eyes. It was the most beautiful cemetery we had ever seen. It was way up on a hill with a view of the town beneath. We parked and just started walking; looking at all the gravestones. Suddenly, we came upon my great grandmother's and grandfather's gravestones and several of their children's. I had no idea they were even buried there. The old stones were there, but next to them had been placed newer gravestones with perfectly legible writing. I'm not sure who replaced the old ones. Maybe it was my grandfather. I felt such a connection to my family at that moment. I stood there until my daughter and niece finally pulled me away. On the way home my niece exclaimed, "That was the MOST FUN I've EVER had at a cemetery." I had to agree with her. We never did find my great Uncle Henry's grave, but hope to in the future. I plan to make the trip again soon, as it brought me such peace and comfort; almost like meeting a long lost relative!

O'Connors, Moriartys and McGhees

William D. McGhee

Waddell family tradition, tells the story of my 2nd great grandmother Mary O'Connor. She was the daughter of Mary O'Connor née Picket and Frank O'Connor, a ship builder of some wealth, both from County Cork, Ireland.

Mary married Martin Moriarty, an Ulsterman. This marriage so angered her parents that they no longer spoke of her as their daughter.

The young couple immigrated to the United States in the early 1850's, settling first in Virginia, where their first son Michael was born in 1853. Martin worked as a laborer, moving frequently, wherever work could be found. Their second child, Ellen Monica, was born in Maryland October 18, 1856. By1870, they had settled in Mason County, West Virginia with their ten children.

In Mason County, Ellen Monica met an English coal miner, John Waddle (born May 27, 1848), who had left Liverpool, England on the Samuel Badger with his parents John and Margaret, older sister Mary, and younger brother William arriving in New York, 3 June 1853. His father then died in February 1856 at the age of 36 and brother William, age 6 a year and a half later. Ellen Monica and John were married in the church parsonage at Point Pleasant, West Virginia in September 1857. On a "Baptismal Blank" for the oldest of their three sons, Martin, was this notation for his father, "John Waddn, protestant born in England & still English". Ellen Monica and her three sons remained members of the local Catholic Church across the river in Pomeroy, Ohio.

Ellen Monica was not blessed with a long marriage, as was her mother. John was killed at the age of 41in a coal mine accident at Bridgeport Ohio, 17 days short of their 14th wedding anniversary. She however lived for another 49 years during which time she helped raise several grand daughters after her daughter-in-law died following childbirth in 1910. Ellen Monica died August 25, 1938; age 81 years, 10 months, 7 days.

George McGhee, with his wife and two sons, lived in County Westmeath, then County Tyrone, before finding it necessary to leave Ireland around 1778. Family tradition tells that one son was killed on their trip to Dublin. A third son, John, was born aboard ship. In 1817, John was indicted by the "July term" grand jury for bringing a deck of playing cards into Jackson County, Ohio and fined five dollars and costs. This did not discourage him or his wife, for they eventually settled there.

John's brother James (1783 –1858), my 3rd great grandfather, learned the milling trade from his father. He and his Irish born wife, Margaret Hazlett, after living in various locations in Pennsylvania, finally settled in Columbiana County, Ohio sometime before 1820. After a period of time, the musically talented McGhee's, who made violins and mandolins, more than likely found their musical activities stifled by their conservative minded neighbors, for they looked for greener pastures and moved. By 1832, James had purchased a large track of land around Vinton, in Gallia County, Ohio to farm. In 1852, James purchased a mill on Big Raccoon Creek, which remained in family operation until 1908, until it was no longer profitable to operate.

Descendants of Margaret and James are still using the McGhee Cemetery in Vinton, Gallia County, Ohio.

McGues Immigration

Thomas McGue Sr.

The McGues also McGough, Gough, immigrated to the U.S. in the years of the late 1850s from Killanny, Monaghan County, Ireland. My great grandfather, grandmother Hugh and Mary Halpin McGue settled in Milan, Ohio on Oak St. off route 113 west of route 250 next to Milan, Ohio. My grandfather Thomas born in Milan married Anastasia born in Cleveland, Ohio, a railroader settled in Toledo, Ohio where my father Charles was born. He married Wanda Ash; they lived most of their lives in Columbus, Ohio. In 1994 we vacationed in Ireland, visited Killanny Parish, County Monaghan and next to a cemetery we meet a 65 year old farmer getting down off a farm tractor; he pronounced his name the same as ours Michael McGough. My Great grandfather Hugh farmed about 600 acres until last great uncle died late twenties.

My wife Janet, her brother David Hartigan, and I have been members of Columbus Irish Clubs since 1986. We have two children Thomas and Mary, six grandchildren Emily, Sean, Kathryn and Benjamin with Thomas, Shelby and Paige with Mary.

279

Some of Zanesville's Irish

Elizabeth Melick

I enjoyed reading that column (Mike Harden's commentary of February 28, 2010 in the Columbus, Ohio Dispatch) referring to tracing the family stories as I have tried tracing my Irish ancestors who settled in Zanesville, Ohio. I think it may have been about 1993 or 1994 I took some classes that Mike presided over about writing memories at the Gillie Center on Morse Road and I remember how much I enjoyed meeting him and the classes he provided.

My great, great grandfather came to the US about 1864 along with his wife, children, brothers and cousins. Some went to work in the potteries in and around Muskingum County. Since I always heard that they were very poor in Ireland one wonders who paid their passages to the US and where they may have landed? The ports I located in my research were Baltimore, Castle Garden (New York) and Montreal in Canada. The surnames I was looking for are Mahaney/Mahoney and McCarty/McCarthy. Some other variations of those names were MahAney and MahOney that we found in our research.

In some of my research I have found that some coal miners' and canal builders' passages were paid to come from Germany and England because they were needed to work in those industries here. Some of the very poor were given free passage paid for by various organizations and companies and that enabled the young immigrants to send some of their earnings home to finance their siblings' passage to the United States. My great grandfather and my mothers' father both made more than one trip from their Zanesville area homes to aid in the development of the coalmines in Perry County. My son and I never researched the Irish in Perry County because the family memories referred to them as "untouchables" because they were Catholics and in the late 1800's and early 1900's they did not associate with them very much.

My son and I found and collected the names of a good many people with the surnames I was looking for in the Zanesville/Muskingum area after looking through repositories that gave information pertaining to the people in that area. The repositories we used in our research pertaining to the Mahaney/McCarty families were city directories, cemeteries, census records (1900-1910), death certificates (Ohio Historical Society Library), and newspaper obituaries. As a result of our research we found that we could make these statements; there were fourteen family groups having the surname of McCarty, McCarthy, Mahaney, MahAney, MahOney and Mahoney. While the given names of these Mahaney/McCarty family members were many and varied the most popular were Mary, John, James, Michael, and, Catherine/Katherine.

After locating as much as we could we gave a copy of our findings, which began with the genealogy of Daniel Mahaney born in in Ireland in the 1820's, to the genealogy room in Zanesville's McIntire Library. Who knows there may be one our readers who are looking someone in these families and this might be a good resource for them.

Timothy McCarty who left Zanesville moving to Clyde, Ohio demonstrated the importance of family. He was one of the descendants of Daniel Mahaney and he had come to the United States as a boy of 12 and we were told that he was a brother of that family. We remember an Uncle Tim coming to the funeral of our Grandpa Charles Mahaney in 1957. Uncle Tim told us that he had worked for the railroad and hitched a ride with a train coming through Zanesville to come to the funeral. We did the math and figured out that Uncle Tim must have been 82 years old when he did his riding the rails. Family will always show up for life's important events.

The Surprise in the Cemetery

Catherine E. Sullivan

My SULLIVAN family is from County Cork, Ireland, in a small area called Fort Grady, near Mallow. Thanks to the research of my cousins, Anna and Ken Johnson (Anna being the granddaughter of Patrick Sullivan who was also my grandfather), I was able to visit the church, St. John's, where my great-great-grandparents, Timothy Sullivan and Julia Cronin-Sullivan, were married.

As Jim Fath and I came around the corner, the church looked like a Chinese pagoda because of scaffolding all around it. There were two men working at the very top, who came all the way down just to talk to us. They were extremely hospitable and showed us how to get in the church through all of the scaffolding, and how to find the old cemetery. The cemetery was overgrown and <u>very</u>, <u>very old</u>. I was looking at a grave marker and suddenly my leg sunk into a grave! I was frantic, thinking absurdly that someone down in that grave might be trying to pull me in! Jim came to my rescue to pull me out, but I had a bruise on my shin for more than six months to prove that it really did happen.

My great-great-grandfather, Timothy Sullivan, was born in 1817 in County Cork, Ireland, Township Dromtarriff, Roman Catholic Parish of St. John's. On Feb. 4, 1845, he married Julia Cronin, born March 17, 1821, of the same Parish. A son, Bartholomew (my great-grandfather), was born on April 6, 1846, followed by John, who was born on March 6, 1852. Another son, Jeremiah, was born on April 11, 1854.

Between the years 1854 and 1859, Timothy and Julia decided that they would like to try a new life in the United States of America. On the trip to America, Julia lost a child, Timothy, named after his father. It is unknown whether Timothy was premature or not, because there was no trace of his birth in Ireland. After their arrival, Timothy and Julia had six more children as follows: Catherine (1859), William (1862), Margaret (1863), Hanora (1864), Mary Ann (1865), and another Timothy (1869).

After remaining in the eastern part of the United States for three years, the family settled in Madison County, Ohio between London and West Jefferson, on the old Washington Marks Farm in Deercreek Township. Timothy died in February 1886, at the age of 69. It is said that three or four children died, along with Timothy, from typhoid fever. They were buried in Mount Calvary Cemetery, Madison County, West Jefferson, Ohio. Most of the children were schoolteachers in the area.

My Ohio Irish Ancestry

Linda Archer Tiffany

Early in Ohio's history as a state, my ancestor James Archer the 1st, and his ten children moved from Marshall County, Virginia and established a small community near East Union, Ohio, called "Archer's Settlement."

James 1 was the son of Patrick Archer, who was born in Ireland around 1717. James was also born in Ireland, around 1747. The family arrived in the United States through Maryland, living in Frederick County, Maryland for a time. By 1774, they settled near Waynesburg, Pennsylvania. Howard B. Leckey, in his book, *The Tenmile Country and Its Pioneer Families*, quoted from the Journal of William Rhodes, a New Englander who bought the trading post at Ft. Jackson, Pennsylvania from James in 1785:

"The first owner of this plantation or Patent called White Oak Bottom was James Archer. His father, Patrick Archer, and mother were Roman Irish, a weaver by trade. Their children were James, Michael, Simon, Joseph, Jacob, Polly, Bett and Nancy. East of the mountains they were Poor Ridge Romans. The eldest son, James, was a roving hunter with the Indians before the colonies revolted from their step-mother, Britain."

At the time of the Revolutionary War, James joined the local militia as an enlisted soldier and rose to captain of one of the units.

James and his oldest sons, James, Jr. and Joseph, bought land and moved to Ohio County, (West) Virginia around 1798. Around 1803 or 1804, they moved to what is now Noble County, Ohio. James was a devout Irish Catholic, but there were no Catholic churches in the area. For many years, traveling priests from Virginia served the faith community. The residents held services in James' home and later in his son Michael's barn. His children described James as a "zealous exemplary Catholic, much given to prayer." Sometime during the 1820s, James' daughter Nancy fell in love with and married a Methodist minister. This created a split in the family as she and her husband managed to convert three of her brothers to the Protestant faith. The other three brothers, including my ancestor, Michael, remained Catholic. In 1841, Michael donated land for a church. Under the direction of Rev. William Peter Murphy, Michael and the community built St. Michael's Catholic Church in Carlisle, Ohio. An article by Silas Thorla in *The Journal and Noble Co. Leader*, bicentennial edition, 3 July 1975, page.6, states, "From the time of their arrival, the Archers maintained religious worship after the rule of the Catholic church. Their little church society has been kept up ever since and in the period from 1803 to the present, they have erected three church buildings. This church society has had an unbroken existence from then to the present and we claim for it, that it is the oldest Catholic Church society in Ohio."

My source for the above information is George W. Archer, an Archer family historian. He states that this Archer family is the only Irish Catholic immigrant family by the name "Archer" that he has discovered so far. He obtained some of his material from an earlier source, a book by Martin Archer, a Probate Judge in Noble Country, Ohio. Martin Archer published the book, "The Genealogical History of the Archer Family", in the early 1900s. Martin Archer collected much of his information in interviews with Archer family members.

Michael's son Abraham, my great-great grandfather, married Mary Sterrett on October 8, 1835 in St. Mary's Church, Temperanceville, Ohio. Abraham died in 1847. His grave is in the cemetery of Old St. Michael's Church. After Abraham's death, Mary remarried and moved to Cass County, Nebraska with her children and new husband. Her son was my great grandfather, Alfred Harvey Archer. His son Melvin Lee, my grandfather, was a rancher in western Nebraska before buying a general store in Wheeler, Kansas. My father, Harold Lee Archer, was a World War II veteran. He and my mother moved to Colorado following the war. I was born and raised in Colorado.

Tracing the Archer Name through County Kilkenny

Linda Archer Tiffany

We do not know where Patrick and his family came from in Ireland. I have been looking into the Archer name in Irish records. One of the sources for the Archer name in Ireland is the old Gaelic, *O'Urcha*. Another is a Norman version, *le Archer*.

Recently when my husband and I were in Ireland, we discovered that the Archer name was prominent in County Kilkenny. We looked up articles at the Dublin library on that family and discovered an interesting history. They were part of a Catholic confederation that tried to stop Oliver Cromwell from taking over Ireland in the 1650s. Since they were unsuccessful, many of the Archers forfeited their land. Those who did not lose their property under Cromwell lost it under William of Orange in 1702 for supporting the Jacobite cause.

An article in the *Old Kilkenny Review* told about an interesting Archer priest, Father James Archer, who was ordained around 1581. He was said to have had great influence over the Irish nobles and chieftains. Following the Reformation, Father Archer refused to adopt the new religion. The nobles who had adopted Protestantism regarded him as a traitor. He was captured and imprisoned in London in 1590, but he escaped. He returned to Waterford in 1596 and took the name of Bowman. He avoided recapture, although he had some narrow escapes.

In 1600, Father Archer was said to be a constant companion to Black Thomas, the Earl of Ormonde, during his imprisonment by O'More, an Irish chief. Father Archer converted the imprisoned Earl, who was a cousin to Queen Elizabeth I, to Catholicism. The Earl claimed regret that he had ruined his country in his youth and that in his old age could not defend it or his religion.

Father Archer was one of the defenders of the Castle of Dunboy when English forces besieged it in 1602. This siege occurred at the end of the Nine Year War waged under Elizabethan rule to conquer Ireland. Father Archer was one of the few defenders who escaped. He went to Spain and founded the Irish College in Salamanca in 1592.

I am proud of my Irish ancestry and look forward to continuing the research. We hope someday to be able to trace our forefathers, Patrick and James, back to the motherland.

Doyle

Peg Doyle Zurface

Bhi `me Beich `me!
"I was and I will be"
Doyle family Motto

The foundation for the family of Thomas Francis Doyle of County Carlow, Ireland and Mary Catherine Flynn of County Tipperary, Ireland began on June 27, 1878. Kate and Thomas were united in Holy Matrimony by Rev. Father Moorissey at St. Mary's Catholic Church in the small picturesque town of An Clolchin, Clogheen, Ireland. There to witness this occasion were Kate's sister, Margaret Flynn and David Condon. We can only speculate that there were others to witness this marriage including the parents of Kate, Mary Fitzgerald Flynn and Edmund Flynn both of Clogheen, Ireland.

Mary Catherine was born Sept. 29, 1859 in Clogheen, County Tipperary, Ireland. Thomas Francis Doyle was born March 1859 in County Carlow, Ireland. Their first child was Kieran Doyle born February 18, 1880. According to records he was baptized in February 1880 at St. Mary's Church in Clogheen. Sponsors were Margaret Flynn and Francis Collins.

During the year of 1880, leaving their son, Kieran in the care of Mary's family, the "Flynn's", Kate and Tom, immigrated to the United States. These hardworking people brought with them their faith, their work ethic and the deep abiding hope for a better life. After reaching America, Thomas and Kate settled in Columbus, Ohio. The September 1880 census documents that Kate and Thomas were living on Hamlet Street. They also lived at 1045 North Fourth St.

During the 1880's their seven children were born:
Kieran b. Feb. 18, 1880, in Ireland
Mary Catherine (Mame) b. Nov. 22, 1883

Helen	*(Nell)*	b. Mar. 26, 1886
John	*(Jack)*	b. Oct. 21, 1887
Edward	*(Eddie)*	b. May 1889
Marguerite	*(Mam)*	b. Jul. 17, 1895
Frank	*(Bun)*	b. Aug. 4, 1897

On Saturday, August 11, 1906 "The Columbus Dispatch" and "Citizen" reported the following: "as the result of a fall from the cornice of a home at 358 Mosette Street, about 10 o'clock Friday morning, Thomas Doyle aged 47 years, died four hours later at his home on 1045 North Fourth Street. Mr. Doyle had been a resident of the north side for 26 years and was a member of the Builders and Traders exchange. He is survived by his widow Catherine and six children: Kieran, Mary, Nellie, Marguerite, Frank and John. The funeral services will be held Monday at 8:30a.m. with the Reverend Father J.B. Eis officiating. The Interment will be made in Mount Calvary."

Catherine Flynn Doyle died at the age of 83 on September 4, 1943 at her home on Wyandotte Avenue in Grandview. She is buried next to Thomas in Mount Calvary Cemetery. My grandmother, Mary Catherine Doyle, was the second child of Kate and Thomas. At the age of 24 she married Robert Dow b. 1879. Robert's parents were Abraham Dow b. May 10, 1831 in Montreal, Canada and Sarah M. Noe b. February 2, 1836. Noe-Bixby Road was named after her family. Abraham, a brick maker, homesteaded what is now the Ohio State Fairgrounds. The property was sold to the state in the late 1800s. Dow Street is located just south of 11th Avenue. The Dow family monument and burial grounds are located in Greenlawn Cemetery. There is still to this day a Dow brick company in Bucyrus, Ohio (connection or relationship unknown).

Mame and Robert had six children:

Delores Fay	b. May 18, 1907	
Robert	b. Jul. 23, 1909	d. Apr. 10, 1989
Catherine	b. Mar. 29, 1913	d. 1993
Margaret Dorothy	b. Aug. 3, 1911	d. Apr. 23, 1912
Charles Albert	b. Apr. 7, 1915	d. Apr. 7, 1915

Helen Ann   b. Mar. 22, 1918   d. Mar. 4, 2002

May 8, 1918 Mary Catherine Doyle Dow passed away due to tuberculosis (TB). She was survived by her husband Robert and four children: Faye, Robert, Catherine, and infant daughter Helen Ann. Robert's mother Sarah Noe also passed away May 16, 1918. Robert and his sister Nell Dow raised Faye, Robert and Catherine. Helen Ann was raised by her maternal grandmother Kate Doyle and her aunt Marguerite Doyle-Dickman.

Helen Ann married Charles Coleman Jones

They had six children:

Sharon Ann	b. Sep. 3, 1945	
Charles David	b. Oct. 7, 1946	d. Jan. 10, 1988
Mary Sandra	b. Jan. 20, 1950	
Paul William	b. Sep. 10, 1951	
Donald Martin	b. Sep. 9, 1952	
Marguerite Patricia	b. Oct. 2, 1953	

Helen Ann Dow passed away March 4, 2002 and is buried next to her beloved Aunt Mame, in St. Joseph Cemetery.

Marguerite Patricia Jones, married Donald Lee Zurface of Fayette Co. on July 29, 1977 at Saint Paul the Apostle Catholic Church in Westerville, Ohio. Marguerite (Peg) and Donald have two daughters:

Hillary Dawn Zurface   b. Jan. 5, 1984

Amanda Marguerite Zurface   b. Mar. 3, 1987

They reside on a farm in Fayette Co., living in the Humphrey Jones house that was constructed in 1902. Marguerite has been teaching art for the past 25 years. The Zurface family has successfully farmed land in Wayne Township, Fayette County, since the early part of the 20th century. The primary products have been corn and hogs.

The genealogy of the Doyle family is quite extensive and widely scattered. Thomas and Kate would be so proud of the many accomplishments of their children, grandchildren, great-grandchildren and great-great grandchildren. Several members of the Doyle-Flynn lineage live in Columbus, Ohio and the surrounding counties. Many others in the Doyle clan are scattered throughout the United States. These states include: Arizona, California, Colorado, Illinois, Florida, Maine, and New York. Many have attended colleges and universities throughout the country and world including Ohio State University, Ohio University, University of Dayton, Cornell University, Ohio Dominican University, and the Pontifical University of Saint Thomas Aquinas in Rome, Italy. There exist a wide variety of vocations amongst all of us. We are teachers, artists, doctors, lawyers, theologians, nurses, and have given ourselves in service to our God, country and world. We have accomplished Kate's and Thomas Doyle's deep abiding hope for a better life. All this because two people fell in love!

This and That

Becky Ellis' Comments on her Irish Links

Becky Ellis

Becky feels her Irish Links are very minimal and yet they must be strong enough to become an active member of the Daughters of Erin

As a child Becky lived in Zanesville over east in Muskingum County and the family often traveled to Columbus via the road through Somerset in Perry County. In Somerset there is a town square in the center of town with a statue of one of Somerset's favorite sons, General Phillip Sheridan of Civil War fame and of Irish ancestry. As the Ellis car would round the Somerset town square Becky's mother would always call out to the children to say "Hello Cousin Phil" as they passed by his statue. Now Becky isn't sure if she is really related to "Cousin Phil" or if her mother was exhibiting Irish good humor, but whatever the situation, she feels Irish.

Speaking about her tenuous Irish links Becky recalls that she was always told to plant lettuce on St. Patrick's Day because Aunt Rosie always did her planting on the good saint's feast day and it was known that Aunt Rosie's was the best green lettuce in Zanesville.

However thin Becky's ties to the Irish are they bind her to them and that's a good thing.

A Questionable Date

J. Michael Finn

In the story about James Gormley, the railroad man, who drove Lincoln's funeral train to Columbus a mention is made about the date of Mr. Gormley's birth as being the same as the date of Ohio's Big Wind. The Big Wind is an event often mentioned in Ohio Lore and is recorded as happening on the night of January 6 and 7, 1839 yet James' birth was recorded as being January 9, 1839 not exactly the same date but close. A story that Mr. Tom O'Keefe, a local historian, never mentioned to us.

The Origin of Grogan

J. Michael Finn

The following obituary appeared in the Catholic Columbian May 21, 1927

John Patrick Grogan, age 72, life-long resident of Columbus, who had been in the grocery business for 44 years on Cleveland Avenue died at his home, 828 East Eleventh Avenue, Monday, May 17.

He was proprietor of the Grogan Community Store at 1355-57 Cleveland Avenue and president of the Columbus Swing Company. The community in the neighborhood of his store was known as Grogan before it was taken into the city, having been named for him, and the post office was known as the Grogan post office.

Mr. Grogan was a charter member of the Knights of Columbus, a member of the Catholic Knights of Ohio, the Ancient Order of Hibernians, and a trustee of St. Peter's Church.

Surviving Mr. Grogan are his wife, Mrs. Julia Grogan; two sons, Joseph D. Grogan and Francis Grogan; two daughters, Mrs. Sylvester Grogan of Columbus and Mrs. Clyde Walters of South Charleston, West Virginia; brother Thomas Grogan of Cleveland, and two sisters, Miss Mary Grogan, of Columbus and Mrs. John Byrne, Shawnee.

Funeral services were held at 9 o'clock Wednesday morning from St. Peter's Church with a solemn requiem Mass. Internment in Mt. Calvary Cemetery.

OLD IRISHTOWN, A Memory of the Past

David H Hartigan

St. Patrick's Church still stands as a monument to those few of the good old days who answered its bell. Dear old Irish folks: they were good old souls; but now they have nearly all crossed the Great Divide. Never again will you meet them winding their way up the old street - Naghten Street - Once called Irish Broadway - towards St. Patrick's Church for worship. Never again at parting will you hear their "Good Bye and God Bless You" an expression so dear to the hearts of all those old Irish born. Those dear old house parties they used to have in Irishtown are a thing of the past. Gone Forever.

The Moon shining through the windows on a Summer's starlight night, and all would be merry within. Boys and girls of the neighborhood gathered together to dance and sing those Irish songs they loved so well. The old folks would join in and dance the Irish Reels upon the parlor floor of their humble homes.

An Irishman having been gone for a long time paid a visit to his old home town. Going out Irish Broadway, passing the old school and church where he studied and worshiped as a boy, he paused to look into the school yard. In fancy he could picture Mike, Jerry, Jimmie and Jack at play. I wonder where they are today. With sadness in his heart and tears in his eyes, he left the scene a sad and lonely old man. Retracing his steps back down the old street, he was impressed with these thoughts:

> There is a street in the town of Columbus,
> They used to call Irish Broadway.
> Where the folks that came over from Ireland
> All settled so happy and gay.
>
> T'was there my old father and mother brought me up
> From a child, but to-day as I walk down that
> Old street, not a soul do I meet.
> My comrades have all passed away.
>
> And I sigh when I think of the changes,
> Now that I am 'feeble and gray,
> When I see my old home,
> As I walk all alone,
> Down that street that they call
> IRISH BROADWAY.

Pat Bloor, Aster Hotel, Columbus, 0

A friend of Past President Dick Bolton, John McLaughen who lives in Urbana, Ohio, passed this well worn copy on to him. It had been written on carbon paper quite some time ago. The

Aster Hotel was located at 32 East Main St. according to the 1940 Polk's Columbus City Directory. I was unable to find Pat Bloor listed in the early Shamrock Club Directories.

"Going Home"
Mary Higgins

Many Americans refer to their visit to Ireland as "going home". My mom sure did. Here's why...

My mother, Carol Devine Higgins, and I were visiting Ireland for the first time in 1989. As we were strolling down O'Connell Street in Dublin on the afternoon of one of their bank holidays, we noticed (we could hear their talk) quite a few visitors from Italy and Germany. Mom turned to me and asked,"What are these foreigners doing here in Ireland?"

Yes, she was home, alright!

O'Shaughnessy's Taunt Brings Green Beer
Published in The Columbus Dispatch, March 16, 1935
By: W. F. McKinnon

There may be no connection at all and most assuredly there is none - but it is something akin to deep coincidence that as water rippled over the crest of the O'Shaughnessy Dam a few days ago beer in vats of the Washington brewery turned green. Therein lies the foundation for whatever follows.

Today there is on sale as a gesture from a worthy German brewmaster toward the patron saint of Ireland, a brew that is as green as the grass that grows along Kilarney's lakes.

It is the result of 20 years of experimentation by Brewmaster John Schott, who conceived the idea of sparkling green beer from a jibe thrust at him at St. Patrick's day banquet by the late Jerry O'Shaughnessy, whose memory has been perpetuated by naming Columbus' largest reservoir for him.

Said Jerry to Schott: "John why don't you produce a green beer in honor of St. Patrick?"

John said little but in the recesses of his memory he tucked away the suggestion. Came prohibition and his experiments in producing a sparkling green beer were halted.

Then when the ban of prohibition vanished Schott returned to his vats and malts and yeast. He recalled that jibe of 20 years ago.

Today or tomorrow if you happen to raise your glass of green beer in toast of Old Erin, you will be drinking a brewed liquid that has as its base, water that one day flowed over the gigantic monument named after the father of the Columbus waterworks system and who in jest inspired Brewmaster Schott to give to the Washington brewery the distinction of being the only firm in the world producing such a reminder that Sunday, March 17, is Ireland's day the world over.

So, Jerry, here's to your memory and the days when, with the Murphys and the Callahans and the Egans and the Ryans you marched, high hat, blackthorn cane and all, rain or shine, to high mass at old St. Patrick's.

The Spirit of Erin - J. J. O'Keeffe

Patricia D. O'Keeffe Ciotola

He came from Carrick by the Suir,
And played a noble part:
With Irish blood still coursing through
His young and manly heart.

The colors of the U.S.A. with distinction
Long he served,
A commissary officer, a rank he well deserved.

O'er many lands he wandered.
To Ireland ever true.
As proudly he pondered on
What Irish men could do.

A splendid type of manhood,
A soul that could embrace

This and That

With all a father's tenderness,
The exiles of his race.

A genial, dear companion,
A true and generous friend:
With sorrowing hearts
We mourn his sad untimely end.

His thoughts were ever turning
To Erin for the West.
And with fond desire was burning
That same day he'd rest.

Kind fate did grant his wishes,
Tho' destined far to roam,
He died just in the prime of his life
On a visit to his home.

In Erin's bosom now he lies,
Where his life came to a close,
In the graveyard of Kilsheelan
He takes his long repose.

The hallowed shades of sweet Gurteen,
And the Suir's lovely view,
Make an ideal; and beauteous scene
For a patriot so true.

This anonymous poem was sent to Patricia D. O'Keeffe from Thomas O'Keefe in remembrance of her grandfather John Joseph O'Keeffe. John J. O'Keeffe was born December 28, 1869 – died December 7, 1909.

A Skillful Teacher

Fr. Jerome P. Rodenfels

My great, great aunt Rose Hanratty Callahan was an Irish immigrant to the United States in the late 1800's. Aunt Rose eventually settled in the Columbus area. She was a skillful seamstress and taught Michael Ryan how to sew. Michael became a tailor and opened his own shop on N. High St. He then decided to change careers and became a funeral director. This anecdote was told to me by my mother, Mary Frances Hanratty Rodenfels.

Dancing Shoes

Fr. Jerome P. Rodenfels

My maternal grandmother Rose A. Hanratty and her sister Kathleen Hanratty would bring down the house in the second decade of the 20th century (1912 – 1916/7). They would get up on the stage and dance at the St. Patrick celebrations in Columbus. They may not have been scheduled to dance and they were likely coaxed to perform but everybody who saw the enjoyed their performances.

I have found it interesting that they never taught my mother's generation any of their dances. The interest in Irish dancing skipped a generation and I started doing Irish dancing in 1980 and kept dancing until 1991. I stopped dancing and then resumed dancing for several more years in 2001-2003. At that time I ended my dancing days.

Irish in German Village

Barb Specht

My family was the "missionary's among" the Germans, as we fondly referred to ourselves. Our grandmother, Nellie Dempsey, ran a boarding house at 925 Mohawk St.. She was in St. Mary's Parish but was buried at the cemetery near St.Patrick's Church at Naghten and Grant. They came to Columbus from Erie, Pennsylvania.

Mark Dempsey, who I think is a fourth generation Dempsey, and I put together the story of the Shamrock clubs' blarney stone. Perhaps he will share it with you.

Slaint

Irish-American Organizations in

Central Ohio

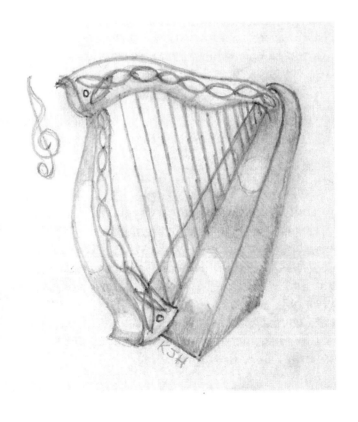

The Columbus Celtic Chorus

Bob Donnelly

I'd like to spend a few minutes talking about our Columbus Celtic Chorus. Like so many things associated with the Shamrock Club there is a long tradition that belongs to singing. If you look on the wall in the pub you will see a picture of the Glee Club, a time when the singing group was a Men-only affair.

I joined the Glee Club almost 30 years ago in 1981 and have been a member since. Bob Cain was Director. We had probably 20 members. We practiced at St. Pats on Monday nights. At that time the DOE was also putting together a group and Bob would lead their practice after he finished with the men.

Jerry Mc Vey was Glee Club President and he somehow embraced the idea that combining practice with the women would be worth a try. From then on we had a combined group with sopranos, altos, tenors and basses. Mariellen and Nancy Russell had served the men as accompanist and librarian for many years and they continue today.

Some memorable people belonged to the singers group; Duke Hinton, Murt Byrne, Pat Walsh, Bob Griffin, Jerry Grady ,and myself, were all Shamrock Club presidents; Marita Surry and Karen Komatsu, DOE presidents. If your name was Jim chances are you were a member; Jim Markum, Jim Maher, Jim Creighton, Jim Moore, Jim McElroy, Some venerable old timers were with the group when I joined; Jim Kennedy, Ted Dempsey, Pat Shane, Al Sheridan, and some stalwarts were long time members, John O'Connor, Judge John Connor, Chuck Wrenn, Ed Norris, Dennis Donovan, and Bill Bannon.

And let's not forget the Ladies; Nora Dorrian, Jeanette Ford, Jeanne McFee, Lynne Gatton, Joanna Brands, Jan McCarty, Maggie(Morrison) Shroyer, Annie(Sullivan) Curran, Jane Garvey, Julie Davis, and Judy Statmiller .

There were lots of husband/wife members; Frank and Betty Curran, Jim and Betty Creighton, Bob and Marilyn Cain, Joe and Mary Hennessey, Matt and Mary Starrett, Al and Irene Cassidy, Ted and Sal Cook, and Bob and Ellie Griffin.

Some were family affairs - Penny Rice and her sons Patrick and David, Frank and Betty Curran's kids Joe and Barb, Bob and Marilyn's son Kevin, Mike O'Keefe, his son Mike Jr. and wife Katie who directed for several years, me and my daughter Katie.

We brought Irish music to many places in Columbus and elsewhere. We were regular performers at numerous community events - Labor Day weekend at the Germania Oktoberfest, Thanksgiving at the Festival of Trees, the spring festival at Maennerchor, The Huron Ohio summer festival. We did opening ceremonies for the Feis both at St. Charles and later Dublin, before it became the Dublin Festival. We performed for the Geantrai at Ohio Dominican, and we were a major part of the cast for Joe Conley's musical Rollie.

In the fall we had a Christmas theme show and in the early spring an Irish show that we took on the road to retirement and nursing homes doing repeated performances at St. Rita's, St. Raphael's, Nazareth Towers, Mohun Hall, K of C kids party, Clearview Convalescent, Friendship Village, Knightsbridge, Eastland Care, and Isabelle Ridgeway.

A few years back Vivien Lermonde help put together our major fund raiser, a Christmas Concert. We continue doing it today with the help of Dawn Peterson.

We are most dedicated to singing for Irish Masses, primarily St. Patrick's Day and Proclamation Day. If we counted all the hours we spent in choir lofts practicing and performing at St. Pat's, the Cathedral, St. Mary's, St. Christopher's, St. Leo's, St. Stephen's, Corpus Christi, Holy Family, Holy Cross and other churches I would estimate it would total over a month's time.

We appreciate the support we receive from the Shamrock Club. This year in 2011 we have sufficient funds available to show that appreciation with this donation of $500.

Mr. President we thank you for all the support from you and the Shamrock Club.

Conradh na Gaeilge í Lár Ohio
The Gaelic League of Central Ohio

J. Michael Finn

The roots of the Gaelic League of Central Ohio began in 1987 when two self-taught Irish speakers, Ron Crow and Larry O'Callan came together to speak Irish. It was Ron Crow's idea to gather a group of Irish speakers and form a group that would begin teaching the Irish language to others in the community.

Pat Flanagan and his uncle, Father Andrew Nugent, joined the small group, who met at the Columbus Public Library. Soon it was decided to organize a beginning Irish language class. Advertising brochures were prepared to promote the class with the slogan, *"Learn Irish Before St. Patrick's Day."*

On January 11, 1988 the first Irish language class was begun. It was a 10-week class and was held at St. Patrick's Social Hall. Over 20 people signed up for the first class. Many Gaelic League charter members came form that class, such as, Anne Daly Flanagan, Michael Finn and Gail Westbrook.

When the first class ended many of the participants continued to meet in order to further their education in the language. On April 11, 1988 an organizational meeting was held. Conradh na Gaelige í Lár Ohio was officially established and elections were held. Ron Crow was elected President (Ard Rí) and Pat Flanagan was elected Treasurer.

The Gaelic League began a period of remarkable success. With humble beginnings and not a lot of members, the Gaelic League began planning its first public event – an Irish language Mass. The first Mass was held on Sunday, June 12, 1988 at Our Lady of Peace Church in Columbus, Ohio. The Gaelic League's good friend and spiritual guide, Monsignor Donal O'Carroll, celebrated the Mass, held in honor of St. Columcille. The Gaelic League members did the readings and provided the music and songs for the Mass. Initial fears by the group that no one would show up were proven unfounded when over 200 people packed the church.

This service was the first Irish language Mass held in a parish church in Columbus.

The first Mass generated considerable public interest in the language. So much so that a second beginning class was scheduled for June 27, 1988 at the Shamrock Club hall in Columbus. It was also a 10-week course and added Paul and Kathy Krumm to the small but dedicated group of Irish speakers.

The Gaelic League continued to grow and became not merely an organization but a group of friends, all working together toward a common goal. More Irish language beginning and advanced classes were scheduled and the group officially became a branch of the Gaelic League parent organization in Ireland. In 1989 the group participated as a unit in the Columbus St. Patrick's Day parade, proudly displaying its homemade banner. That year it also issued its first newsletter, *An Páipéar Bán*. A trip to Ireland followed in July 1989. Its first Irish Language Masses held outside of Franklin County were held at Dayton (1989) and Steubenville (1990). By 1992 the group had organized a total of five Irish language Masses.

On January 17, 1992 the first Douglas Hyde Birthday Party was held at St. Patrick's Social Hall. Named for Douglas Hyde (1860-1949), Irish Language scholar, who co-founded the Gaelic League in 1893. A dinner was held, followed by a Traditional Music session. It was the public response to this music session that would convince the Ancient Order of Hibernians to add Irish traditional music to its regular entertainment schedule at Tara Hall. Traditional music has since become a staple of Irish groups in Columbus.

On January 23, 1992 the first Irish History Roundtable was held at the Grandview Municipal Building. For the next four years this began a Gaelic League institution that met in many places, most often at Ohio Dominican College. It is no longer in operation.

In May 1994 the Gaelic League sponsored its first Gaelteacht Weekend at the P.I.M.E. Seminary in Newark, Ohio. The three-day Irish immersion weekend drew over 23 participants. On November

14, 1998 the Gaelic League conducted its first out of state Mass held in Wheeling, West Virginia.

Each year the group schedules new beginning Irish language classes. In recent years the demand for the language has been sufficient that two beginning classes can be held. Also, the group began doing demonstrations of Irish wake activities at the annurl Dublin Irish Festival. Now the Wake Tent is a regular festival feature.

The Gaelic League of Central Ohio continues as a smaller but no less active group teaching Irish, gathering together to speak the language and holding Gaeltacht Weekends.

Ron Crow's idea has become a major part of the Columbus and Ohio Irish cultural scene. Those who were around before 1988 know that this small band of friends has forever changed the Irish cultural landscape of Columbus.

The Gaelic League has trained over 1,500 people in the Irish language, exposed many to Irish History, conducted over 25 Irish language Masses and is responsible for the revival of Irish traditional music in Columbus, Ohio.

"Gaeilge Abu!"

The Irish Living History Society of Central Ohio

Lynne Cahill Gatton

The Irish Living History Society of Central Ohio was formed in 1997 by Lynne and Don Gatton, along with other interested folks in the Irish community in an effort to further educate themselves and the public about life as it was in Early Medieval Christian Ireland. Our time period (950 A.D. - 1014 A.D.) is the time of Brian Boru, and is also called "The Viking Age". Our first members included Fr. Stephan Hayes as authenticity officer and Ron Crow our Irish linguist and the first meeting was held at the Ancient Order of Hibernian's Tara Hall Pub, located on the top floor of the old Social Hall at St. Patrick's in downtown Columbus, Ohio. This had become a gathering place for those interested in Irish Culture.

Irish-American Organizations in Central Ohio

Our talented group of re-enactors include: blacksmiths, woodworkers, textile workers, a seanachie (Irish Storyteller) and herbalist, musicians, cooks and bakers, warriors, and scripters and religious.

The first activity the group participated in was the Dublin Irish Festival in Dublin, Ohio in 1998. Our goal was to portray an Irish community with demonstrations and displays of various household, martial and artistic activities. At the time, our "home" consisted of two tents rented for us by Dublin: a 39ft round tent and a 10' X 10' "abbey". Since that time, our area has expanded to include many more tents, props, and wattle fencing, including period beds, weapons, a currach (small fishing boat) and even a king's throne! Most of our props were lost in a fire in 2009, but were redone in time for the Dublin Festival in 2010.

Although the Dublin Irish Festival continues to be our main event, we have also participated in a smaller way at these venues:

- OSU Medieval and Renaissance Festival
- Rio Grande Tri-Valley Celtic Festival
- Cashman Celtic Festival
- Shamrock Club Music Festival
- Memphis in May
- Pittsburgh Irish Festival
- Granville Irish Festival
- Lancaster Irish Festival
- Ashville Viking Festival

Some of our other activities include various workshops to further educate ourselves in the crafts that we demonstrate, and participating in the Columbus and Dublin St. Patrick's Day parades. We also have a bonfire in September. One of our most popular events is the 12th Night Feast in January, which includes music, dancing and storytelling along with mead and a potluck of delicious medieval dishes.

Our past presidents: Lynne Gatton, Mia Gatton, Thomas Powers, Terry Griner, Pete Gerrity, and Bob Tatz.

The Daughters of Erin
Maggie Grove and Mary Grady Strickland

Mary Kathleen Grady and Mary Margaret ("Maggie") Grove co-founded the Daughters of Erin. They attended grade school and high school together and are both from very Irish families. For years they celebrated St. Patrick's Day with the Shamrock Club – by watching the parade from the sidelines and standing at the back of the church during the Mass. But that was not enough for them. At the July, 1978 Shamrock Club picnic, they were informed that a vote had been taken on whether or not to admit women to the Shamrock Club. The women lost. Next a vote was taken on whether or not to allow non-Irish, non-Catholic men into the Shamrock Club. The men won. Needless to say, Mary and Maggie were not happy. That was when they decided that there must be other women out there who also wanted to join together to share their Irish heritage.

The first step was to find out how many women would be interested in an Irish women's organization. What better place to start looking than their own families! And there they found Helen Daughtery Grady; Mary Daugherty Fowle; Patty Grove and Dorothy Gallen. Together with Helen Burwell, Mary Foley Underwood, Ruth Sweetman and Mary Sweetman Ferguson, the ten Charter Members created the Daughters of Erin ("DOE").

Hundreds of fliers were sent to women of Irish heritage announcing the formation of an Irish women's organization. The first meeting was held on October 15, 1978 at 2 p.m. in St. Patrick's Social Hall. On that day the Charter Members established the goals of the Daughters of Erin; to establish an organization for women who want to share their Irish heritage, to increase our knowledge of the customs of Ireland, and to help make contributions to charitable organizations within our community.

Janet Scanlon, grandmother of Maggie, Patty and Dorothy, provided us with our name – the Daughters of Erin.

During our first year we accomplished many things. Our membership grew from 10 to 184. We had our first picnic, began the newsletter and gave $1,500 to the Vinton County St. Francis

Center. And, on March 17, 1979, the ladies marched for the first time in the St. Patrick's Day parade and when they entered St. Patrick's Church, they were led down the aisle to the front pew!

The support of Bob Griffin, then president of the Shamrock Club, and his officers, Joe Byrne, George O'Donnell and Tom O'Keefe, was invaluable. They welcomed the DOE to the Irish community even though there were quite a few men at that time that thought the organization just didn't belong. These men made our road a little less rocky by involving the DOE in all the Irish functions around town. As time has shown, not only did the DOE benefit by the help of the Shamrock Club but the Shamrock Club has accomplished more because of our joint effort to make Columbus a true Irish community.

The DOE has continued to grow and carry out the goals of the founders. The Daughters of Erin works together to raise funds for those who have needs and over the years, the Daughters have given $ 320,000 over the last 32 years to charitable causes in our community. We have given to over 50 non-profit organizations since 1978. The members volunteer in the name of the DOE for many worthy causes, scholarships have been granted to the Irish Way program, high school and college students, events promoting Irish culture and heritage or raising money for charity are sponsored on a regular basis. Annually the entire membership works to adopt families in need providing a Thanksgiving meal and Christmas gifts and dinner. Our fund raisers have included yard sales, style shows, raffles, parties, OSU football games, numerous plays and the annual Irish Breakfast.

The DOE has been compared to a garden. Mary and Maggie planted the seed, but the members have watered, fertilized, weeded and cultivated that seed to ensure that it will continue to blossom and flourish for years to come.

Shamrock Club Pipes and Drums

David H. Hartigan and Mic Trenor

February 12, 1961: During a General Meeting of the Shamrock Club of Columbus, Jim Foley raised the motion of raising the dues to $2.00.

Thus started the Shamrock Club Pipes & Drums. Pat Canty had a vision for a grand Irish Pipe Band here in Central Ohio. I am proud to report that Mr. Canty's vision is alive and well. Like any great organization, the Shamrock Club Pipes & Drums had a slow start. Over the next four years, votes would be carried and passed, objected and tabled, and discussions would be had over a Pipe Band. As irony would have it. Mr. Canty never had the chance to see the fruits of his labor but on the 17th of March 1964 the physical presence of The Shamrock Pipes & Drums took to the streets with a single piper – Francis Patrick McGuire leading the parade. The following year Mr. McGuire would be joined by piper Dave Hartigan. In 1966, on the 17th of March, The Pipes & Drums of the Shamrock Club of Columbus had arrived. Its members consisting of Patrick McGuire, and Dave Hartigan on pipes, Tom Enright on snare, Bill O'Conner on tenor and Chuck Bell playing bass.

In its early days, in accordance with Irish tradition, the Pipe Band was called the Drums and Pipes of the Shamrock Club of Columbus. Many have forgotten the history, but in fact the bagpipe was the national instrument of Ireland and the Harp the national instrument of Scotland. Somewhere in the early days of history the two countries had adopted each other's instruments as their own. Today, we call the Pipe Band the Shamrock Club Pipes & Drums purely based on modern tradition.

The Shamrock Club Pipes & Drums have been fortunate enough to have many great members of the piping community enter and influence their ranks. The likes of Bob Ryan, Dave Gettinby, and John Rechnagle have benefitted the band. Drummers the likes of Ed Cotter, Roger Brown and Tom Enright have certainly helped us keep our beat. We have a deep gratitude to our Scottish cousins in the Capitol City Pipes and drums with whose support and the encouragement and influence of people like David Daye, Glenn Harriman and the Father of Piping in Central Ohio, Robert Bobby Peters.

The Pipe Band consists of 28 musicians from all walks of life. We practice weekly and perform throughout the year as various venues. So that today you have The Shamrock Club Pipes & Drums here in Central Ohio.

The Shamrock Club of Columbus
Update on the History of the Shamrock Club

David H. Hartigan

The conceptual meeting of the Shamrock Club occurred in the back room of the Egan–Ryan Funeral Home on March 10, 1936. There after some discussion, the new organization was named the "Shamrock Club" by Anthony J. Scanlon in the presence of Michael J. Ryan Jr., George P. Ryan and Joseph E. Ryan.

The original purpose of the Shamrock Club was to celebrate Saint Patrick's Day in a Catholic manner. In order for a gentleman to be eligible to join the club it was necessary that he be "a practicing Catholic of Irish descent".

On Saint Patrick's Day March 17, 1936 about twenty (20) men marched behind the Friendly Sons of Saint Patrick in the parade. George P. Ryan had made a pasteboard sign with SHAMROCK CLUB written on it and George attached it to a stick and it was carried in the parade by Paul Sullivan, son of Ed Sullivan, then about fourteen (14) years old.

On April 20, 1936 the Shamrock Club was organized in the Blind Room of the Knights of Columbus building, at Sixth and State Streets. At this meeting it was decided that a group of five men should leave the meeting and go to James A. Devine's home to plead with him to be our first president. These men were Hugh McGrath, Joseph P. Ryan, John McGlynn, Frank McCourt and Anthony J. Scanlon. They returned to the meeting with the good news that Mr. Devine had accepted.

At this same meeting it was decided to draw up a constitution for the Shamrock Club. Those appointed to complete this task were Ed Kirwin, Francis Howard, Gene McCurry, Charles Eberly and Francis Eberly.

James A.; Devine was a very prominent attorney in the city and he had been very active in prior Irish organizations. In addition to having one of the leading citizens of Columbus to represent our organization, he was most generous with his financial assistance for the new club. Mr. Devine paid for the band which marched in the first parade of the Shamrock Club as an organized group in 1937, and also took care of many other expenses in connection with the breakfast following the parade, etc.

At a meeting held at the Knights of Columbus Club, Columbus, Ohio. On the 21st day of April, 1936, for the purpose of organizing THE SHAMROCK CLUB, the following were present: Messrs: John J. O'Keefe; James A. Devine; Vincent Donohue; Charles A. Eberly; J.A. McGrath; Francis F. Howard; Edward J. Kiewin; Anthony J. Scanlon; Thomas B. Devine; John Devine; R.P. Devine; William P. Bresnahan; Hugh McGrath; James E. Grace; Joseph Sheeran, James F. Bourner; Auther Cannon; Eugene L. Dodd; Carl Kekky; Ed Sullivan; George Bower; Tom Duffy; Robert P. Kirwin; Michael J. Ryan Jr.; Walter O'Grady; Ed A. Moriarty; Gene McCurry; Joseph E. Ryan; James Neilan; C.J. McDonald; James Welsh; Robert E. Archibald; John McGlynn; Frank McCourt; Bud Murphy.

The above thirty five (35) men shall be known as the Charter Members of the Shamrock Club.

The First elected officers of the Club, 21st Day of April 1936, were:

> James A. Devine, President
> Anthony J. Scanlon, Vice President
> Francis P. Howard, Secretary
> Walter O'Grady, Treasurer

In 1940 Saint Patrick's Day fell on Palm Sunday, and there was no Saint Patrick's Day Parade per se. This chronometry event caused reverberations that could still be detected on Saint Patrick's

Day 2008. A March 10, 1940 article in the Columbus Citizen said "There will be no Parade because the religious observance of Palm Sunday calls for greater respect, but Ruey W. Rhodes, Grand Knight of the Knights of Columbus, has very kindly asked the members of the Shamrock Club to act as escorts for those making the annual K. of C. retreat which ends at the Cathedral on Palm Sunday". As reported by Shamrock Club President Anthony J. Scanlon.

The 1940 Stealth Parade was a very short jaunt from the K. of C. Building at the corner of Sixth & State Street West one block to Fifth Street and three blocks to Saint Joseph's Cathedral at the corner of Fifth Street & Broad Street and back to the K. of C. after Mass. Not much of a stretch of the leg. An article in the Columbus Journal stated that the "IRISH WILL PARADE WITHOUT SHENANIGANS". St. Patrick's Day on Palm Sunday, So March Will Be Shorter and Quieter.

The weather for the Saint Patrick's Day Parade on March 17, 1941was bitter cold, temperature was 8 degrees above zero. In spite of the cold the Club still had a big procession and parade (The Columbus Dispatch recorded the marchers at 1,000), and a grand breakfast afterwards at the Neil House Hotel. The parade was led by the Boys Ranger Band of the Catholic Order of Foresters, the Band also provided entertainment at the breakfast.

The first Membership Drive other than word of mouth was conducted by Anthony J. Scanlon who spent many hours going through the Columbus City Directory at the K. of C. where he lived, picking out names of Irishmen and sending them cards inviting them to become members of the Shamrock Club providing they met the eligibility requirements of "a practicing Catholic of Irish descent".

There was no Parade in 1942 because of the war effort. The 1942 Breakfast was the first that the Ladies and Families were allowed to attend. This decision was made in order to increase the crowd since so many Shamrock Club Members were in the service of their Country. Jim Grace and his wife, Lucille, made a tremendous effort during this period to keep the Shamrock Club alive.

The OBJECTIVES of TODAY'S SHAMROCK CLUB;

The objectives of this Club shall be to promote and encourage the awareness and appreciation of Irish Culture, History, and Traditions; provide educational and entertainment opportunities relative to Irish Culture, History and Traditions, for membership and community; participate in community service and charitable activities; coordinate and cooperate with other Irish organizations in an effort to unify the Irish American voice.

Since this Club was formed to venerate the memory and teachings of Saint Patrick, who is also the Patron Saint of the Shamrock Club, the Club shall promote the public veneration of Saint Patrick on March 17 of each year by sponsoring and engaging in a procession to a Catholic church in the City of Columbus and participating in the Holy Sacrifice of Mass by the Bishop of the Diocese of Columbus or his designee.

Since then, we have eliminated the gender and religious requirement for membership in the Club so we could be more inclusive of all Irish traditions and accept all who love and enjoy our Irish culture.

FAMILY TRADITIONS and DEDICATION to the
SHAMROCK CLUB

The Club's 1946 President Michael J. Ryan is the Father of the 1956 President Joseph E. Ryan and the Grandfather of the present proprietors of the Egan-Ryan Funeral Service.

The Club's 1955 President Edward A. is the Father of the 1968 President Michael E. Moriarty and the 1990 President Edward Moriarty.

The Club's 1959 President Jerry P. O'Shaughnessy is the Uncle of Maryellen O'Shaughnessy, Franklin County Clerk of Courts.

The Club's 1964 President Edward M. Dempsey is the Grandfather of the 2008 President Mark Dempsey.

The Club's 1970 President Murdith P. Byrne is the Father of 2001 President Patrick W. Byrne and the 2006 President Thomas P Byrne. He is also the Brother of 1980 President Joseph H. Byrne.

The Club's 1971 President Frank McCabe is the Uncle of 1985 President Andrew M. Connor.

The Club's 1986 President James C. Graham is the Uncle of 2009 President Patrick W. Graham.

The Club's 1989 President William T. O'Reilly is the Father of the 2007 President Brendan P. O'Reilly.

The Club's 2004 President Timothy E. Feeney is the Grandson of the 1946 President Michael J. Ryan.

The Club's 2001 President Patrick W. Byrne is the Husband of the 2011 President Molly C. Stapleton-Byrne who is the first female President.

The Club's 1972 President Patrick L. Fallon is the Father of the Patrick M. Fallon who will be the President of the Club in 2012

The Club's 2nd President John A. Connor is the Grandfather of Judge John A. Connor II who will be the President of the Club in 2013.

The Emerald Society of Columbus

Michelle Henry

The Irish brought the ancient Celtic tradition of playing the bagpipes at the funeral of a fallen comrade to this country. This tradition of playing the "pipes" has been continued by the pipe and drums corps of the Emerald Society's police and fire departments in the Columbus, Ohio Emerald Society.

The first known Emerald Society was formed by the New York Police Department in 1953 and in 1956 the New York Fire Department started their Emerald Society. There are now more than 50 Emerald Societies in the United States whose members are working in many different municipal departments relating to the safety and well-being of our citizens.

The Emerald Society of Columbus, Ohio was founded in 1990 by Thomas Hayes and Dennis Cassidy, who were both Columbus Police Officers. At it's founding it was decided that to foster camaraderie among its safety forces the Columbus Emerald Society would be a joint Police and Fire Emerald Society, one of only two such groups in the country.

The Emerald Society of Columbus is a non-political social organization of active and retired police officers and fire fighters of Irish descent. The group has had as many as 100 members during the twenty years of its existence. The earliest records from October 2, 1990 show that Dick Callahan, Sean O'Reilly, Mike Millay Tom Hayes, Tim Dempsey and Dennis Cassidy attended the first organizational meeting and the group has continued to be an important part of the Columbus Irish-American community.

The Emerald Society of Columbus provides financial assistance to the families of police officers and firefighters when necessary and donates to several charities, both local and national on an annual basis.

Ladies Ancient Order Of Hibernians, Columbus, Ohio

Julie O'Keefe McGhee

The Ladies Ancient Order of Hibernians was organized in Omaha, Nebraska, in 1894 as the "Daughters of Erin," which pledged itself to God and Country. At the National Convention of the Ancient Order of Hibernians (organized in 1836 in New York) held in Saratoga Springs in 1906, the name of the organization was changed to the Ladies Auxiliary to the Ancient Order of Hibernians and functioned as a separate organization" At its founding, the primary purpose of the LAOH was to protect young immigrant Irish girls, assist them in securing employment, and provides social interaction with Irish and Irish Americans to help them from becoming homesick and discouraged.

The motto of the Ladies Ancient Order of Hibernians is "Friendship, Unity and Christian Charity." St. Brigid is the patron saint of our organization. Our purpose is to promote Friendship, Unity, and Christian Charity among our members, to foster and sustain loyalty to our country and community, to aid and advance by legitimate means the aspirations and endeavors of all Irish people for a Irish Republic which shall include all 32 counties of Ireland, to promote Irish history, traditions, and culture, and to support the Church through mission work and Catholic action activities.

Shortly after the 1894 National Convention at Omaha, Nebraska there was a meeting called of all Irish Catholic women in Columbus. AOH County President Jerry O'Shaughnessy called the meeting and presided at the installation. Quite a number of Columbus women responded. The Right Rev. Bishop Watterson, Bishop of Columbus was also at the meeting and gave the new organization his blessing. Catherine Mooney Hart was elected President. An early Columbus history states that this was the first division of the Ladies Auxiliary of the Ancient Order of Hibernians in the United States. Catherine Hart was the first president of a Ladies Auxiliary Division in the US.

By 1923 there remained five of the original division charter members, Mrs. Charles Conroy who was the first County President; Cecelia McEvoy, then President of Division No.1; Alice Rourke, Mrs. John Christe and Catherine Mooney Hart. In 1923 there were two divisions. The two ladies divisions eventually met the same fate as the early men's divisions, dying out in the 1930s.

Fortunately for Hibernianism, on April 26, 1981 the Ladies Auxiliary of Ancient Order of Hibernians was reestablished in Columbus with the installation of the Countess Constance de Markievicz Division #1. That name was chosen by the members, for her name represents the spirit of a strong Catholic faith and the belief of a united and free Ireland that all members work towards. At the 1984 National Convention in Albany, New York the name of the organization was changed to its current title, the Ladies Ancient Order of Hibernians.

Since 1981, our division has made financial contributions to local and national charities, including: Sacred Heart Church, St. Patrick Church, Holy Rosary Family Shelter, Holy Family Soup Kitchen, J.O.I.N. (Joint Organization for Inner City Needs), the Dominican Sisters of the Sick Poor, the Columban Missions (our principal charity), St. Paul's Church in Belfast, Ireland, All Hallows Seminary in Dublin, Ireland, the St. Brigid Altar at the Shrine of the Immaculate Conception in Washington, D.C. and S.O.A.R. (Save Our Aging Religious). We also promote and support Right to Life activities.

The members of our division have supported and promoted Irish culture by participation in the Dublin Feis, the Dublin Festival, the Gaelic League (Conradh na Gaeilge), the Oireachtas, the Celtic New Year celebration (sponsored by the AOH), the Irish Cabaret (sponsored by the AOH and the Shamrock Club), the Columbus Celtic Dancers, Irish language masses, the Irish Way Program and performances by Irish musicians and artists visiting Columbus.

THE ROCKS ON WHICH HE SPLIT

Rev. James Meagher and the Early Years of St. Patrick Parish,
Columbus
by Donald M. Schlegel

St. Patrick's Church, Columbus, as it appeared in 1952

It did not go as smoothly as the published histories make it appear. The historical sketches of Columbus St. Patrick Parish, which for the most part are based on the works of Jacob Studer and Rev. Dennis Clarke, state that Father Furlong came to Columbus in 1851 or 1852; he was replaced in 1852 by Rev. James Meagher, who left in 1857 to be replaced by Father Fitzgerald. Not a ripple was in the current, to all appearances, and certainly no mention is made of the treacherous "rocks," such as those on which Father Meagher "split."

By 1852 the English-speaking Catholics in Columbus and vicinity were numerous enough to be formed into a new congregation separate from. the Germans, who had long been the dominant nationality at Holy Cross Church. Rev. Jonathan Furlong was sent to organize the new congregation, which would still meet at Holy Cross until they could build their own edifice. It was not long before Rev. Caspar H. Borgess, the pastor at Holy Cross, was writing to Bishop Purcell in Cincinnati concerning the irregular actions of Father Furlong. (1) The Irishman was offering weekday Mass only irregularly, the German priest reported; he would take no advice; he had presided at marriages between Catholic and Protestant before the altar at Holy Cross in surplice and stole, rather than in the rectory. In May, Father Borgess wrote again to the bishop, not wishing to interfere but considering silence to be sinful. Father Furlong's acts, he reported, were "to the Catholics scandalous & in the estimation of the Protestants disgraceful." Furlong was speaking against the bishop, both privately and publicly, and was at the same time disrespectful of the members of his own Irish congregation.

We have no documentary corroboration of Father Borgess' statements, but Bishop Purcell's quick removal of Father Furlong lends them credence. In July of 1852 Rev. James Meagher arrived as second pastor of the new congregation.

Father Meagher (pronounced Mahar) was a native of Mallow, County Cork and Diocese of Cloyne, Ireland, where he was born in August of 1814. (2) He attended the Irish seminary at Maynooth (3) and was ordained in 1836 or 1837. (4) He first came to the Diocese of Cincinnati 1851 and early the next year was sent to Urbana to organize a parish. After his assignment to Columbus he continued to visit Urbana irregularly well into 1853. (5)

The new congregation in Columbus had made little progress under Father Furlong, but Father Meagher "entered upon his labors with an enthusiasm that inspired his entire flock." First priority was given to the church. Father Meagher negotiated for and purchased the present site at the corner of what was then Seventh Street and North Public Lane. On Sunday Sept. 5, 1852 the cornerstone of the church was laid by Bishop Purcell.

Father Meagher took up residence in a house at Seventh. (Grant) and Long, two blocks south of the construction site. (6) In this house (Father Borgess implies in a postscript) Father Meagher heard confessions and offered Mass and may have performed baptisms. For want of a church, and apparently wishing to avoid the German church as much as possible, Father Meagher (the same letter implies) performed marriages and baptisms in private homes. For want of money for a better vessel, he consecrated in and distributed Communion from "a vessel, which to the people appears a tin box." (7)

"The obtaining of means was a wearying task among the Catholics who were generally in very poor circumstances," but the church was completed in just over a year. On Sept. 25, 1853 the bishop again was in Columbus, this time for the dedication of the building to Almighty God under the patronage of St. Patrick. High Mass was sung by Father Blake of Xenia; the two Columbus pastors assisted, and the Holy Cross choir under Mr. Kronenbitter provided the music. (8) St. Patrick's bell, with its particularly beautiful deep and mellow tone, blessed and hung in 1855, was the first in the city to ring out the Angelus to God and Our Lady.

The next task was the school building, which was opened in 1854. Father Borgess asked Father Meagher to join him in requesting the Sisters of. Notre Dame in Cincinnati to send teachers for the two parishes' schools. Father Meagher was reluctant to agree to this, since St. Patrick's already had heavy debts, but when he learned that the Sisters would require no salary but would be compensated only by what the pupils could pay, he agreed. When the time drew near for the Sisters to arrive, the arrangements were left largely in his hands. (9) He found a suitable house to serve as their convent in a secluded spot east of Washington Ave. and north of Broad Street, near the State Insane Asylum. On their arrival at the railroad station on August 27, 1855, they were conducted to Father Meagher's residence for dinner before going to their new home. The Sisters taught the girls' school at St. Patrick's, while lay men were employed to teach the boys. A School Society was formed to which dues were paid by parishioners to help defray the expense of the teachers' salaries.

The presence of the Sisters caused Father Meagher and the congregation to take up another building project, a convent, which is the present rectory behind the church. This, however, was not yet completed when Father Meagher left the parish in 1857.

Despite the fact that Father Meagher was genuinely well liked by the congregation, there had been vexing problems from the very start of his pastorate. Father Meagher insisted, even from the pulpit, that he was the pastor of the English-speaking congregation, and they were to come only to him for the sacraments. (10) In Delaware, where Father Borgess had purchased a lot and collected money for a church, Father Meagher told the people not to give to the "Dutch" priests. (11) Father Meagher, however, often was absent visiting his missions when the services of a priest were required in Columbus. From the time of Father Meagher's arrival in Columbus until December of 1852, Father Borgess had attended and buried forty-two Irish, in addition to attending many who had not died and of whom he had no record. Since Father Meagher had begun complaining, and Father Borgess had therefore refused to answer such calls, thirteen had died without the sacraments. (12) This situation seems to have cleared up, but soon the pastors were arguing about the graveyard. Father Meagher had requested and received from Bishop Purcell use of the graveyard for his congregation. In 1854, on the suggestion of Father Borgess, the graveyard was divided between the two parishes by the bishop, but it was reported that Father Meagher ignored this division. . This situation does not seem to have been resolved until after Father Meagher's departure.

In February of 1856, the relations between the two pastors boiled over again. Father Borgess had silently observed what he considered to be scandals and had borne personal abuse, meanwhile avoiding criticism of the Irish priest, he wrote, because of the archbishop's attitude. But now Father Meagher had crossed the invisible line by interfering in the work at Holy Cross: he was complaining because Father Borgess had begun instructing the children of the German immigrants in English, which they understood better than German. Father Borgess understood a rule of "the Council" to apply, whereby membership was established by pew rent, not by language. However, Father Meagher's understanding of his assignment, apparently, was that if the German children understood English better than German, then they automatically became members of his congregation! Father Borgess' letters to Archbishop Purcell at this time fell on unsympathetic ears, but there is no doubt that the majority of the German immigrants did not entrust their instruction to the Irish parish. Borgess wrote prophetically, quoting Meagher, "When the fall comes, it will be the greater, - & it is to be feared, 'that God's curse will be pinned to (a different) tail' as one is said to have said on the altar." (13)

That spring, it was alleged that Father Meagher had been seen drunk on the railroad cars, a charge never proven and which he vigorously denied. He said that he never drank before dinner, even in Ireland where it was common to do so. Other reports and complaints about him were apparently reaching the archbishop. (14) At one point Purcell came to Columbus to question Notre Dame Sister Mary Augusta about the situation. Sister, it is said, tried to excuse appearances that were unfavorable, though she could not deny them. (15) In the summer of 1857, Archbishop Purcell suggested to Father Meagher that he resign his pastorate in Columbus, and the beleaguered priest did so on August 13. (16)

On the evening of Sunday, September 13, 1857 Archbishop Purcell administered the sacrament of confirmation at St. Patrick's. At the end of the ceremony, he announced that he was withdrawing Father Meagher from the parish and would send in his place the newly ordained Rev. Edward Mary Fitzgerald. He also wished the new convent under construction to be used instead as the parish rectory. After word of these announcements had spread,

> ... a number of ignorant and violent persons, who
> seem to have been well trained in low groceries

320

[saloons], proceeded, with vulgar brawling and gesticulations, to strike the doors with their clenched hands, insisting that the appointment of the Pastor and the control of the church property belonged to them. They appeared to think the Blessed Sacrament also belonged to them, for they became its jailers, having nailed up the church and allowed no priest to approach the Tabernacle for several days. On Monday morning, the Archbishop, from the altar of the Church of the Holy Cross, declared the church and all the congregation who should not sign a protest against, and condemnation of, those sacrilegious and schismatical proceedings, interdicted, and excommunicated all who had any hand, act, or part in shutting up the church, or opposing ecclesiastical authority. (17)

During the following week, the ringleaders of the opposition to the archbishop held meetings in the school house and collected money, ostensibly on behalf of Father Meagher. The names of only three of the ringleaders have come down to us, namely a Mr. Collins, a Mr. Mahoney, and Mr. William Kehoe. Mr. Kehoe was the organist for the parish and also was the teacher of the boys' school. (18) For at least three weeks the opposition held out against the archbishop, opening the church only on Sundays and leading prayers in defiance of him. The majority of the people wished to carry out the wishes of the archbishop but were confused as to whose signatures were required on the "protest." The situation began to clear up on October third when the Catholic Telegraph ran an article explaining the chain of events and the archbishop's requirements. On Sunday, October 4 the keys of the church were turned over to Rev. Bernard Hengehold, the representative of the archbishop, and on October 6 the letter in which the people asked forgiveness of the archbishop was mailed. (19)

On October 5, the Ohio State Journal published a letter from William Kehoe, the organist, school teacher, and ringleader of the opposition, addressed "To the Congregation of St. Patrick's Catholic Church in this city."

Ladies and Gentlemen: You are all well aware of the several societies which have been instituted and most carefully arranged and carried out by the unparalleled energies of our late respected pastor, Rev. Jas. Meagher. The benefits of such societies you all know were sanctioned and organized with your consent, to defray the expenses of the school, &c., &c. I shall confine myself to one of these societies, namely, the St. Patrick's Literary and Library Society. I wish to place before you the following statement relative to it. In the organization of this society, it was proposed, and unanimously agreed to, that there be twelve dollars per month paid out of the Treasurer's funds, for the support of the schools. The Treasurer, you all know, is Mr. John Clark, (boss mechanic) who has funds in his hands amounting to over forty dollars, for the months of July and August. He (the Treasurer), has not paid this money. The President of said society waited on him to demand it; the school teacher, also, waited on him with his order and receipt; and Mr. Clark openly denies having any money in his hands to cash the order. Now, if such notorious rascality, and swindling of the public moneys be sanctioned or favored by the President or members of said society, I say, and can maintain, that honesty and justice is no more than a mockery to any community.

This apparently was answered by a private letter from the president of the society, in reply to which Mr. Kehoe had another letter published in the Ohio State Journal of October 10, addressed "To the President of St. Patrick's Literary, Library, &c., &c., &c., Society, Columbus." This letter, which is of such quality that it will not be published here, in essence made two points. First, it attempted to turn the tables on the president and his allies, alleging that they "scandalously assumed the power of governing our late zealous Pastor, the church and his flock, and through such schismatical and vile midnight concoctings, you have brought the curse and the vengeance of Heaven...on your heads, which will sooner or later overtake you." Secondly, the real reason for the meanness of the letter appeared when he stated, "You have openly declared to me that you received the monthly contributions from the members of your society for the months of July and August last, and that you did not hand such moneys into the hands of the Treasurer, having received it in his absence. ...As you are a copartner in Clark's concocted schemes of swindling, I have no necessity to give an answer to his premeditated and ridiculous reports which you have bungled together to send before me and the public." The officers of the society apparently had conspired in such a way that the money could be denied to the rebellious teacher without any lies being told, strictly speaking, but the trick did not fool him for long.

This letter of Mr. Kehoe was dismissed but not really answered by William Naghten, probably the president of the society, in a letter published on October 12:

Editors of the Ohio State Journal:

In the Journal's issue of last Saturday appeared a communication
addressed to the "President of St. Patrick's Literary, &c., &c.,
&c., Society," over the signature of that specimen of the genus homo known by the name of Wm. Keogh. That filthy mucilage of lying incongruities, the production of his morbid mind, which you thought fit to insert in the columns of your paper, deserves no notice at my hands. This pseudo Adonis, its author, like the scorpion when set upon by his adversaries, and seeing no manner or chance of escape, turns round and stings himself, and expires, the victim of his own poison. So has this master-mind of intellectual genius, this self-constituted representative

of the congregation, taken leave of his friends. Poor defunct Mr. Keogh, (alias Kehoe) peace to thy shade. May thy slumbers be as calm as thy tongue would be scandalous. In dismissing this subject, I remain yours, &c.,

WILLIAM NAGHTEN

Father Fitzgerald, the new pastor, arrived in Columbus some time before October 16th and went to live temporarily with Father Borgess at Holy Cross. He found the people of St. Patrick's good, honest, sober, and industrious, and in general very warmly attached to Father Meagher. He foresaw some difficulty from the school societies and from a large body who bore ill will against those who, they thought, had caused Father Meagher's removal. By the 21st, Mr. Collins and Mr. Mahoney had both been reconciled with the archbishop. On October 26th the school was opened; Father Fitzgerald himself taught the boys, for he thought continued employment of Mr. Kehoe would be improper (20), even though the Sisters believed that he had always been an upright and pious man. Father Fitzgerald soon obtained the services of the Brothers of the Holy Cross from Notre Dame, Indiana for the boys' school. (21)

With prudence and charity, Father Fitzgerald was able to reconcile the opposing factions within the parish, the relationships between the two city parishes, and those between the Irish parish and the archbishop.

Father Meagher at first seemed helpful to Father Fitzgerald, before his departure from Columbus about October 22. He tried to warn his successor of "the rocks on which he split." By the 27th he had left the diocese, exeat in hand, and had been received kindly by an old friend, Bishop O'Connor of Pittsburgh. His cooperation with Father Fitzgerald was not all that could have been desired, for Father Fitzgerald later wrote that he was expected back in the city after Christmas and had offered but "did not exactly promise" to bring the old parish account books with him. (22)

Father Meagher eventually went to Illinois, where he died at the town of Mendota in the Diocese of Chicago on August 6, 1860.

It was expected that his remains would be brought to Columbus immediately and the Irish-Catholic military unit, the Montgomery Guards (which had been formed at St. Patrick's by Father Fitzgerald), postponed a picnic excursion to Pleasant Valley, which had been scheduled for the eighth, in order to meet the casket. However, he was interred in Illinois and it was not until the week of January 27, 1861 that the remains were brought to Columbus for burial in the old Catholic Cemetery. (23) His body was removed to Mt. Calvary, "some years ago" according to the 1918 diocesan history, and was found to be in a remarkable state of preservation. His final resting place at Mt. Calvary is unknown at this time.

NOTES

The letters to Archbishop Purcell noted below as the sources of many statements used in this article can be found in the Archives of the Archdiocese of Cincinnati; copies can be found at the Archives at the University of Notre Dame; copies of many can be found in the Archives of the Diocese of Columbus.

1) Borgess to Purcell, Feb. 14 and May 8, 1852.

2) The Crisis, Feb. 7, 1861 (Columbus newspaper)

3) Diary of Bishop James Donnelly, in the Clogher Record Album; Enniskillen: Cuman Seanchais Chlochair, 1975; page 336. The name is spelled phonetically, "Maher.".

4) Lamott, History of the Archdiocese Q[Cincinnati, page 362; if true, he was only about twenty-two years old at the time of his ordination.

5) Champaign Democrat, June 15, 1905 (Courtesy of Mark Gideon). Here the name is spelled "Mahar."

6) C. H. Borgess to Purcell, Dec. 6, 1852.

7) ibid.

8) Hartley, The First Fifty Years, pages 176-179.

9) Feth, Sr. Vincent, S.N.D., thesis (Xavier University), "A History of the Sisters of Notre Dame in Columbus, The First Fifty Years, 1855-1905," pp 13 ff.

10) Borgess to Purcell, Dec. 6, 1852

11) O. H. Borgess to Purcell, Jan. 4, 1853

12) Borgess to Purcell, Dec. 6, 1852

13) Borgess to Purcell, Feb. 12 and Feb. 21, 1856. The allusion may have come from the ancient Irish practice of plowing by the tail, wherein the pole of the plow was tied to the tails of several horses.

14) Meagher to Purcell, Apr. 22, 1856

15) Feth, op. cit., page 34

16) Meagher to Purcell, Aug. 13, 1856

17) Catholic Telegraph & Advocate, Oct. 3, 1857

18) Fitzgerald to Purcell, Oct. 16 and Oct. 21, 1857

19) Catholic Telegraph, Oct. 10, 1857

20) Fitzgerald to Purcell, Oct. 16, 21, and 26, 1857

21) Hartley, page 179. The 1860 City Directory lists Brother Gregory and Brother Edmond as teachers of the "Irish Catholic School."

22) Fitzgerald to Purcell, Oct. 21 and Dec. 28, 1857; Meagher to Purcell, Oct. 27, 1857.

23) Ohio State Journal, Aug. 8, 1866; The Crisis, Feb. 7, 1861.

Chart and Map Showing

Family

County Origins

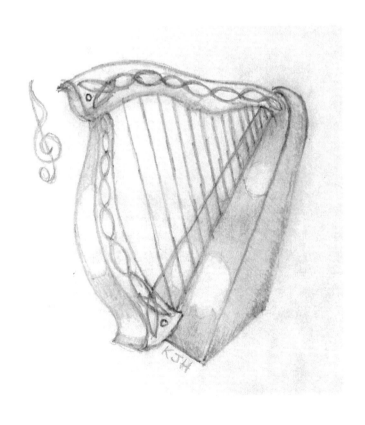

Irish County Origins of Central Ohio's Irish-Americans

Antrim	Doyle (J. Flanagan), Duffy/Rodgers (M.G. Lovell), McAllister (Kelley), Erwin, Doyle(Flanagan), McAlister(Kelley)
Armagh	Gillespie (M.G. Lovell), Erwin
Carlow	Doyle (Zurface)
Cavan	Brady (Issenmann, Quinn) Tackney-Sexton (Hayman), MacGahan (Harden)
Clare	Jeffers (Browning), Gallagher (Driscoll), O'Brien (Krutsch)
Cork	O'Connor (2), McGuire (Browning), Brady, Sullivan, Stack (Ardrey, Douglass, and de Oliveira), O'Connor (McGhee)
Derry	O'Neill (Grove), Erwin
Donegal	Griffin, Noon, Erwin, Gallagher (Gatton)
Dublin	Kelley (Wright-Stover), Caulins (Wohlfrom), Madden (Ziccardi)
Galway	Flaherty (J. Dorrian), Fallon (Durbin), O'Toole (Flanagan)
Kerry	Scanlon (Grove), O'Connor, Canty (Adkins), Morans, Donohos (Robinson), Cronin (McGhee, O'Keefe), Brosnan/Bresnahan (McGhee, O'Keefe)
Kildare	Graham
Kilkenny	Cody
Limerick	McKearny (Dalton), Kiley, Hynes(Nelson)
Longford	Doyle, Hourican (Fath), Goodwin (Devine), Conway (DeVoe), O'Farrell (DeVoe)
Louth	Cook

Mayo	Gaughan (Brammer), Mellet (Minor) Power (Proffitt), Barrett (Brammer), Hoban (Martin), McNulty (Lavelle), Clery (Clark), Toolen (Shanahan), Varley, O'Brien (Henderson), O'Grady, Grady (Strickland), Durkin (Carpenter), Shanahan
Meath	McCarty (Krutsch)
Monaghan	McCough/Gough (McGue), Duffy (Hoffman)
Offaly	King's Handiboe (Hoffman)
Roscommonn	Byrne (Martin)
Sligo	Finn, Toolen (Shanahan), O'Tarpey (Tarpy), Scanlon (Kelley), Cahill (Gatton)
Tipperary	O'Keeffe (Ciotola), Meehan, Keenan (Gueth), Flynn (Zurface), Morrissey
Tyrone	McKearney (Collette M.), Gallagher (Hoffman)
Waterford	O'Keefe
West Meath	Gormley (O'Dell), McGhee
Scotland	Dorrian (by way of Donegal)

Names without parenthesis indicate that the immigrant's name and that of the descendant are the same: a name in parenthesis is that of the 2011 descendant.

26 counties represented
47 stories did not indicate from which county the immigrant family member came.

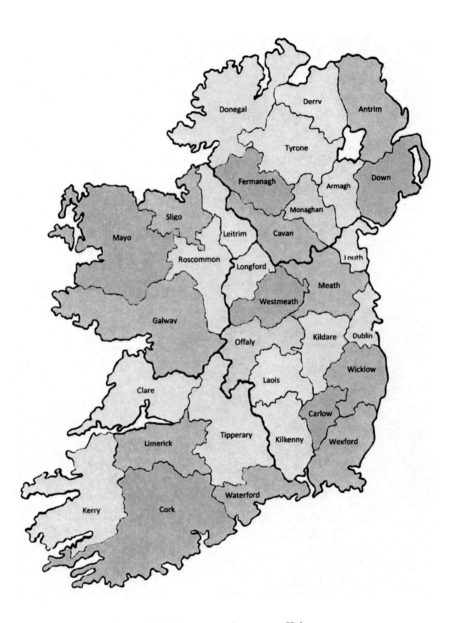

claire@irish-genealogy-toolkit.com

Title and Submitter Index

Title and Submitter Index

Title and Submitter Index

Thumbnail Sketches of the Anthologists

J. Michael Finn

 J. Michael Finn is the Ohio State Historian for the Ancient Order of Hibernians and Division Historian for the Patrick Pearse Division in Columbus, Ohio He is Chairman of the Catholic Record Society for the Diocese of Columbus, Ohio. He writes regularly on Irish and Irish-American History. In addition he writes a monthly column for the Ohio Irish American News.

Kathryn McConnell Hess

 A Columbus, Ohio native with an art background, Kathi is proud of her Irish heritage. She believes in the preservation of our culture and is especially interested in the fables and lore of Ireland.

Julie O'Keefe McGhee and William McGhee

 Julie and William together have 62 years experience as teachers and have an interest in genealogy and history. Julie is active in Central Ohio Irish-American groups and is currently Division Historian for the LAOH Countess de Markievicz Division. Julie is a professional storyteller focusing on Irish and Ohio History. William's math and computer skills have been a major aid in the production of this book.

Anne O'Farrell DeVoe

 Ann was born and raised in Central, Ohio. She has a Bachelor's and Master's degree in Nursing and has worked as an advanced practice nurse in the mental health field. Ann has been involved in Irish organizations and is an ongoing student of the Irish language, Irish history and culture.

"The measure of a man
was the stories he could tell."
(*Unknown Source*)

CPSIA information can be obtained at www.ICGtesting.com
Printed in the USA
LVOW131404200912

299625LV00005B/46/P